The Complete Real Estate Adviser

By Daniel J. deBenedictis

New Revised Edition

CORNERSTONE LIBRARY, NEW YORK

The Complete Real Estate Adviser is a new revised expanded and updated
compilation of The Family Real Estate Adviser, copyright © 1966, 1967;
Practical Ways To Make Money In Real Estate, copyright, © 1967; Laws
Every Homeowner and Tenant Should Know, copyright, © 1968; Ten Ways to
Make A Killing In Real Estate, copyright, © 1967, 1973. All of the above titles
are copyrighted in the name of Daniel J. deBenedictis.

This edition also includes a complete unabridged reprint of the booklet entitled
Settlement Costs, prepared, prescribed and approved by the U.S. Department
of Housing and Urban Development and which is in the public domain.

Manufactured in the United States of America

ISBN 0-346-12212-0

CONTENTS

PART II
Laws Every Homeowner and Tenant Should Know

PART III
Practical Ways to Make Money in Real Estate

ESPECIALLY FOR THE BEGINNER OR SMALL INVESTOR

PART IV
10 Ways to Make a Killing in Real Estate

PART V
How the Broker Makes His Money

The Family Real Estate Adviser

Chapter 1

HOW TO FIND THE RIGHT PROPERTY FOR YOU

Many people have looked for years in the hope of finding the right house for their needs and desires. Some have never found it, and have given up in disillusionment and despair. This tragic waste to the unfortunate persons involved, and to the economy, probably never should have occurred.

The tremendous task involved should never be tackled alone. Certainly you would not dare to practice medicine, or law, or engineering without being licensed and qualified. But if you are like most people, you will wade right into looking for your house, certain that you understand enough about real estate.

Fortunately for you, the market is filled with a large number of legitimate professional brokers who are only too glad to lend a helping hand, if you will only let them—and at no charge whatever to you.

Be sure to enlist the aid of brokers in the towns surrounding the specific area you are seeking. Brokers normally cover all areas adjacent to their office. Frequently an out-of-town broker holds the exclusive right to sell the very house you want.

Don't expect to find "For Sale" signs on most houses on the market. Also, many sellers are too proud and too foolish to admit that their house is up for sale even though all their neighbors already know it and they are dying to make a sale.

Place ads in the "Real Estate Wanted" columns of the local as well as the big paper. You will receive calls from both brokers and owners selling direct. Remember, according to a recent survey of the National Association of Real Estate Boards, 27 percent of all buyers and sellers deal directly without a broker.

Look for "Owner" ads in the local as well as the big city paper. Many penny-wise and pound-foolish owners never advertise in the big city paper, where the real action is. Also, many brokers place ads in the local newspaper that never appear in the big papers, for the following reasons: 1. Their advertising budget is too limited. 2. They are trying to fulfill their obligation to advertise "exclusives" and "multiple listings" as cheaply as possible. 3. They are trying to dominate the columns of the local paper to impress the local residents—with their eyes looking more toward securing listings than actually selling houses—through the local paper.

Don't keep a secret of the fact that you are looking for a house. Today, with over one million licensed brokers in the United States and Canada, plus hundreds of thousands more who have not paid for license renewals, you are apt to find many eager brokers among your neighbors, relatives, friends, fellow workers, tradesmen, delivery people, etc., any one of whom might just have the right house for you. Often, one of these people might be trying to sell his own house.

It is up to you to get as many people helping you as you can, especially where many are so eager to do it without pay from you. Never forget that in a good area the demand far exceeds the supply of houses for sale. If you find an abundance of homes for sale, be very wary of buying in that area.

Chapter 2

HOW MUCH YOU SHOULD PAY FOR IT

Surveys have proved that in large urban areas an informed, experienced broker can get the house for the buyer at actually less money than the inexperienced buyer can get it for himself. Part of the reason for this is that often a broker is so hungry for a sale and a commission that he will be more persuasive in getting the seller to come down in price—especially since he is looking down the seller's throat with knowledge of all the hidden shortcomings of the house, and many of the personal problems of the seller.

All things being equal, the price of the house should equal its "fair market value." The trouble comes because all things are seldom equal. But first let's see what "fair market value" really is. Appraisers define it as the highest price a buyer is willing to pay and the lowest price a seller is willing to accept when both are operating in a free market, with full knowledge of all the facts, and acting voluntarily without any compulsion. Now, the actual sales price rarely coincides exactly with the fair market value of the house for the following reasons:

1. Sellers are quick to take advantage of the fact that they have a unique commodity for sale, which the law says cannot be exactly reproduced any place on the face of the earth. In good areas, today, fine older houses are as scarce as hen's teeth.

2. Buyers who are transferring from one area to another are seldom in a fair bargaining position, but rather must act under great compulsion.

3. Some hungry brokers, eager for an easy sale, will sell a distressed owner down the river at too low a price.

4. Both buyers and sellers are usually abysmally ignorant of the "replacement cost new" of the bricks and sticks and the land that comprise the used parcel of real estate and know even less about how to measure the physical, functional and economic depreciation of the property.

5. Many brokers will snap up a house themselves, if they feel they can wheedle it from an unsuspecting widow, or under other distress circumstances, at a price considerably below value.

6. Other brokers will take advantage of an unwary buyer, especially where the broker is to receive "all over a fixed net amount to the seller."

For these reasons and many more, too numerous to relate here, every buyer should be protected by a professional appraisal of the house he intends to buy. This does not mean a "seat of the pants guess" by an ordinary untrained broker. Nor does it mean a "windshield" or "horseback" appraisal given on the spot for a low fee or gratis, even though it comes from a seasoned broker. It does mean a careful, thorough, scientific appraisal made by the Veterans Administration, Federal Housing Administration, or qualified independent fee appraiser. Also, a growing number of bank mortgage officers are becoming qualified appraisers rather than mere mortgage takers.

It would be very helpful for a buyer to buy "subject to V.A. or F.H.A. appraisal approval," even though the buyer intends to buy through conventional bank financing. This protection to the buyer against such hazards as a leaky roof or basement, cracked foundations, settlement, illegal or unfit wiring, plumbing or heating, termite damage, etc., as well as functional or economic obsolescence is certainly well worth the very small charge by the V.A. or the F.H.A. Think it over. Today the

F.H.A. guarantees to make the appraisal in 5 days. For a V.A. appraisal allow about 10 days. You may request your bank to order in the V.A. appraiser by telephone and have the appraiser there within 24 hours. Previously these appraisals frequently required several weeks.

Now, the V.A. and the F.H.A. buyer can always proceed to negotiate the sale at a price higher than the V.A. or F.H.A. appraisal, if he wishes to. Formerly the V.A. buyer could not legally proceed to negotiate a sale at a price one penny higher than the V.A. appraisal.

Remember to be always wary of an appraisal that the seller has received "from a broker." Too often the broker was more interested in trying to please the seller into giving him an exclusive right to sell the house. Again, if the broker was sandbagged into giving the appraisal free or for a nominal sum, the concluded price may not be accurate or valid.

Remember that top authorities on residential appraising round off appraisals to the nearest $500. The F.H.A. allows local authorities to change an appraisal by 3 percent without even ordering a reappraisal. The fact is that price will always be higher than value in an inflated market, and lower than value in a depressed market.

Finally, bear in mind that most sellers start a thousand or two, or even higher, than the price they will finally accept. Also, on top of this there is superimposed the broker's 6 percent, plus the leverage of several hundred dollars more that the broker wants you to be able to chisel from him to keep you happy, while still protecting his full commission. Just today, a client requested my counsel on his purchase of a new house. The owner was "asking" $65,000. The broker suggested to the buyer that he thought a $57,000 offer would be quite acceptable to the seller. The client was pondering whether or not he could afford any more than $48,000; he was beaten out of the purchase by another buyer dealing directly with the seller at $49,000. In this case the seller had allowed himself $16,000 for a $3,000 brokerage fee, plus plenty of leverage. When my client asked his broker how come the other buyer could do this when the broker had his "exclusive agent" sign on the premises, the Realtor merely shrugged and admitted that his exclusive agency had terminated some time ago.

Don't offer what you are willing to pay; always start with an offer of less than you are willing to pay. This will compensate for the high start by the seller and the broker, and allow for levelling out at your price.

Chapter 3
HOW TO CHOOSE A BROKER

Make up your mind at the outset that there is absolutely nothing to gain by shifting the big burden of finding your house onto the shoulders of only one broker—no matter how good he is. Remember, if this broker is really any good he is already extremely busy. Also any seasoned broker knows he must stick with the house, rather than with the buyer. For sooner or later somebody will buy the house which will always be right there. But experience shows that the buyer can be lost by the next day to any one of a hundred other areas. So, you must depend on many brokers, just as the broker knows he can safely depend only on many buyers.

You don't need to be over-choosy. After all, the broker does not charge the buyer. And you never know who the lucky broker is going to be who will just happen to have the listing on the very house for you. On the other hand, common sense would dictate that you spend the greater portion of your time with brokers who have high caliber background and training, plus adequate experience in the area in which you are looking. For example, you would not use a new broker from one town to show you around other towns not immediately adjacent. This would be too much like the blind leading the blind. You would be much better served by a broker with twenty or thirty years of experience within the distant town.

There is no substitute for experience, background, and training. Make it a point to check the broker's qualifications on these points. Use the broker who is willing to help you personally, not the one who sends out a new salesman to learn on your time and at your expense. Don't spend your valuable time with an obvious greenhorn who will take you right by a thousand good homes to show you a white elephant.

As buyer or seller, it is essential for you to understand that a broker's "exclusive right" to sell is exactly that; it means that the houseowner has given up the right to sell his own house. Further, it is no contradiction for an "exclusive" to be on a "multiple listing." If the broker with the exclusive is a member of a multiple-listing group or board, he may share his exclusive with his fellow multiple-listing members. If he sells his exclusive himself he gets full commission; if another member of multiple listing should make the sale, then the commission is split and the listing broker gets the smaller share. And thus the "exclusive" often turns out to be rather nonexclusive after all.

You can tell a lot about the broker's integrity and ability from the way his "ad" reads, the way you are handled when you telephone him, and the way you are treated when you reach his office. Drop him fast if: 1. He has practically no listings. 2. The few listings he has are obviously overpriced, indicating either ignorance on his part or, worse yet, lack of honesty with his principal, the seller, when he took the listing. 3. He has mostly multiple listings or co-broker listings. Often, the seasoned brokers only put their "dogs," or overpriced houses on multiple listing. Few brokers, indeed, will share a "hot" listing by putting it on multiple listing or co-brokering it with another broker. 4. He is obviously more interested in high-pressuring you into buying what he already has, rather than trying to find out what you really need and then trying to locate it for you.

Stay with the broker who gets most of his business by referral, rather than by high-powered promotion. The woods are full of promoters. You should rely on the dedicated, sincere real estate broker. Promoters will take only a commercial interest in you. They depend on volume and turnover, rather than rendering service to you.

Find out if the broker can get you a big enough mortgage on the house he is asking you to buy, and on the terms you need. He should be able to tell you why you should buy the house before he even shows it to you. Your inspection of the house should merely be for corroboration and proof of his advice to you. He should insist on your careful thorough inspection of the entire house, inside and out, plus a close examination of the houses on either side, and across the street, and the entire immediate neighborhood. After all, this is what the bank or V.A. or F.H.A. appraiser would want to know.

Finally, the broker should ask you if you like the house. If you say no, he should forthwith show you something else or arrange a subsequent meeting. If you say yes, you do like the house, he should immediately suggest you go back to his office to execute an offer with a deposit, before you lose the house. If he fails to do this he is incompetent. He will never sell you anything. The sooner you drop him, the sooner you will buy a house.

Chapter 4

HOW TO KNOW IF A BROKER IS REALLY TRYING TO HELP YOU

No broker is helping his principal, the seller, or himself, if he does not screen the buyer to determine his needs and ability to pay. Now, if he can't help his principal, or even himself, how can he possibly help you? So, if he does not check your credit rating, don't take him seriously. This would constitute gross ignorance or incompetence on his part, or even worse a callous disregard for your needs and requirements.

A good broker will counsel you as to areas and neighborhoods, styles of houses, types of construction, size of house for your needs, whether it should be a single or a two-family house, or one with a separate in-law apartment (that is, a home with self-contained quarters for a relative, and meeting all the legal requirements for a two-family house), the right price range for you, whether you should finance conventionally, V.A. or F.H.A., the amount of down payment which will be required, what the total monthly carrying charge will be, facilities available for you, your wife and your children, and other things too numerous to mention here. He will recognize that if you are like most people you will be trying to put your best foot forward and improve yourself. Furthermore, he will know that some particular motive will be the key issue with you. He will search out that key issue. He will try to determine if it is more space, peace and quiet, trying to get closer in, or a little farther out, or more land, or less land, or if you have a teen-age daughter and you want the right neighbors and environment to enhance her marriage opportunities. If he does not probe for that key issue with you, he's not going to find out about it. If he does not know the "hot button" to lean on with you, he's not going to satisfy you and sell you. In short, he is not trying to help you. He is probably like too many brokers, completely self-centered, trying to pressure you into buying what he happens to have on hand, regardless of your needs or desires.

A good broker will move heaven and earth to search out the right house for you. He will be willing to go to other brokers for help. He will be able to command their best listings. He will be willing to look into other nearby towns offering the same housing amenities. He will keep in contact with you, advising you of the progress he is making and inviting you out for subsequent briefings and inspection trips. In short, the paramount issue with him will be that you get the best house for your needs, rather than guaranteeing that he earn the biggest possible commission.

Just be sure you are not misplacing your confidence in him. Test him a couple of times for the completeness and the accuracy of the information and advice he is giving to you. If he measures up, count yourself lucky, and stay with him.

Chapter 5

HOW TO GUARD AGAINST A "CON-ARTIST" BROKER

You will recognize him first from his phony advertising. For example: "Gentleman's estate, treed grounds, sun-splashed living room, festive dining room etc." All for $7,900! You know it has to be a converted summer camp in the middle of a swamp. And of course it actually is. Indeed, many times the house turns out to be nonexistent, a mere figment of the imagination of the "connie" who is using it just to bait you in.

The next chance you get to spot him is over the telephone. He is selling the house to you before he has ever met you, or has the slightest idea of your needs and requirements. But the instant you enter his office, you are sure he is a phony. The big bargain he advertised has "already been sold." The "brand new" houses his huge outdoor signs hawk at bargain prices turn out to be sold out as well, or available, but only in a distant one-horse country town. The "free consultation" so blatantly offered on his billboards, on all matters from appraisal to finance, turns out to be a fast third-degree as to how much cash you have, and whether you brought your check book with you.

The amazing truth is that many buyers return again and again to continue to deal with these bandits. You must never forget that the only protection you have is the integrity of the broker. After all, the law says that he is under no legal obligation to volunteer any factual information to you in this arms-length transaction. Consequently you must be on your guard, and question the broker, and evaluate his integrity very carefully. You can't even depend on the advance opinion of his reputation you received from a third party. That person may not really know the broker, or may be hoping to receive a finder's fee. A jealous competitor might deliberately scare you away from the very broker who could help you the most. After all, it is your money you are spending, and any mistakes made will quite definitely be only your loss. So, judge for yourself.

Don't accept personal opinions or seller's puff. The law says neither the agent nor his principal, the seller, will be liable for these "opinions" if they should cause you loss. Question the broker often and thoroughly, and make him commit himself, with positive statements of fact. Then, and only then, can he or the seller become liable if he is wrong and you lose. In fact, under a landmark Massachusetts case two decades ago, even if the broker makes an "innocent" misstatement of a material fact you may be able to rescind the contract, although it is completely executed and you have already moved in. The case that started this significant and radical departure from the old basic doctrine of *caveat emptor* (let the buyer beware) happened to involve an increased tax assessment. But you could safely protect yourself against any number of otherwise hidden hazards such as: misplaced boundary lines, termite damage, water leakage from a roof or into a basement, inadequate heating system, faulty, insufficient or illegal wiring, bad plumbing, broken or defective appliances, windows that don't work, settlement, foundation cracks, lack of water pressure, clogged septic tanks, obnoxious odors from adjacent properties, nuisance easements (an easement being the right of any particular person or party to use the property of another), illegal zoning and building code violations—to mention a few hazards that a worthy broker would protect you against.

Don't let the broker rush you, or distract you, evade you, or artfully camouflage bad conditions. You are always responsible for having noticed conditions which are readily apparent. So, stop, look, question, and demand positive statements of fact, or insist on seeing the proof. In later chapters you will see why these things and others should be covered in your Purchase and Sale Agreement, and why you should never, never sign this agreement before consulting your lawyer.

Other protections readily available to you are:

1. The broker often tries to keep the seller away from you for fear he will spoil the sale with his big mouth. Be sure to talk to the seller as much as possible, as he frequently blurts out the truth.

2. Talk to the neighbors. They love to tell the truth, especially if they think it might hurt.

3. Inspect the neighborhood.

4. Check the town building inspector, and the assessor's office.

9

5. Find out at the Registry of Deeds exactly how much the present owner really did pay for the property.

6. Find out if he really did add all those improvements he claims, or whether a previous owner added them.

7. Beware of the broker who goes out of his way to knock a competitor or a competitor's listing. This is the hallmark of the "con artist."

Chapter 6

THE BIG WINDFALL YOU GET FROM WORTHY BROKERS

Surveys have shown that over 95 percent of the time the home seeker does not buy the house he looks at in response to an advertisement. At this point the broker's service to the buyer begins. Armed with the knowledge of why the buyer was not satisfied with the advertised property, the broker quickly suggests other listings he has, or can get from fellow brokers, which will more closely suit the now apparent needs and desires of the buyer. This kind of help is invaluable to the buyer. It greatly accelerates the speed at which the buyer can now reach his goal.

A worthy broker saves you much time and money in many ways. He advises you as to the right location, the lowest tax bill, the best construction, the resalability of the house, the price to pay in a low, high, or normal market for the particular house and location. He gets you a better price than you could get for yourself. He advises you on matters of zoning, restrictions, easements, building codes, neighborhood influences, and scores of other important considerations you would never think of, if left on your own.

He not only appraises the property for you, but he also evaluates your ability to qualify for the necessary financing. He then proceeds to supply that financing, generally at better rates and terms than you could get for yourself.

The broker does not stop at quickly producing the house and the financing. His most crucial help to you comes when the going gets rough. When the seller will not budge an inch for you, the broker gets him to give up yards. When the appraiser lets you down, the broker finds a way to keep the deal together and get the financing. When the lawyers make demands the buyer and seller cannot meet, the broker satisfies those demands. Invariably, retaining a broker pays in time, effort and money, over and over again, so that in the end you move into the house of your dreams, instead of having that dream dashed to bits by the seller, appraiser, banker, lawyer, town official or a dozen other potential obstructionists. If it sometimes appears to take him a little time to accomplish all this, please try to remember that the "difficult" is usually easy for the qualified experienced broker, and that many "impossible" situations that come up are apt to take "a little longer."

Chapter 7

BROKER TRICKS YOU SHOULD RECOGNIZE AND AVOID

1. A stranger to both real estate practice and the local area sets up his office with the following false fronts:
    a. His name is an alias, adopted to conform with the dominant nationality and religious group of that area.
    b. Although he is a brand-new licensed broker, he pretends to have lifelong practicing experience in real estate.
    c. The decor of his office suggests that he has been there a long, long time.
    d. Typical props of the con artist are phony portraits of his "ancestors," and an out-of-date, musty set of old law books to give the false impression of dependability and professionalism.
    e. The billboards offer brand-new houses at unusually low prices, which are really not available, just to bait you in.
2. He will try to sell you a house he knows you are already considering with another broker. This is not only patently unfair, but may also be illegal.
3. He will "knock" the house because you are already considering it seriously through another broker.
4. He will go out of his way to "knock" his competitor to try to frighten you from doing business with him; if only you knew the truth, the other broker might be twice as ethical and successful.

5. An older broker in the area will often quite unfairly try to cut the throat of a newcomer broker to that area. Frequently, the newcomer is much more qualified, and might have the very house you want.

6. He will go out of his way to criticize other geographical areas which he personally does not cover.

7. He will take a $5 binder, or even your wrist watch, just to "tie the house up for a while so nobody else can get ahead of you." If he can be this unfair to his principal, the seller, imagine how little consideration he will have for your welfare.

8. He keeps high-pressuring you to buy his listing which will give him a full commission when you would really be better off with a "co-broke," which would mean a split commission with another broker.

9. Any relationship between the house he shows you and the house described in the ad is purely accidental. When this happens, drop the rascal immediately, before he sticks you with a lemon.

10. He persistently interrogates you about other houses you have seen, so he can steal his competitors' listings after he leaves you.

11. He prominently displays membership in a respectable and worthy organization as a false badge of respectability to cover up his shady operation. Local real estate boards have grievance committees if you need them.

12. He has signs up, or otherwise pretends to have the exclusive right to sell the house he shows you, when in reality he never did have the exclusive right, or it has long since expired. If he will injure the seller this way by unfairly limiting the exposure of the house to a sale, or if he is trying to frighten buyers from approaching the seller directly, imagine what he would be willing to do to you.

13. He offers to get the house for you F.H.A., with minimum down payment, even though you do not intend to live in it. This is illegal. Under these circumstances, you are entitled to only 85 percent of the mortgage money a resident owner could get.

14. He makes you pay bonus points to one bank, when another bank would give you the same mortgage without extra charges.

15. He makes you pay extra financing charges on the house, when you could get a better house for the same price and one which a bank would be willing to finance without bonus payments.

16. If there are extra financing charges involved due to tight money, make sure he has really tried to get a bank which would be willing to forgo bonus payments.

17. If there are mortgage bonus points to be paid, why can't the seller or broker, or both share the added financing expense? Remember, it is

illegal to charge a V.A. or F.H.A. buyer more than one point (one percent of the amount of the mortgage).

18. Normally, high bonus points paid to the bank to secure a mortgage are paid by the seller and added to the price of the house.

19. He "kites" the price of the house above the true price to illegally gain a higher mortgage from the bank. You could be getting less than fair market value under these circumstances. Remember, this is illegal.

20. He "kites" the price to deceive a V.A. or F.H.A. appraiser. This is also illegal. Remember, if the government appraiser is on to him, the house will be rejected. If the appraisal is approved you are getting less than fair value. Either way you lose.

21. You are asked to pay the difference between a "low" F.H.A. appraisal and the seller's price. Obviously, this difference is not a true loss to the seller when measured in terms of fair market value and should at least be negotiated by the parties, if not borne entirely by the seller. You are free, of course, to refuse the deal. By law, your deposit must be returned in full, if you were properly protected by an honest F.H.A. escape clause in your contract of sale.

22. Remember, under new public law, you now have the legal option to pay a seller more than the G.I. appraisal value, if you wish to do this. If you do not elect this option, when the appraisal is lower than the price, you must receive your deposit back in full—if you are protected by an honest G.I. escape clause in your contract of sale.

23. You are asked to satisfy conditions dependent upon F.H.A. or G.I. approval when these deficiencies, or improvements, etc., are actually the responsibility of the seller. You are always entitled to fair market value. You are not acting wisely when you connive with a broker to circumvent the protection offered you by a V.A. or F.H.A. appraisal. If the government appraisal appears unjustifiably low, the proper procedure is to request a re-appraisal and furnish proof of alleged discrepancy or mistake.

24. He pressures you into placing your mortgage with his bank so he can get a finder's fee (usually one percent of the mortgage) when you could get a lower rate and better terms from another bank.

25. He gives you a "Preacher's Discount" by raising price first, then letting you beat him down to a price where you think you are stealing the house.

26. Knowing he is legally responsible for actual misrepresentations of material facts, he avoids making any positive statements of fact, dwelling instead on personal opinions and seller's puff. He deliberately withholds information which is important for you to have in order to reach a sound

decision, whenever he feels that your decision might become negative if you had the full facts.

27. Remember, your lawyer should see your Purchase and Sale Agreement before you sign it. Don't let anybody fool you about this.

Chapter 8

SELLER TRICKS YOU SHOULD RECOGNIZE AND AVOID

1. The seller claims that he made improvements to the house to justify the higher price he is asking, when in reality these improvements were made by the previous owner.

2. He starts at a higher figure than he is willing to take, hoping that some lucky broker will find a "live one" fresh in from the country, who might be unwary enough to pay it. He figures he can always come down when time begins to run short. He also wants to give the tough buyer a chance to take a lot off, and think he is stealing the property. This is precisely why most sellers are only too happy to list with any broker who comes down the pike.

3. He frequently demands a higher price in return for giving some broker the exclusive right to sell the house, or the exclusive right to share the commission under a multiple listing with many brokers. Under these plans, in return for a good price, the seller agrees that he will not sell his house himself, or through any outside broker, without paying a full commission to the listing broker. Experience shows that "exclusive" or "multiple" listings generally sell at significantly lower prices than the listing prices. In other words, the seller winds up kidding nobody but himself.

4. He wants to hold the deposit because the broker who is selling him a new house tells him he is entitled to it, and can use it as a deposit on the new house he is buying. This would be all right if every deal were certain to go through. Actually, the deposit is much safer in escrow, at least until such time as the house and the buyer are approved for mortgage purposes.

5. He wants time to consider your offer so he can use it as a wedge to

14

drive other interested buyers up in price. So always give very short periods—usually one or two days—for acceptance.

6. He suggests to you on the side that you come back and see him personally and directly (obviously suggesting that you could do better in price if there were no broker commission involved). This kind of double-crossing seller would be quick to double-cross you, and is flirting with a lawsuit for a commission from the broker, which could tie the house up, anyway.

7. At the eleventh hour, the seller refuses to go through with the deal. He is trying to force the buyer to go higher, or the broker to cut his commission, or both. This "hungry" rogue will swear that the broker never had the listing, or that the listing was qualified in some way such as, the seller would be bound only if he could find some other house to move into, etc. Hence, you must be sure to have a signed acceptance by the seller.

8. Remember, under the Statute of Frauds every real estate transaction must be in writing in order to be enforceable.

9. The seller, or his lawyer, puts unacceptable and unfair clauses in the agreement of sale, such as "seller will close on a certain date but only if he has purchased another house by that time." A buyer would be silly to change his position and be at the mercy of an unfair clause like this.

10. The seller hides a water leak in his basement by painting the floor and walls so the stains will not show. He also camouflages or conceals his water pump from view.

11. He hides roof leaks by redoing an inside ceiling or wall.

12. He does not explain the "easement" or use rights that others have in his property.

13. He does not tell you about illegal zoning violations, such as a "bootleg" two-family house, etc.

14. He does not tell you about illegal building code violations that exist in his wiring, plumbing, kitchens, entrances and exits, etc.

15. He claims to have four bedrooms, and the house might be listed this way by a big reputable brokerage firm. Yet it will never be appraised for the necessary financing, perhaps because it really has only two bedrooms instead of four. One of the alleged bedrooms may be under minimum size requirements and without a closet, another may in reality be nothing more than a converted sun porch.

16. Frequently, a seller is trying to hide his true boundary lines due to a dispute with his neighbor, or lack of sufficient room for a needed purpose, such as getting into the garage. Make him identify his boundary lines quite definitely, and see to it that they are indicated in your written agreement.

17. The seller gives you his last year's tax bill, knowing that this year the bill is much higher.

18. He hides an unacceptably high assessment.

19. He misleads you into thinking that you will be able to continue some very low assessment that he has had as a disabled veteran, or something similar.

20. Always find out if in that town the house is immediately reassessed higher upon a sale to conform to the new higher sales price. Massachusetts has recently ruled this practice illegal for lacking in uniformity of assessment practice.

21. Always ask for the actual assessment and tax bill. Then if it is given to you materially lower than it turns out to be, you may rescind the sale and get your money back, even though the seller or broker was innocent of deliberately trying to misrepresent the fact.

22. The seller hides serious defects in his interior walls, like cracks or holes, with furniture, or pictures, etc.

23. He hides bad flooring with wall to wall rugs or linoleum.

24. Don't be misled by fences and hedges, etc., which actually are on your neighbor's land.

25. Insist on seeing the "plot plan" of his property which shows where the house actually stands in relation to his boundary lines.

26. Read the measurements and boundaries as described in his deed and walk over the property lines yourself.

27. Make sure you actually have heat in all of your rooms.

28. Find out where his septic tank or cesspool is and where the leaching lines are. Make sure you have no problem in this regard. Don't be misled into thinking you have town sewerage when you have only a cesspool.

29. Find out at the Registry of Deeds how much the seller paid for the property when he bought it. Federal tax stamps on deeds recorded prior to January 1, 1968 when they were abolished, were purchasable at the rate of $0.55 for each $500 or fraction thereof of the sale price. Remember, if the house was previously sold "subject to a mortgage" the stamps paid were on the previous owner's equity only. For deeds recorded after January 1, 1968 use your state excise tax stamp rate in a similar manner. Most states charge a stamp rate of two or three dollars per thousand of the sale price. Massachusetts has recently enacted a law requiring the actual sale price to be spelled out in the deed.

30. Be sure you have the true heating bill.

31. Be sure the seller will actually move on closing day. Otherwise, you are entitled to be reimbursed on a per diem basis for your expenses or refuse to close. It is no more than standard procedure for the buyer to

insist that money be held in escrow (usually about $1,000.00) to guarantee that the seller will in fact move on the subsequent date he has promised.

32. Make yourself known to the neighbors of the house you are about to buy. They frequently come up with a gold mine of important information, plus some surprises that you otherwise would not know in time.

33. Never forget that the basic law is still *caveat emptor*. The seller is under no duty to speak. In a famous Massachusetts case the buyer who afterwards found he had termites could not collect damages from the seller because the seller never told him the house was free of termites. So be sure to ask about these important things. A wise buyer would demand that the seller furnish a termite report. The Veterans Administration insists upon this protection to a buyer.

34. Professional buyers always leave themselves an "out" in their agreement to protect themselves from surprise tricks by a seller or broker. Most common of the outs are specific financing clauses and making the offer subject to a later inspection, etc.

35. Always be wary of the seller who insists on a "conventional" buyer because he does not want to wait around several months for a closing. Today, G.I. sales, and F.H.A. sales, can be closed in reasonably short periods of time. What this seller really fears is that a V.A. or F.H.A. appraiser will appraise his house for much less than the unrealistically high price he prefers to kid himself into thinking that some sucker will pay him, whereas the bank will be satisfied with its safety margin of a big down payment by the conventional buyer.

36. Be careful of the clause in the agreement of sale which states that "time is of the essence in this contract." A seller who happens to get a better offer after he goes into agreement with you will take advantage of his clause to refuse you any extension of time, however short, that you may find yourself needing in order to close. On the other hand, you may want this clause in your contract because you have the protection of the financing clause you need, and you do not want the seller to be able to extend the time for closing.

37. Don't be misled into thinking you are getting certain appliances or furnishings etc. which the seller intends to take with him. Be sure to specify these items in your agreement.

NOTE: As a practicing real estate attorney, I hope that the reader will gather from the above enumerated seller tricks that there is really no substitute for the qualified worthy broker. This good broker will insist on legal, ethical, and fair treatment to the buyer, as well as on fulfilling his fiduciary duty to act in the seller's best interest.

Chapter 9

WHAT YOU CAN DO TO HELP YOURSELF

1. Wait for the "exclusive" or "multiple" listing to expire. The exclusive may be for a very short period of time. The minimum duration of a multiple listing is usually sixty days. This is the time when the seller breaks his price and comes closer down to earth and reality. Also, he can now sell to you direct. If you are well enough informed as to his true "net" price to himself, you may save the brokerage commission.

2. Houses come on the market at their highest price in early spring. The lowest price is reached in mid-winter. Wait if you can.

3. Some towns actually have lower tax bills for the same type of house. Find out where these towns are.

4. Some towns will enable a builder to sell the same house for a considerably lower price. Search out these towns.

5. Remember that tax and heating expenses go down the drain, because you can never get this money back. Be sure these expenses are as low as possible.

6. Make sure that the seller, or broker, is comparing the price he asks you to pay with the actual "sales prices" of recently sold similar houses in that area, and not quoting you the "asking prices" placed on those houses.

7. Always consider your chances of resale from the standpoint of both price and time.

8. If the house is on "open listing," and several brokers have it, then the owner can sell it to you direct. This is a privilege he gives up when he gives the "exclusive right to sell" his house to an exclusive broker.

9. Remember you cannot assume that once you inspect a house with, or through, one broker you can no longer buy it directly or through another broker. New Jersey now makes a broker commission unenforceable unless the sale actually took place. Massachusetts has just held that a purchase and sale agreement calling for a broker's commission cannot be enforced unless the sale actually took place. So check for this modern view in your state.

10. Never buy the house as soon as it comes on the market. The seller always allows himself a big lead in time and price.

11. When you see a "For Sale" sign by a broker don't be afraid to contact the owner direct. The chances are great that the broker has merely an "open" listing, or an expired exclusive.

12. Never let a seller or broker bluff you with untrue statements and claims. Always check him for truthfulness and accuracy.

13. The "pros" in the business know that buyers buy houses on an emotional basis. Try to restrain your emotions. Don't let yourself become carried away. Go back to reinspect the property several times. Each time you will see things that you did not notice before. These things could be important to you. Remember, you are buying "as is." So be sure you know what you are buying.

14. Be sure you are exposing yourself to the seller who insists on selling direct without a broker. Otherwise, you would be missing 27 percent of the market. Look for "Owner" ads in all the papers. Look for "For Sale by Owner" signs.

15. Always remember that while the seller and the broker are anxious to close the sale as quickly as possible, you are the one who will have to live in and pay for the house for many years to come.

16. Are you making allowances for a smaller or a larger family which may be in the cards for you, perhaps sooner than you ever imagined?

17. Is the area you have selected:
    a. close enough to your work?
    b. convenient enough to facilities for your wife and children?
    c. quiet enough for you?
    d. zoned to protect you?
    e. provided with the right schools and churches for your needs?
    f. in the path of growth and increasing value rather than in a direction destined to be by-passed and thus with decreasing value?
    g. free from infiltration of injurious influences?

18. You should always buy the house subject to a qualified appraisal value equal to the price you are paying.

19. Can you really afford the house? Remember, total housing expense means more than the often quoted bank payment of principal, interest and taxes. It also means insurance costs, heating costs, utilities costs, and costs for maintenance and repairs. Remember, too, that your total debt service is important. Obviously, if you are already overburdened with loan payments, car payments, tuition payments, etc., you may have less room for total housing expense than you think.

20. A great many people should buy a two-family house instead of the single that they actually buy. This one decision alone could well make

the difference in whether they ever get ahead financially, or spend their entire life in debt.

21. Never sign anything or turn over money without consulting your lawyer first. The layman cannot possibly imagine how heavily weighted and rigged most broker-drawn contracts of sale are in favor of the broker first, the seller second, with the buyer running a poor third. I have seen all too many of these contracts drawn by brokers so that the buyer cannot get out of the deal—no matter how much he may stand to lose—without the broker keeping his deposit. It is unbelievable that buyers would sign these unfair contracts, but they do.

Chapter 10

HOW TO MAKE AN OFFER AND BUY FOR LESS

It is an indisputable fact that most sales are made for less than the asking price. It is my contention that there are still many sales being made at the asking price which could be made for reduced prices, and that present reduced prices could be further reduced. Buyers get so excited when they finally see a house that they like, or one that they find at least tolerable, that they forget that the price is merely an asking price.

Of course, the seller is entitled to try to get the very highest price he possibly can. But it is equally true that the buyer is entitled to try to get the house for the lowest possible price. This lowest price should be his offer, not the highest possible price, which is the seller's asking price.

The buyer should always seek out the seller's bottom dollar. It is useful to work backwards from the broker's quote. If the price tag includes a $900 figure above a certain number of thousand dollars, remember the true gross price is usually at least $900 lower than the quoted price. And this gross figure still includes a full 6 percent commission for the broker. However, often there is still another one, or two, or even several thousand dollars that can still be lopped off the price. How can the buyer know?

One thing the buyer can do to probe for rock bottom is to make a low verbal offer. If the broker or seller is a fool, he will accept this low offer without insisting on a written statement to make it binding—and many of them *are* this foolish. The buyer now knows that he probably has not reached rock bottom yet. What the buyer should now do is to treat the verbal acceptance as a counter-offer. The buyer should take some time to consider this new low price, then come in at a still lower figure, or insist upon some further concessions. If the seller balks and will not accept, then the buyer should offer to compromise the difference, but giving in only $100 at a time, until he finally reaches the seller's bottom price.

If the seller or broker is smart enough not to tip his hand and reveal his bottom price for a mere verbal offer, then the buyer will have to come in with a written offer, which will become legally binding upon acceptance. This gives the seller some protection for revealing his lowest acceptable price. However, since it will become binding upon the seller's acceptance, the buyer must be certain that he has come in at the lowest possible figure.

Remember you can always come up a little more to gain acceptance. But once your written offer is accepted, you can no longer reduce the price.

Of course an offer can be revoked anytime before acceptance.

Another advantage in starting low enough with your offer is that each time you come up a little more, you have the opportunity to try to exact some further concession from the seller.

Many tough professional buyers leave themselves an out when making a written offer, which would otherwise become immediately binding upon the seller's acceptance. This out usually consists of a clause which makes the offer subject to unattainable financing, or to further inspection and approval, etc. The real reason for this out is that the buyer will not be satisfied that he ever did reach rock bottom price if the seller should accept his offer too easily. The buyer will then threaten to exercise his available out unless the seller gives him either a lower price or further concession.

The whole point is that too many amateur buyers give in too quickly and too easily to the first demand made by a seller or broker.

Buyers should remember that it is most important to buy right—at the very lowest possible price. It is better to keep looking rather than to pay a premium price. Few buyers realize just how low a seller or broker may actually go. It is a rare seller or broker, indeed, who will not cut his price. Furthermore, the seller or broker who gets his full price from the buyer often tends to consider the buyer somewhat of a fool rather than to respect him for being a good fellow.

Actually most buyers would be much better off if they paid a fee to a seasoned professional as a consultant, or to do their negotiating for them.

Chapter 11

YOUR DEPOSIT: HOW BIG IT SHOULD BE, HOW YOU CAN PROTECT IT

The sharp seller or seller's lawyer demands as big a deposit as he can with an agreement of sale favoring the seller all the way. This means that if the buyer defaults for any reason, the seller can keep the entire deposit, even though it may be several thousands of dollars. The buyer deserves a better break than this. Even the standard realtor agreement form calls for a forfeiture of the entire deposit to be split equally between the seller and the realtor in the event of the buyer's default.

Consequently, it is most important for the buyer to do two things. First, he must keep his deposit as small as the seller will let him. Second, he must make the deposit in a way that will give him the best chance of getting it back if trouble should arise.

We shall discuss the size of the deposit first. While some geographical areas have developed the custom of a 10 percent deposit, the general practice is that the seller is entitled to at least a $1,000. deposit in return for taking his house off the market. Good brokers will protect their principal's interest by demanding at least $1,000.

The point to remember is that it is not necessary for a buyer to tie up several thousand dollars on a deal which may never ultimately go through. Also, if the buyer does not have $1,000. on hand when he wishes to make his offer, it is quite acceptable practice for him to give a binder (earnest money) in a modest amount, anywhere from $200 down to even $25, if necessary. The broker simply fills in a standard offer form which provides for this type of situation by stating that if the offer is accepted, then the buyer will make an additional deposit of so many dollars. This additional amount to be made either upon acceptance, or upon a specified early date, should be an amount which would bring the total deposit up to at least $500.

As a general rule, it would be best all around for the buyer to put $1,000. on the line, along with the lowest offer that still makes common sense. At least, the seller and the broker both know he means business.

Now, as to protecting the deposit, the buyer should normally insist that the broker hold it in escrow. This prevents the seller from using it as deposit on the house he is buying. Also, it is safer to depend on the broker returning it, if necessary, rather than the seller. An average full-time, commercially located office will have an overhead of upwards of $1,000 per month, plus a capital investment of several thousand dollars. The broker's knowledge and experience are tied in with that area. He is not about to leave the area, as a seller is. Moreover, the broker is subject to pressure from your attorney, local business bureaus, chambers of commerce, broker associations and the State Licensing Board. Also the broker is bonded by law for $1,000. On top of all this, the broker must depend on a referral business and the goodwill of all those with whom he does business. On the other hand, the seller or the seller's attorney are normally not quite so vulnerable to pressure from the buyer or the buyer's attorney.

Buyers should always remember that in every case of a G.I. or F.H.A. transaction where either the house or the buyer fails to meet approval, the deposit does not necessarily have to be returned in full, by law. Actually, the public law states that the deposit should be handled in accordance with the terms of the agreement. Now, many, many crafty and overreaching brokers fail to protect the buyer with a proper and complete escape clause, which these buyers only assume that they are getting. However, when a buyer happens to be lucky enough to be dealing with a broker of integrity, or, better still, when the buyer has his lawyer draft his contract of sale, then he can get his deposit back if the G.I. or F.H.A. appraisal is less than the sale price. This is another reason why it makes a lot of sense for even a conventional buyer to avail himself of the protection offered by a V.A. or F.H.A. appraisal clause in his agreement of sale. Just be sure that the offer form as well as the agreement form recites the G.I., or F.H.A. escape clause—complete with an automatic return of buyer's deposit.

If the buyer is proceeding strictly on a conventional basis, that is, just a bank mortgage is involved with no V.A. guarantee or F.H.A. insurance to the bank, then the buyer must protect himself especially; otherwise, in case of his inability to perform, he will lose his deposit.

The conventional buyer can protect himself when making an offer by specifying that the offer is subject to the specific financing in terms of interest rate and number of years which he will require in order to be able to perform on "closing day."

When the buyer comes in with a low offer he is merely fishing to see for how little he can buy the house. He is being assured by the broker and seller that, in the event his offer becomes accepted, he will be "stealing" rather than buying the house. As this point, the buyer is in no position whatever to become completely and finally bound to the entire complicated transfer of the real estate by a mere acceptance of the offered price by the seller. There are certainly many more critical considerations than price alone in the purchase and sale of real estate. These other critically important matters should be fully treated in a complete, properly drafted purchase and sale agreement.

The buyer should protect himself when making an offer and deposit by reciting in the offer form that "this offer, if accepted, is subject to the formation of a full and complete purchase and sale agreement, mutually acceptable to both parties."

Chapter 12

WHAT SHOULD BE IN THE PURCHASE AND SALE AGREEMENT

The Statute of Frauds requires every real estate agreement to be in writing in order to be enforceable. Therefore, the following clauses should appear in every agreement:

1. The buyer should insure that he will be getting as much land as he expects. Since most buyers do not know for a fact that the approximate total square feet recited in the agreement actually measure up to what they think, or were led to believe, they will be getting, a special clause should be inserted to protect the buyer, such as: "The actual delineations of the boundary lines shall coincide with existing fences in the rear and on either side." This clause would cut down the numerous boundary dispute cases and guarantee that the buyer will actually get as much land as he thinks he is going to get. It is a fair clause, and should be in every agreement.

2. All appliances, furnishings and anything which might be considered to be personal property which the buyer expects to get should be spelled out in the agreement, so that he will wind up with as much house as he expects.

3. The purchase price must be subject to the buyer's ability to arrange the specific financing he will require; that is, the amount of the mortgage which will be needed, plus the rate of interest needed, plus the number of years required. This will guarantee that the buyer will actually have as many dollars as he thinks he will have in order to perform on closing day.

4. If it is important for the buyer to close by a certain date the

following clause must be inserted: "Time is of the essence of this contract." Otherwise the seller might be entitled to an extension of time which could be costly to you. Provision for specific damages in the event of delay should also be provided.

5. Since a suit in equity for specific performance against a defaulting seller is not always the most practical solution for a buyer, the following clause should be used: "If the seller defaults, he agrees to pay (a specific amount of damages—usually as much as or double the buyer's deposit)." Unfortunately, most sellers will refuse to sign this clause—fair as it is. They are simply spoiled by the custom that has grown for a defaulting buyer to lose at least his deposit, if not more; while the defaulting seller rarely has to do more than return the buyer's deposit. Most pre-printed contracts of sale are too one-sided in this regard and need to be changed to at least require the seller to use reasonable efforts to perform on closing day.

6. The buyer should insist that the seller keep the premises insured until closing day in an amount equal to the sale price. The seller's existing insurance protection probably only equals the amount of his old original mortgage—usually much lower than the present sale price. At the very least the insurance clause should read, "sufficient to protect buyer." Just be careful of the usual seller's clause which reads, "as now insured." Most pre-printed contract of sale forms give the seller the election, in case of fire, of turning over the insurance proceeds to the buyer or restoring the premises. Restoration does not require the seller to replace anything new in a house that is not new. Thus, the seller actually winds up with the chance to give the buyer the insurance proceeds when they are not enough, or restore second hand and pocket the difference when the insurance proceeds are high. Accordingly, the buyer must at least have the protection of the following clause: "in the event of fire or casualty damage exceeding $3,000 (or some reasonable minimum) the buyer shall have the election of cancelling this contract and receiving his deposit back without recourse to either party."

7. A "possession" clause should protect the buyer against the seller who holds over illegally, after the closing date. This clause should provide for per diem damages equal to the buyer's out-of-pocket costs, plus some penalty to make it unattractive for a seller to linger on the premises beyond the closing date. This clause should also excuse the buyer from performance in the absence of immediate access to the premises.

8. Every buyer should be protected with a clause guaranteeing him that, "when he moves in all appliances shall be in working order, the heating system shall work effectively to all parts of the house which are alleged to be heated, that the plumbing and wiring systems conform to

the local building codes and are free from major defects, all windows shall function, that the roof shall be free of leaks, and the basement free of water seepage."

9. In the event of a brand-new house, the remaining work to be done and all other responsibilities of the builder should be carefully spelled out in detail, with provision for specific damages in the event of default. This will nullify the builder's claims that you agreed to forgo various needed work due to a price concession, or that "after all the builder does not insure the house."

10. All parties who will have to sign the deed must sign the agreement to sell, otherwise no power on earth can make them sign the deed.

Minimum as the above protections are, some of them are normally absent from the usual purchase and sale agreement. In addition, for each individual case, any number of other contingencies should properly be provided for. Hence the importance of the next chapter.

Chapter 13

WHEN YOU NEED YOUR LAWYER: WHY YOU NEED A REAL ESTATE COUNSELLOR

Ninety percent of your problems as a buyer or seller must be solved before you can logically go to your lawyer. For these problems you need a real estate counsellor, not a lawyer. This is because your lawyer is expected to know the law, but he is not presumed to have specialized knowledge of real estate problems, and normally does not possess such practical knowledge and experience.

Furthermore, most buyers secure mortgage money to help them buy and the lending institutions taking the mortgages insist upon their own attorney searching the titles and preparing closings.

Therefore, your lawyer can help you as purchaser in only one area of your many problems, and usually only at one time. This is not to minimize the absolute importance of using your lawyer, for you need him at a vitally critical period in your negotiations with the seller and the broker. It is of paramount importance that you see your lawyer before signing any offer you make, which might bind you immediately upon acceptance by the seller and possibly cost you your deposit, or, even worse, force you to go through with a deal to your great disadvantage. This is because a contract is formed the instant of acceptance. While it is possible for you to revoke your offer any time before acceptance, once the seller accepts, you become bound. Only a fool would make such an offer without having his lawyer check it to insure proper protection, in the event it should become accepted and a binding contract ensue.

As we noted before, any proper offer form calls for the parties to enter promptly into an agreement of sale. Since the law grants the extraordinary remedy of "specific performance" for a purchase and sale agreement for real estate, it is again imperative for you to have your lawyer review it before you sign it.

Few buyers go to their lawyer before signing the agreement. This puzzles me, because I can't readily think of a more important time for one to consult one's attorney. Most buyers who run into trouble see their lawyer for the first time after they get hurt, when it is often too late.

But—what about the 90 percent or more of your difficulties, ranging from appraisal to zoning? All important problems, such as: whether you are getting into the right neighborhood, whether the house you picked really suits your needs, whether you are getting fair market value for the price you are paying, the best financing available to you, resale value, whether your buyer is actually going to be able to perform on closing day, and a score of other vitally important questions you face as a buyer or seller. If the average lawyer cannot be expected to answer these questions competently, who can? A relatively small percentage of properly trained, qualified and experienced brokers possess this kind of specialized knowledge and ability. If you are not dealing with this kind of broker, you should be. You need a qualified real estate counsellor. The ideal real estate counsellor would be a worthy broker, attorney, and appraiser all wrapped in the same person. In most cases, the best you can hope for is a good broker. Obviously, then, you must make separate use of an experienced real estate attorney, plus a competent, qualified appraiser.

Beware of the broker who tells you that you do not need an attorney or an appraiser.

The code of ethics of the National Association of Real Estate Boards includes a duty upon all Realtor members to never advise a client against the use of an attorney in any real estate transaction. One of the official rules and regulations of the Massachusetts Board of Registration of Real

Estate Brokers and Salesmen reads as follows: "No broker or salesman shall advise against the use of the services of an attorney in any real estate transaction."

Chapter 14

HOW TO GET THE BEST FINANCING AVAILABLE

The first question you must answer is whether you should buy through G.I., F.H.A., or conventional financing. Since the rates, terms, and regulations may vary quite rapidly and suddenly, you must depend for advice on this matter from a competent broker or bank mortgage officer.

You should know that each bank has its own policy as to terms and types of mortgages it will take. The bank is quick to change this policy depending upon the availability of its funds. Once you have properly made this decision as to which of the three methods of financing is best suited to your needs and qualifications, do not be bluffed into a change by a broker, or seller, who prefers a different method. Many times the seller or broker knows full well that a particular house would never measure up to a G.I. or F.H.A. appraisal, especially at the price asked. In these cases, you are told that you must make a large down payment and go "conventional." Even if you can afford to do this, are you not much better off at least to know that the government appraisal apparatus believes you are getting fair market value for your money?

It is not enough for you to merely get mortgage money, after you make a very substantial down payment. The fact that the bank feels it has a wide enough safety margin, and that your credit is excellent, does not guarantee that you are getting fair market value. You need an appraisal.

Under normal market conditions, many banks pay a one percent finder's fee to the broker. It is only natural for a broker to channel your mortgage to such a bank. However, often you could get a better interest rate, or better terms, such as "no penalty charges for early payment," if you yourself were to go to your bank where you are known as a depositor or a mortgagor. Some bank attorneys charge less than others for closing costs. The point to remember is that the choice of the bank and the method of financing are your prerogatives. Never let a seller or broker bluff you out of the best possible choice for you.

The only safe thing to do is to check a few different banks and ask them questions. Remember, the broker takes his commission and moves on to the next one, and the seller takes his money and moves away. You are the one who must stay and pay that mortgage through hell and high water for a long time to come. You are entitled to the best rate in terms for *you*, not for the seller or the broker. Remember that in the final analysis you must expect that the seller is primarily concerned with the best deal all around for him, especially as to the certainty and swiftness of your financing, so that he can get his money as soon as possible.

The broker, quite naturally, feels the same way. You must be sure that you do not wind up losing a great deal of money over the years of your mortgage because they were on the ball and you were not, especially in this matter of financing.

A few points to remember are:

1. Normally you can't beat G.I. financing. Check with the V.A. to see if you are entitled to it. Many more people than realize it may avail themselves of this government munificence. Others besides the veteran himself can sign the mortgage deed and note, and become part owners on the deed. Those veterans who have used only part of their entitlement, or who are included for the first time by recent expansions of the law, should be sure to contact the V.A. for particulars.

2. In periods of high rates for conventional mortgages, F.H.A. financing is excellent for the buyer. The trick is to keep looking until you find a bank that will take an F.H.A. mortgage without charging a substantial bonus payment for the privilege. F.H.A. financing is, of course, one-half of one percent higher than V.A. financing, the extra one-half of one percent going to Washington. Also, F.H.A. charges one percent for prepayment or if resold within ten years to a non F.H.A. buyer.

3. While many banks will not be bothered handling V.A. or F.H.A. mortgages or both, there are always some banks in every area who will. It is important for you to know that while most banks who will take these mortgages will want several bonus points for accepting the lower interest rate, invariably some one good bank in your area will grant a V.A. mortgage to a veteran without charging any extra points. A "point" is one per cent of the face amount of the mortgage, paid one time as part of the closing costs. Banks have it figured out on special tables that each point they charge to grant these special low interest loans makes up for ⅛ of one per cent interest.

Few buyers appear to realize that many times the banks have escalation clauses in their mortgage instrument which permit them at their discretion to increase the interest rate on the mortgage at any time in the future. Fortunately most banks have not exercised this prerogative. However, the important thing for the buyer to know is that it is likely to be in the fine print—he should read it, he should be aware of it, and he should ascertain for himself whether or not the particular bank handling his closing has actually increased its rates on existing mortgages in the past. Some banks do.

The most important thing of all for you always to keep in mind about financing is that the banks treat each mortgage application on an individual basis. The bank considers all pertinent information regarding each individual property and each individual buyer before making a decision on the particular application. In periods of tight money local banks still try their very best to take care of local residents, veterans, present depositors, and present mortgage holders.

Dedicated, sincere bank mortgage officers recommend that an applicant check a few different banks to be certain that he is getting the best bank for his particular needs.

Chapter 15

THE CLOSING AND CLOSING COSTS

After sitting in on a couple of thousand closings, I find that a few things stand out as worthy of note. I mention them here in the hope that more buyers and sellers will thus be better prepared for ever-increasing actual closing costs. I am convinced that, at present, few people fully realize all that actually took place at their closing.

First, it should be understood that while banks, their closing attorneys, the F.H.A. and the V.A. usually make a technical distinction between closing costs and prepayable expense items, such as advance tax payments etc., the buyer is primarily interested in the total cash he is called upon to part with.

The buyer's total costs would normally include the bank attorney's fees for the title search, preparation of papers, etc. Previously, you could allow roughly one percent of the amount of the mortgage for this. Now, the schedule of fees has been revised by The Massachusetts Conveyancer's Association as follows:

Amount of Mortgage	Fee Rate Per Thousand
up to $10,000.00	$15.00
$10,000.00–$15,000.00	$10.00 additional
$15,000.00–$30.000.00	$ 5.00 additional
$30,000.00 and up	$ 2.50 additional
Minimum Fee is $85.00	

(Thus, for example, a $25,000.00 mortgage would be computed as follows: $150.00 for the first $10,000.00 plus $50.00 for the next $5,000.00, plus $50.00 for the last $10,000.00 of mortgage.)

Fees for examination of title to registered land are usually three-quarters of those for unregistered land; minimum charge $75.

However, since each bank sets its own policy, or permits its closing attorneys to set their individual charges, you must ask the attorney selected for your closing, in advance, what his charges will be so you will not be surprised on closing day. Also banks today are demanding plot plans which show the location of the house on the lot. The buyer should be sure to get his copy of this drawing for his own personal records. Banks usually charge between $25 and $50 for this. The bank attorney must get a "Certificate of Municipal Liens" from the local city or town hall, to be sure that there are no outstanding taxes, or water bills, etc. The charge for this certificate is usually $3. On a conventional mortgage the bank will want three months taxes paid in advance, so that it can pay the full year's tax bill to the town on October 1 of each year. Of course, in some towns the taxes are paid November 1 instead of October 1, so then the bank would only need to collect two month's taxes in advance at the closing in order to have enough money to pay the tax for the full year. With the growing pinch for money in the cities and towns, many of them are collecting taxes every six months; for example, collecting on April 1 for the first six months of taxes due, and on October 1 for the last six month period. Effective July 1, 1975 in Massachusetts, under new law the banks must pay their mortgagors interest on this tax escrow money. On an F.H.A. mortgage this advance tax payment could run as high as four months or more due to the lead time it takes to get an F.H.A. mortgage on the billing cycle, and the day of the month or time of the year the closing takes place. The buyer is expected to have a fire insurance binder for at least as much as the amount of the mortgage. In F.H.A. cases, the buyer needs a paid premium receipt for the first year in addition to the binder. It is the practice of insurance brokers to

31

accommodate with these policy binders, and even paid receipts for first-year premiums, before they actually issue the policy itself, bill and collect for it. Of course, the buyer is expected to pay for any fuel oil the seller leaves in his tank. Often there are extra charges for items of personal property which the buyer wishes to buy from the seller. These things could be and sometimes are handled separately by the seller and buyer. The buyer pays about $10 to have his deed recorded and $10 to record the mortgage on the public records. Some banks require a security committee fee which usually varies between $15 and $50, as well as a credit report fee between $4 and $10. All other items are adjusted by appointment.

The buyer is expected to have a bank check, certified check or cash for the balance of his cash down payment; that is, the difference between the price, less the deposit, and the mortgage. His closing costs may be paid by personal check or cash.

It is important for the buyer to have his spouse at the closing, if he is married, even though the buyer may be putting the deed in his or her name alone. The bank taking the mortgage wants both the husband and wife to sign the mortgage deed and the mortgage note.

It is worth noting that although the buyer pays for the services of the bank attorney, the attorney is responsible only to the bank, and not to the buyer. For this reason some buyers like to have their own personal attorney at the closing, or pay a token amount to the bank attorney and ask him to look out for their interest as well as the bank's. In about 90 percent of the cases, buyers are not represented by any attorney having any responsibility towards them. Due to the efficiency and integrity of bank attorneys, everything normally works out perfectly well for these buyers, but not always. Moreover, as pointed out earlier, and will be explained later, the buyer desperately needs his personal attorney at the time he first signs an "offer" or a "contract of sale," and when he turns over money to a broker or seller.

As to the seller's cost and responsibilities, he must, of course, give a deed to the buyer. The seller may of course elect to have his own personal attorney draw his deed, whether or not he has his own attorney at the closing. The charge for representing the seller in a sale is usually one percent of the amount of the sales price up to $30,000, and upwards of this amount by agreement. Of course, the seller really needs his attorney at the beginning, before he signs "accepted" to an "offer" or a "contract of sale" and accepts money or allows his broker to accept a deposit from a buyer. The seller must know, as will be explained more fully later, before he takes his house off the market that he is properly protected against both a defaulting buyer or a selfish broker.

The seller does not have to be at the closing. He may sign his deed in advance, and arrange to be represented. The seller normally pays the broker's commission, the amount of which is a matter of agreement between the parties.

When a seller refuses to budge one inch, and a buyer is absolutely limited in his ability to pay, the broker gets caught in a bind whereby he winds up having to absorb all disparities and deficiencies which may arise, such as: low governmental appraisal, inability of buyer to meet unanticipated high closing costs, the difference between the seller's price and the buyer's offer, assumption of special expenses to get a delayed deal closed before the agreement expires, etc. Most brokers will sacrifice part of the commission rather than lose the deal altogether, and cause undue hardship to one or both of the parties. But it is extremely unfair for any seller, buyer or attorney to expect a broker to make this type of concession. Contrary to popular belief, the broker normally has earned his commission twice over in time, effort, expense and overhead. NEW FEDERAL RESPA INFORMATION IS INSERTED AT THE END OF THE SUPPLEMENT AT END OF PART I OF THIS BOOK.

Chapter 16

HOW TO BUY A MULTIPLE DWELLING

Many people buying a single house cannot really afford it, or in order to pay the total cost of keeping it, strap themselves to the point where they will never become financially independent. Others are presently shut out of the single house market due to low income. These two segments of the market should join those wise people who are already buying and profiting from two-, three- and four-family houses.

The following tips should be helpful:

1. Deal with a broker who has sufficient listings and experience with multiple dwellings.

2. As a general rule, you are better off with a conventional building, that is, one built for the purpose, rather than a converted single house.

3. Heat and utilities should be separate for each tenant.

4. Use fair economic rentals for the area as a guide to fair market value, rather than the actual rentals, which may be abnormally high or low.

5. Be sure to allow for higher cost for maintenance, insurance, repairs, and vacancy.

6. You may allow for lower heat and utility costs if these expenses are separate for your tenants, as they should be. Your tax load will always be lighter than in a single house.

7. You should normally raise tenants' rents only a small amount, say $15.00 at a time to discourage turnover of tenants which is always costly.

8. A good, helpful tenant is entitled to a lower rental.

9. The F.H.A., or V.A. will help you to buy a multiple up to four units, with lower down payments. However, if you do not actually reside in the multiple, you are entitled to only 85 percent of the normal F.H.A. insured mortgage. Remember, the F.H.A. is trying to help the homeowner, and should not be expected to finance nonresident speculator investors. The V.A. has no provision for a nonresident buyer.

10. Always try to buy in an area where the demand exceeds the supply so you will not experience a resale problem, and your investment will be sure to appreciate.

11. You must be more careful than you are with a single in your inspection of heating, wiring, plumbing, and overall condition of both exterior and interior. If you are not an expert yourself, you should have an expert check these things for you. Always make your offer subject to the inspection and approval of this expert.

12. Be extremely careful that the building conforms:
   a. to zoning ordinances
   b. to building codes
   c. to bank, F.H.A., or V.A. location requirements for mortgage purposes. Many towns today have the same strict regulations for in-law apartments as they do for two-families.

13. If it is only a two- or three-family house, be sure your apartment is big enough for your subsequent needs. A two- or three-family house normally does not appraise out for an absentee owner. This is due to the high expense to income ratio for a nonresident owner.

14. The ideal location for a two-family house is different from that for a single house. You will need to be more centrally located and handy to public transportation, stores, schools and churches. Your tenants will require and demand these facilities.

15. Never accept a verbal agreement which is a mere nullity at law.

16. No matter how good the deal may look always protect yourself

with a clause which will give you an out if you need it, due to inability to obtain financing, or for any other reason.

17. Never, never be in any haste to buy, and never accept the seller's first price. This marks you as a novice. Set a price in your mind and do not vary from it, unless the seller is also willing to compromise.

18. Do not be afraid of property that needs some upgrading. Many fine buys are made in this way. However, if this is your first purchase, be wary of property that needs extensive repairs. In time you will become experienced enough to buy this type of property and find it to be very profitable. But you must be able to get financing, which is most difficult to come by on multiples in poor condition. Also, you must be able to make some repairs yourself, or else be an astute enough bargainer to contract the work yourself, and still come out ahead.

Many fortunes have been made in real estate. For the average person, whether educated or not, this can sometimes be the quickest way to a fortune. If you are faint-hearted, keep your money in the bank. However, the foreclosure rate is something like 400 to 1 in your favor. What other business offers you such favorable odds?

Chapter 17

IF YOU ARE NOT FINDING THE HOUSE YOU NEED

If you have been using the previous chapters of this book as a guide and have still not found the right house for you, the following tips should be helpful.

Perhaps you are just a "looker" and do not intend to buy just at this time. You could be influenced by a spouse, family, in-laws, etc., who do not really want you to buy, so they are sure to find some fault with every place you find.

If you are really sincere about buying, chances are you will have to pay more to find the house you want. Start looking in a higher price bracket. Every thousand or two increase in price means a large number of additional houses opened up to you. A lower tax bill may more than offset a higher price in your total monthly bank payment. You may get a thirty-year mortgage if you go V.A. or F.H.A. Also conventional mortgages are now available for 30 years at some banks. Again, the lower monthly payment will enable you to raise your price sights. After all, the average mortgage, today, only lasts for about six years.

Offer a cash bonus to each broker or salesman serving you. Remember, he normally has twenty times more prospects than he can properly serve. It is up to you to convince him that you mean ready cash to him. If possible make him understand you are a conventional, fast buyer with a big cash down payment, and easy to finance.

Consider new areas. Get more brokers working for you. Run an ad under "Real Estate Wanted." This will attract more brokers as well as owners selling direct.

If you have been limiting yourself to new houses only, start considering the advantages and savings of a modern house already broken in, or even a fine older home that has been modernized.

If you have been afraid of brand-new houses, don't be. Generally speaking, modern building codes, materials and techniques provide for a better built and more functional house than those of yesteryear. Besides, it is always easier to finance a new home.

Never forget that in a good area, demand far exceeds the supply, and listings are extremely scarce. You must still have the patience to keep looking in the good areas even though the going is a lot tougher. In the end you will have a sounder investment, while you are enjoying more amenities.

Chapter 18

HOW TO FIND THE RIGHT BUYER AND SELL FOR MORE PROFIT

Everything will depend on just how good a buy you are offering to the public. If your house is well located on a good lot without site problems, in a good neighborhood, free of structural weakness, in good condition both outside and inside, has three good size bedrooms, more than one bath, a modern kitchen, a large fire-placed living room, a formal dining room or large enough formal dining area, a finished playroom or family room, a garage, low taxes, is under ten years of age, is appraised by a qualified appraiser and priced at the fair market value, and you are in a town where demand exceeds the supply, your house will sell the day you place your ad or put your sign on the front lawn. You will probably even save a broker's commission.

However, if any one or more of the foregoing conditions is absent, you need not one broker, but as many worthy brokers as you can get to help you, in your town and in the surrounding towns.

Every broker and seller of a house knows that 95 percent or more of the buyers who answer their ad are destined to be greatly disappointed once they see the house. The reason for this is that buyers' needs and desires are so complicated and highly evolved that only the extraordinary house could possibly satisfy them. How is it then that so many houses are sold?

This is where salesmanship comes in. And this is why the worthy broker will always be sorely needed, just as any other middleman in any business transaction. The broker who has screened his prospect, has already shown him the house he answered the ad on, plus some other more suitable houses for the buyer's actual needs, begins to know the buyer and his problems well enough to be able ultimately to steer the right buyer to your house.

Your house probably will not answer all of even this selected buyer's requirements. But the broker has prepared the buyer in advance to accept your deal as the best one available at the time, in the area, for his needs. When the buyer begins to discount for the shortcomings of your house and makes a low offer, it is the broker who is in the best position to explain why the offer will have to be higher to have any chance at all for acceptance.

The good broker is a skilled negotiator; he has tact, diplomacy, sales talent, experience, the know-how to bring a buyer to an acceptable price. He knows and can prove fair market value. This enables him to convince you, the seller, to forget about your original, inflated, unrealistic asking price, and accept a fair market price which still gives you a fair profit, even after paying a commission to the broker.

Normally, you cannot do the negotiating with the buyer, yourself, as well as the broker can. In fact, surveys prove that in an urban area you get more money for yourself on an average when you deal through a broker. This is the main reason why three quarters of all sellers use brokers.

Here are some of the reasons why the broker can accomplish the difficult feat of selling at a profit to you when you may not be able to do so for yourself.

1. You are too emotionally involved.

2. You are "up on cloud nine" thinking of your neighbors' asking prices rather than what they actually sold their houses for.

3. You reveal the weak points of your house to a buyer, out of a feeling of guilt, and fear of subsequent reprisal or law suits.

4. You just don't know how to build up the value higher than the price before you ask the buyer to buy.

5. You do not know how to show your house to its best advantage.

6. You do not know whether your buyer can really afford the house, or whether he has any real chance of getting a conventional mortgage, or F.H.A. or G.I. approval.

7. You would probably tie your house up, take it off the market for long periods of time, for minimum deposits by hopeless buyers.

8. You do not have the time to do the job right, yourself.

9. The right buyer for your house probably will never answer your ad. He will have to be steered to you most times by another person, usually a broker, and sometimes from another town.

If you do not use enough good brokers, and make it interesting for them to keep plugging for you when the market is on the closed side, and financing is practically unavailable, you will probably lose a great deal of time and money in one of the following ways:

1. Your overpriced house will become shopworn, a white elephant on the market.

2. Hundreds of lookers, curious neighbors, etc. will drive you to distraction without one single bona fide offer.

3. Eventually, some shrewd buyer will get you to reveal your rock bottom price, verbally only. Then he will come in with a written offer, and deposit, at a still lower figure which you simply cannot afford to take. If the buyer cannot accomplish this directly, he will trick you into this impossible bargaining position through the use of confederates.

4. Sorehead brokers will use your house for a football, even going out of their way to knock it while showing buyers in your area.

5. The time may come when you have to "close" on your new house and continue to support the old one. Your problems and expenses now multiply themselves.

6. You have changed your position and are relying on a hopeless buyer. Now you are really in trouble.

7. The buyer insists on a price "less the broker's commission" because you are dealing direct and saving the commission. So all your time, expenses, and effort were wasted, at best.

8. You gave up the "exclusive right to sell" your house for too long a period of time, maybe with even an automatic extension of time in fine print—to the wrong broker.

9. Some broker has a "hot" buyer for your house. The only trouble is the broker who holds the "exclusive right to sell" refuses to share his

commission with him. The exclusive broker believes the paramount issue is that he receive a "full" commission, not that your house must be sold, as soon as possible, to the best possible buyer, at the highest possible price.

10. You can finally sell the house, yourself, on acceptable terms, but your "exclusive" broker, or "multiple listing," will not release you from their exclusive contract, and by the time you pay them 6 percent, you can not afford to sell it yourself to your own buyer.

All of this brings us to the importance of the next chapter.

Chapter 19

HOW TO LIST WITH WORTHY BROKERS AND AVOID THE "CON ARTIST"

The foregoing chapter served to point up the necessity for you to list your house on the right terms, and only with brokers whose ability and integrity can be depended upon.

Remember, even after you go into an "agreement of sale," your problems really just start. The following list includes a few of the more commonplace problems that come up between the time of agreement of sale and the closing:

1. Several banks refuse to agree to the price, the buyer, the terms, or the house itself.

2. The F.H.A. or V.A. appraiser comes in so much lower in evaluation than your sales price that you and the buyer might just as well be dealing from the earth to the moon.

3. Zoning or building code problems rear their ugly head.

4. Boundary disputes crop up.

5. Either you or the buyer were less than completely truthful in your representations. Now you are in trouble.

6. You become extended to the point where you just plain need help. Or your buyer needs help.

Will your broker still stand by you, and see the sale through to a conclusion in the face of hardships, loss of time, and the personal sacrifice of a considerable sum of money? Unfortunately, too many brokers just will not measure up to this test. So, very late in the game for you, suddenly you find that your house is not really sold at all.

The kind of broker you want working for you is the broker who is glad to get your listing, and will advertise it, and show it, and try to sell it for you, even though you retain control over it yourself. You should not have to give an exclusive right to sell to a broker, either for himself alone, or for purposes of getting it on multiple listing, unless you are trying to milk an overprice out of it, or the house has some serious drawbacks. The only exceptions to this rule would be:

1. You cannot or do not want to be bothered with the selling effort even if it costs you some money.

2. Your house is so unusual in size, style, or price that no broker can afford to be bothered with it unless he has an exclusive listing.

3. You want to help a broker friend even if it costs you some time or money.

Give an "open listing" to any good broker who deserves it. This arrangement ripens into a contract, legally, only when the broker finds a buyer ready, willing and able to buy on the terms of the listing, or when you "accept" the broker's customer at a lower figure.

The moment the house becomes sold by the first broker who is the "efficient procuring cause of the sale," or by yourself, all other brokers are automatically fired. It is common courtesy to let them know, but you are under no legal obligation to do so.

Some shrewd sellers give the brokers a "net listing." This means that the broker must guarantee the seller a certain net amount out of the proceeds of the sale. The big advantage to the seller is that when the broker's customer comes in with a low offer, the broker realizes that he alone must suffer the loss, as the net amount to the seller is both fixed and guaranteed in advance.

Since most sales are made as a result of offers made under the listing price, and most sellers still pay the full 6 percent commission out of this lower sale price, it is easy to see why the net listing is better for the seller, while the open listing is better for the broker. However, some unscrupulous brokers have used the "net" listing to take advantage of ignorant or desperate sellers, and it has now become illegal in some states.

Now, the con artist is the broker who comes to your house for a listing and brazenly lies to you. He will tell you that he belongs to an association, and that under the rules of his group of brokers he is obliged to accept only exclusive listings for a minimum of sixty or ninety days. Or, he gets you to sign an "exclusive right to sell" your house over to him, while leading you to believe that you are signing a paper permitting a large number of additional brokers to sell your house.

Never forget that a great many brokers who have permission to sell your house under a so-called multiple listing arrangement will never equal the combined effort of a few well-chosen brokers who actually took the listing themselves. The reasons are:

1. That these multiple listing brokers may never actually get to see your house. They cannot sell what they have not even seen.

2. Brokers do not relish working for half a commission.

3. Brokers' salesmen are not eager to work for half of a half commission.

4. Too many brokers will put only their "dogs" on multiple listing. The best of them usually want a little time, all to themselves, at the full commission, on a house that they believe can actually be sold at the price.

5. Moreover, in spite of the fact that some good buys do go into multiple listing, and that overpriced houses actually do eventually sell at much lower and realistic prices, many buyers are so sophisticated that they order the broker not to show them multiple listings on the mistaken notion that they are all dogs, or all overpriced.

6. Buyers do not like to be taken to the same houses by every broker they visit. They hope that each new broker will have something different, or a new to the market listing to show them.

Multiple listing works out very well in some areas where it is clearly understood and appreciated, and all the brokers put all their houses into it and honestly support it.

Chapter 20

HOW TO KNOW IF THE BROKER IS REALLY TRYING TO HELP YOU

First, you should evaluate the broker's attitude. The paramount issue, after all, is that your house must be sold, not that he must be guaranteed to receive a full commission from you. Accordingly, he should be more than willing to try to sell your house whether or not you favor him with an "exclusive right to sell."

You can advertise your house yourself; you can quote a lower price than the broker and the magic word "owner" should produce results. The main reason you are giving a listing to this broker is to reach his ready-made file of waiting customers.

Check him on the following things:

1. Is he advertising your house? If not, be sure to complain.

2. Is he screening his buyers? Listen to their remarks and you can tell. If he is not, register protest.

3. Is he explaining the right price for your house to you?

4. Check with someone he shows your house to as to what price he is actually quoting to the buyers.

5. Determine if he is merely showing your house or if he is really trying to sell it when he shows it.

6. If you give him an exclusive, check him through a friend to see if he is willing to "co-broke"; that is, share his commission with another broker who thinks he has a sure buyer.

7. If you give him an exclusive to get it on multiple listing, be sure you date the contract when you sign it. Don't let him keep it to himself for a while before he dates it and sends it to headquarters. It will take about a week anyway before all the other brokers on the circuit get the full information on your house. Make him promise to advertise in the big-city paper. Be sure that he will invite his fellow brokers to come at once to a special showing by him for the purpose of insuring that the other brokers will know why they should concentrate on your house.

8. If you have given him an open listing, put a For Sale sign up if he does not. Don't keep your house a secret from someone who might buy it from you direct, or prevent other brokers, who may have a ready buyer for you, from knowing that you are selling. As you now know, on an open listing basis you are free to sell the house yourself, or hire any other broker you want to.

9. If you give him the exclusive right to sell your house so that you can no longer sell it yourself, or hire any other agent during the term of the exclusive, be sure he posts a For Sale sign. No one else may. The sign may cause the sale. The broker may not want to post the sign, for fear that some buyer might wait until the exclusive is up to approach you directly, or that other brokers will find out your house is for sale and also get the listing when the exclusive is terminated.

10. If you give him a multiple exclusive, be sure his sign carries the additional multiple listing notice. You are entitled to this service. He should be protecting you; you should not be protecting him.

11. Does he report to you after showing your house, so you know what the buyers think? He should do this. It is important. After all, in the final analysis, you can only get for the house what some buyer is willing to pay. Also, you may be able to take corrective steps, if you know what the buyer reaction is. Never, never let a con man broker extend you to such a point that you are forced to accept a low offer which you really cannot afford.

12. If the broker asks you to suffer with an unexpectedly low offer, ask him what he is willing to do for you.

Chapter 21

BROKER TRICKS YOU SHOULD RECOGNIZE AND AVOID

The following is merely a partial listing of the more common tricks practiced by the high pressure boys, the con artists, the rascals and the rogues. Regrettably, many established brokers, apparently big, impressive and successful, operating behind various shields of respectability such as association memberships and alleged codes of ethics, are apt to try these same tricks whenever and wherever they think they can get away with them.

1. The tricky broker will offer to list your house only if you give up your right to sell it yourself. This privilege, whenever granted, should only be extended by you to a worthy broker—never *demanded* by the broker.

2. He goes right along with your price, even though you know you are starting far above fair market value. This rascal is not being duped by you into spending his time and money to find you a sucker. He simply intends to let you suffer a while, keep other brokers from really trying to sell your overpriced house, then break the price when he has an offer. This rogue does not want your house on the market at a salable price for fear some other broker will sell it ahead of him. In similar cases, where the seller is actually ignorant of the true market value, he may mistakenly think this self-serving broker is his friend.

3. He pretends that he is trying to sell your house at your price, when all he ever does is to beg for a low offer.

4. When he knows you are really extended, and over the barrel, he will encourage the buyer to come in with a low offer, assuring him that you will have to accept it.

5. He will not co-broke your listing and share his commission with a fellow broker, when he knows that broker has a buyer who will be sure to buy your house.

6. You never gave him an exclusive but he takes it anyway by putting a Sold sign on your house with a $5 binder from a shaky, undecided buyer.

7. His exclusive has run out but he leaves his sign there just the same to mislead other brokers or direct buyers into thinking that his exclusive is still in effect.

8. He puts automatic continuations—in fine print—in his exclusive contracts.

9. The bad broker ties you to a multiple listing exclusive for a minimum of sixty days, then sells you short in the following ways:

    a. Instead of you getting the kind of big advertising and promotion you expect, you actually receive an occasional blurb in the local newspaper.

    b. The other allegedly contributing brokers are not even invited, by your listing broker who gets your exclusive, to come and inspect the house themselves. No wonder that you sometimes are discouraged by the inactivity that follows. Of course there are many good brokers who use multiple listing exclusives properly to help the seller sell his house faster through wider exposure.

10. He knocks your house to every buyer who is foolish enough to listen to him because you favored a competitor with an "exclusive listing."

11. He knocks a harder working, more qualified and more successful broker for fear you may give that better broker the listing, too. The one thing the phony broker and trickster can't stand is competition!

12. He keeps you ignorant of problems that arise for fear you will dump him or his buyer.

13. He uses a phony direct buyer to smoke out your rock bottom price.

For the above reasons and many more, while you need the help of all the good brokers you can find, you certainly cannot afford the hindrance and irreparable harm you will suffer from bad brokers. You must make it your business to detect the difference between them.

Chapter 22

BUYER TRICKS YOU SHOULD RECOGNIZE AND AVOID

Shrewd buyers try to steal a house rather than buy it. They offer less than they are prepared and willing to pay. Consequently, a seller should never accept in haste, and never the buyer's first offer when it is unexpectedly low. Some unscrupulous buyers send confederates along in advance for two reasons: first to find out your bottom price with offers so low they do not expect you to accept them; and secondly to find you through a broker, then subsequently deal with you direct to save the broker commission. Be careful that the buyer does not have unacceptable and unfair escape clauses in his agreement such as:

1. Subject to inspection and approval, without reasonable time limits.
2. Subject to the sale of the buyer's house.
3. Subject to unobtainable financing.

The buyer is apt to use a V.A. or F.H.A. appraisal for the sole purpose of beating you down in price. These appraisals do tend to be somewhat lower than sale prices in a rising market.

He uses delaying tactics to get you extended to the point where he can now force a lower price or other concessions from you which you would have initially refused.

He comes to you direct, makes you do all the work a broker would normally do, then demands that you shave from your price the amount of a regular broker commission which he contends you are saving. Even at the closing a bad buyer will threaten to back out unless you give in to unreasonable demands.

Again the use of worthy brokers and attorneys can shield you from both the unscrupulous buyer and the bad broker.

Chapter 23

WHAT YOU CAN DO TO HELP YOURSELF

Throughout this book my whole thesis has been that a buyer would be foolish indeed not to avail himself of all the free help he can get from the many good brokers that stand ready to serve him and thereby save him time and money.

In the case of the seller, he can benefit, too, from the help of all the good brokers he can get to work for him. But one bad broker can harm the seller immeasurably. This is why you must choose the brokers who represent you with thought and care.

Remember that once you relinquish your right to sell your own house, you cannot get it back until the termination of the exclusive you have given. Therefore, think twice before you give up the exclusive right to sell your house to a stranger. You should retain control of the sale as long as you can. There is no need to be hasty about such an important decision. There are many unselfish, topnotch brokers who would be very happy to have an "open listing."

If your house is free of major problems, it may sell faster and easier than you think. One thing is sure: normally when the house is put on the market at a price equal to its fair market value a sale almost automatically follows. To help you know what the fair market value of your house is the V.A. will appraise it for you for about $50.00, the F.H.A. for about the same amount. Get your house in condition before you have it appraised. You do not have to be a veteran to get a V.A. appraisal if you are the seller. Any seller may get either a V.A. or F.H.A. appraisal.

As soon as you place a "For Sale by Owner" sign on your house you will be flooded with inquiries and offers of help by many brokers. Also, as soon as you place your first "Owner" ad in the papers, you will get all the inquires and offers of broker help you can handle. If you are not getting this response, this is the first time you should consider giving an exclusive or multiple listing exclusive.

After you put up the sign and place the ad, any broker you have to go after, yourself, to give your listing is asleep on the job. Do not expect too much action from him.

If you have real selling problems, it may pay you to offer a special cash bonus to a broker to induce him to concentrate on your house.

Owners, particularly, can benefit from advertising in the local papers.

If you do give an exclusive or multiple listing to a broker, make it for the shortest period possible, at first. You can always extend the exclusive after you are sure you are getting enough action from the broker. One month is a long enough period for him to show what he can do.

Keep your expenses down. Save your time for your own business, which you understand and know; you still need to make a living. Selling a house is an eighty-hour-a-week job, week after week after week. Can you afford it? Would you really be doing it as well as a "pro"? The broker's commission is microscopic compared with what your own total selling expenses could amount to.

Never accept a contingency sale. It is probably easier to sell your own house than be at the mercy of your buyer's getting a sale on his house. Remember, a contingency sale is no sale at all. No self-respecting or honest broker would have any part of tying you up this way, without any protection for you whatsoever. The only honest reason he could possibly have for doing it would be that he is too lazy to try to make a real sale that you could depend on.

Make sure that you, or the broker, actually have at the very least $500 in cash, not a rubber check or a promise, before you accept any offer and take your house off the market.

The next day a good sale could be lost, if you are tied up by a phony sale. Make the buyer do all his checking up first, then demand a firm unqualified offer, the only kind of offer that has legal significance and that you can dare to change your position on.

Straighten out any boundary disputes with your neighbors in advance. Be sure that you are legally zoned. Don't make any positive misrepresentations of material facts. If you do this deliberately or your broker does you can be sued in tort for deceit for all resulting damages. If you or your broker make innocent positive statements of material facts which turn out to be wrong, like taxes, etc., the buyer may rescind the sale and get his money back, even after the closing. Consequently, do not volunteer anything. If you are asked, give an honest answer or admit that you do not know. Never put your mouth into high gear until you are sure that your brain is turning over. Remember, words are your slaves until you have spoken them. Then you become their slave. The basic law is still *caveat emptor*. Don't you do anything to lose this tremendous protection which the law affords you.

You may, of course, always indulge freely in seller's puff; that is, your own personal opinions about general things. Just avoid any positive statement of a material fact that you do not have to make.

In states where the "net listing" has not been declared illegal, one way you cannot lose is to make the broker sign an agreement that you will in

47

any event receive a certain specified net amount from the sale. Then he is on notice that any low offer that he accepts will cost him part of his commission; you will not have to pay him a full commission for an unexpected and unacceptable low offer which you really cannot afford to accept. Otherwise, an unscrupulous broker will be quick to pressure you into the acceptance of an unfairly low net amount to you, especially if he knows that he has you stretched to the breaking point financially. This kind of broker will then brag that he always gets his full commission. Any decent broker will freely admit that he has taken less than a full commission, at the closing stage of some sales, in order to avoid undue hardship to a seller, or buyer, or his salesman, or all of them if the only possible alternative would be no sale at all.

Chapter 24

WHAT SHOULD BE IN YOUR PURCHASE AND SALE AGREEMENT

It is important for the seller to enter promptly into a full purchase and sale agreement with the buyer. At the moment of acceptance of the buyer's offer the seller does not have enough information and safeguards to properly protect himself for taking his house off the market. The law recognizes that whenever the parties indicate an intention to further agree, then they still have not made their final agreement, and they will not be able to use "Specific Performance" as a remedy for default. This means that, based on the usual "offer and acceptance," and prior to the execution of the formal complete agreement of sale, default by either party can bring on a suit for damages, or loss of a buyer's deposit, but neither party can be forced to go ahead with the deal.

In the agreement, the seller is entitled to know just how the buyer intends to raise his financing, so that he may evaluate the seller's probable chances of being able to perform. At this critical point, before the seller gets married to this buyer, he should receive basic credit information on the buyer from the broker. The seller should know that the broker, or the buyer, can actually get the intended financing. A shrewd seller, not acting under time or financial compulsion, would demand a letter of committal from a bank, or at least give himself a two-week escape clause in the event the buyer has not obtained his financing by that time. This would prevent the seller from getting burned months later by a buyer who just cannot get financing. The good selling season and several other potential good sales could be lost in the interim. Likewise, the seller should not permit the broker to post a Sold sign on the premises until at least the financing has been concluded by the bank, and also the F.H.A. or V.A. if necessary.

The seller should be sure that the deposit money is substantial, and should never take even a modestly priced house off the market for less than $500. The deposit should be in cash, bank check or certified check. If it is a personal check clear it promptly to be sure it is not made of rubber. Be wary of a promissory note. The broker or some third party should hold the deposit in escrow whenever there is a chance that it may have to go back to the buyer. In an F.H.A. or V.A. deal, the law unfortunately does not guarantee that the buyer will get his deposit back in full if he does not receive final approval by the governmental agency. One of my many pet peeves about brokers is that more and more of them are having their own distinctive contract of sale forms printed which deprive V.A. and F.H.A. buyers of a return of their deposits when the appraisal comes in lower than the sales price. These outrageous and disgraceful purchase and sale agreements should be declared illegal. This is another reason why only lawyers should be permitted to draft purchase and sale agreements. Realtors split forfeited deposits with their sellers. Some hungry brokers try to keep the defaulted deposits themselves. A few good brokers solve the problem by reselling the house and returning the deposit to the buyer. I know this can be done effectively, because I have never failed to accomplish this solution on the occasions when it became necessary. Prompt action on the part of the broker is the all-important factor in this type of unfortunate situation.

The closing date should be specific and in time for the seller's needs. If time is important, then the seller must insert the clause "time is of the essence of this contract." Otherwise, an extension of time is freely granted by the courts for reasonable and necessary delays.

The seller should be sure that he will merely have to keep the premises insured until closing "as presently insured." This will keep him from having to take out a new higher policy until closing day.

The seller should also be sure he has a clause excusing him from clearing the title of any "restrictions or easements of record," since he would not have such power.

The broker's commission to be paid by the seller should be specifically spelled out, and always the seller should be called upon to pay it "only if, as and when" the deal is consummated.

Finally, the seller should never, never sign the agreement without having his lawyer review it first.

Chapter 25

HOW TO SELL A MULTIPLE DWELLING

If you are selling a two- or three-family house, beam your ads and your sales effort towards the buyer who is going to live in it rent free, or at very little expense.

Most nonresident, investment buyers will know full well that this is not their cup of tea and will not give them a good enough return on their investment. So do not waste your time trying to fool them or kid yourself.

On the other hand, if you are selling four units or more, go after the purely investment buyer. This type of buyer is interested in only one thing. You can skip everything else and save yourself a lot of time and effort. He wants to know how much cash he will get back each year on his investment, that is, his percentage of return on cash invested. Therefore, you might just as well be honest. He is going to find it all out anyway. Admit all your expenses, and tell him your true income. This is better than to have him assume that the income is lower than it really is, or that the expenses are higher than they really are, which is exactly what he will do out of distrust alone if you try to deceive him.

You are entitled to fair economic rental income for the area. You are entitled to fair, average expenses spread over a period of years, if you have recently experienced inordinately high expenses.

If your cash flow is reasonable, and your building can be financed reasonably, then you can start talking about extras like:

1. Potential increased rental income due to present housing shortage and lack of available mortgage money.

2. Appreciation in value over the years ahead.

3. Tax shelters and savings available to the investor, depending upon his circumstances.

4. Best hedge against inflation, etc.

In periods of tight money the properties which suffer first and hardest due to lack of mortgage financing from regular sources are older frame, multiple dwellings. This is aggravated by inferior locations or poor condition of the building.

Chapter 26

IF YOUR HOUSE IS NOT SELLING

Check this list of the most common causes for sales failures:

1. House is overpriced. Buyers are out digging up the facts in today's market; and they know how much too much you are asking. If you are not absolutely sure that you are down to fair market value in your price, get a G.I. preappraisal or an F.H.A. conditional commitment. These excellent appraisals cost only about $50 today. They are a tremendous bargain. Remember, you are still free to set your own price. At least now your starting point is reality, rather than "cloud nine."

2. A lazy, penny-pinching, incompetent, or con-artist broker has a stranglehold on you. He holds the exclusive right, which you carelessly gave to him for too long a period, to sell your house. Now he is doing nothing for you, and he will not release you so that you or some good broker can sell your house. Usually you can complain to a local grievance committee. However, your only real protection is the integrity of the dealer. If the house is an exclusive on multiple listing, appeal to the local multiple listing board. They may not release you from your burdensome contract, but you can ask them to appeal to the member brokers to at least go to see your house, and try to give you some action in return for the stranglehold they have on you. Give them some price reduction to help them help you, if you possibly can. It would probably be too complicated, and against their rules, for them to reduce the size of their

commission. If the broker who is holding you up is an independent agent, try to negotiate a more attractive arrangement with him in regard to price and commission, which may help the sale of the house.

3. If you are lucky enough to be still in control, give more open listings to more brokers. Cover the surrounding towns. If this still does not work, consider an exclusive or multiple listing for a short period, but only with a very deserving broker.

4. If your brokers have only open listings or net listings and they are not producing, place an owner sign on your house, and run your own owner ads. This is your prerogative. Make your own deal with a direct buyer, if necessary. Just be sure to consult your lawyer before you sign anything.

5. Remember the paramount issue is that your house must be sold.

Supplement:

THE HOME BUYER'S CHECKLIST

GENERAL QUESTIONS TO CONSIDER ABOUT THE NEIGHBORHOOD, COMMUNITY AND EXPENSES

☐ Does the community in general seem to reflect your way of life?

☐ Are the schools good? (Important if *you* have children. Important on resale of house if buyer has children.) Is school within walking distance? If not, is there free school bus? Does school system include a high school or does the community share high school facilities with another town?

☐ Is there adequate public transportation to your job? Will you need a second car to get around?

☐ Is there adequate police and fire service? (Fire service can be checked by asking your insurance company. Bad service is reflected in a higher insurance rate.)

☐ Is there free garbage collection? How often?

☐ What kind of water: city-furnished or well? Does water require expensive softeners?

☐ Are there: churches, synagogues, libraries, park, shopping centers?

- [ ] Does the surrounding neighborhood seem to be the kind of place you would like to live in?
- [ ] Is there much traffic on the street you are looking at?
- [ ] Are there sidewalks for the children to play on? If not, is there a playground and are the streets quiet and relatively safe?
- [ ] Is the house the largest on the block? (Is it a $30,000 house in a $20,000 neighborhood? This leads to possible resale problems.)
- [ ] Are the houses next door well maintained or will you get stuck with a slovenly neighborhood?
- [ ] Check zoning of your area very carefully at the town zoning board. Any unfavorable change in zoning can cause a serious depreciation in the value of your house. Here are some typical pointers:.

1. If you are buying a one-family house, is the immediate area composed of one-family houses exclusively? If there is a mixture of one-, two- and multiple-family dwellings your purchase price should reflect this weak zoning structure.

2. Check zoning of vacant lots nearby. The vacant lot next door could be zoned for a gas station. The rolling meadow behind you could be zoned for an industrial park.

3. Are any new roads or superhighways planned? You could be moving next door to a future traffic jam.

SPECIFIC QUESTIONS ABOUT THE HOUSE

Outside:

- [ ] Are the grounds well kept?
- [ ] Are the walkways and driveways free of cracks and holes?
- [ ] If there are fences or walls are these in good order?
- [ ] If there is a hedge on property line, who owns and maintains it?
- [ ] Does the roof have missing shingles or slates?
- [ ] Do rain gutters and downspouts seem in good order and free of debris which causes run-overs (check sides of house for stains which show run-overs)?
- [ ] Do downspouts go into drywells or spill over onto lawn, walks and driveway? (Spills in winter cause slippery conditions.)
- [ ] How is outside paint on siding and trim?
- [ ] Is window putty smooth, or chipped and broken?
- [ ] Are there city sewers; or septic tanks or cesspool? If the latter, ask owner to show you where fields are and see if ground is absorbing properly. Important: Check if town is putting in sewers which can sometimes make for a ruinous assessment.

Inside: Bring a flashlight and screwdriver for proper inspection

- ☐ Shine flash on attic floor—look for stains which indicate roof leak.
- ☐ Can you store things in attic? Is there a stairway or ladder for easy access?
- ☐ Do windows open and shut properly? Can they be locked?
- ☐ Is plumbing in bath in good shape? Does water come on full pressure? What happens when you run shower and flush toilet at same time?
- ☐ Is there hot water?
- ☐ Are there shut-off valves to all sinks?
- ☐ Does tub drain? Does shower work? Does toilet flush without galloping?
- ☐ Are tiles properly grouted and sealed around tub and sink?
- ☐ Are there adequate closets?
- ☐ Is there adequate ventilation in every room?
- ☐ Is there adequate heating in every room?
- ☐ Are floors level? If they sag, go to basement and find out why.
- ☐ Is furnace relatively new? Converted coal furnaces are notoriously inefficient and expensive to operate. Is oil stored inside or out? If inside, check storage tank for leaks. Also, find out how much heating costs per year.
- ☐ Scratch pipes with screwdriver to see what kind of pipes are in house—iron, brass or copper tubing. Copper tubing is best—shows more modern plumbing techniques. Brass is long-lasting. Iron can rust out after long service—check this especially in an older house.
- ☐ What kind (110v, 220v) and how many amps electrical service does house have?
- ☐ Can you run TV, air conditioner, electric dryer on present circuitry?
- ☐ Are there sufficient outlets in every room?
- ☐ What goes with house? Window air conditioner? Refrigerator? Stove? Washer? Dryer? Light fixtures? Sconces? Carpeting? Storm windows? Screens?
- ☐ Shine flashlight in corners of cellar. Are there any stains indicating water leaks? Is cellar dry? If you see a dehumidifier, cellar will be damp.
- ☐ Shine flash at beams over foundation walls. Are they in good shape?
- ☐ Poke screwdriver into sill beams to see that lumber is sound and free of termite damage (get termite report on condition anyway).
- ☐ Any signs of vermin, droppings, dead bugs?
- ☐ Are there adequate supporting columns for first floor? Beware of strange looking jacks or lally columns which indicate previous trouble with sagging floors.

- ☐ Is there a separate door to cellar, or do you have to go through house to reach cellar?
- ☐ Check all exposed pipes for leaks or stains.
- ☐ Is there an operable drain at low points outside cellar door or garage doors so cellar will not get flooded in heavy rain?

CAN YOU AFFORD THE HOUSE?

Estimated Annual Expenses:

Interest and Amortization	$_____
Town Tax	$_____
School Tax	$_____
Water Tax	$_____
Heating and Hot Water	$_____
Gas and Electricity	$_____
Repairs and Improvements	$_____
Garden and Lawn Expense	$_____
Total Estimated Annual Expenses	$_____

And don't forget the initial moneys required to buy the house:

Down Payment	$_____
Legal Fees (which include your lawyer and bank's lawyer)	$_____
Title Policy Costs	$_____
Fire Policy Costs	$_____
Bank Charges for Mortgage	$_____
Escrow Fund Required by Bank	$_____
Cost of Moving	$_____
Total Expenses	$_____
Annual Income Available for Housing	$_____

Settlement Costs

A HUD Guide

Revised Edition

U.S. Department of
Housing and
Urban Development

Office of Consumer Affairs and
Regulatory Functions

CONTENTS

SETTLEMENT COSTS

Introduction

For many people, buying a home is the single most significant financial step of a lifetime. The Real Estate Settlement Procedures Act (RESPA), a Federal statute, helps to protect you at this step.

Settlement is the formal process by which ownership of real property passes from seller to buyer. It is the end of the home buying process, the time when title to the property is transferred from the seller to the buyer.

RESPA covers most residential mortgage loans used to finance the purchase of one- to four-family properties, such as a house, a condominium or cooperative apartment unit, a lot with a mobile home, or a lot on which you will build a house or place a mobile home using the proceeds of the loan.

RESPA was not designed to set the prices of settlement services. Instead, it provides you with information to take the mystery out of the settlement process, so that you can shop for settlement services and make informed decisions.

This information booklet was prepared as provided in RESPA by the Office of Consumer Affairs and Regulatory Functions of the U.S. Department of Housing and Urban Development.

Part One of this booklet describes the settlement process and nature of charges and suggests questions you might ask of lenders, attorneys and others to clarify what services they will provide you for the charges quoted. It also contains information on your rights and remedies available under RESPA, and alerts you to unfair or illegal practices.

Part Two of this booklet is an item-by-item explanation of settlement services and costs, with sample forms and worksheets that will help you in making cost comparisons. Remember that terminology varies by locality so that terminology used here may not exactly match that used in your area. For example, settlement is sometimes called closing and settlement charges are frequently referred to as closing costs.

PART I

What Happens and When

Suppose you have just found a home you would like to buy. In a typical situation, when you reach an agreement with the seller on the price, you then sign a sales contract. The terms of the sales contract can be negotiated to your benefit, as the booklet explains below.

Next you will probably seek a mortgage to finance the purchase. This booklet suggests questions you should raise as you shop for a lender.

When you file your application for a loan, the lender is required by RESPA to provide a good faith estimate of the costs of settlement services and a copy of this booklet. The lender has three business days, after written loan application, to mail these materials to you.

Between loan application time and settlement, you usually have a chance to shop for settlement services, to ensure that you will obtain good value for your money.

Finally, one business day before settlement, if you so request, the person conducting the settlement must allow you an opportunity to see a Uniform Settlement Statement that shows whatever figures are available at that time for settlement charges you will be required to pay. At settlement, the completed Uniform Settlement Statement will be given to you.

Note: In some parts of the country where there is no actual settlement meeting, or in cases where neither you nor your authorized agent attends the closing meeting, the person conducting settlement has the obligation to deliver the Uniform Settlement Statement to you by mail.

There is no standard settlement process followed in all localities; therefore, what you experience, involving many of the same services, will probably vary from the description in this booklet.

Shopping for Services

When settlement arrives, you are committed to the purchase of the property and may have made a partial payment, sometimes called earnest money, to the seller or his agent. Services may have been performed for which you are obligated to pay. Unless a seller fails to fulfill a legally binding promise or has acted in a fraudulent fashion, you are normally obligated to complete your part of the contract and pay settlement costs. Thus the time to decide the terms of sale, raise questions, and establish fair fees is not at time of settlement services. By the time of settlement, any changes in settlement costs and purchase terms may be difficult to negotiate.

You can also negotiate with the seller of the house about who pays various settlement fees and other charges. There are generally no fixed rules about which party pays which fees, although in many cases this is largely controlled by local custom.

Among the many factors that determine the amount you will pay for settlement costs are the location of your new home, the type of sales contract you negotiate, the arrangements made with the real estate broker, the lender you select, and your decisions in selecting the various firms that provide required settlement services. If the chosen house is located in a "special flood hazard area," identified as such by HUD on a flood insurance map, the lender may require you to purchase flood insurance pursuant to Federal law (See page 81). Information on flood insurance availability, limits of coverage and copies of maps can be obtained through the National Flood Insurers Association servicing company for your State or by calling HUD toll free numbers 800-424-8872 or 73.

Role of the Broker

Although real estate brokers provide helpful advice on many aspects of home buying, and may in some areas supervise the settlement, they normally serve the interests of the seller, not the buyer. The broker's basic objective is to obtain a signed contract of sale which properly expresses the agreement of the parties, and to complete the sale. However, as State licensing laws require that the broker be fair in his dealings with all parties to the transaction, you should feel free to point this out to the broker if you feel you are being treated unfairly.

A broker may recommend that you deal with a particular lender, title company, attorney, or other provider of settlement services. Ask brokers why they recommend a particular company or firm in preference to others. Advise them that while you welcome their suggestions (and, indeed, they probably have good contacts), you reserve the right to pick your own providers of services.

Negotiating a Sales Contract

If you have obtained this booklet before you have signed a sales contract with the seller of the property, here are some important points to consider regarding that contract.

The sales agreement you and the seller sign can expressly state which settlement costs you will pay and which will be paid by the seller although some may be negotiable up to time of settlement. Buyers can and do negotiate with sellers as to which party is to pay for specific settlement costs. The success of such negotiations depends upon factors such as how eager the seller is to sell and you are to buy, the quality of the house itself, how long the house has been on the market, whether other potential buyers are interested, and how willing you are to negotiate for lower costs. If the contract is silent on these costs, they are still open to negotiation.

There is no standard sales contract which you are required to sign. You are entitled to make any modifications or additions in any standard form contract to which the seller will agree. You should consider including the following clauses:

● The seller provides title, free and clear of all liens and encumbrances except those which you specifically agree to in the contract or approve when the results of the title search are reported to you. You may negotiate as to who will pay for the title search service to determine whether the title is "clear."

● A refund of your deposit (earnest money) will be made by the seller or escrow agent, and cancellation of the sale will occur if you are unable to secure from a lending institution a first mortgage or deed-of-trust loan with an amount, interest rate, and length of term, as set forth in the contract, within a stated time period.

● A certificate will be provided at time of settlement, stating that the house is free from termites or termite damage.

● A certificate will be provided that the plumbing, heating, electrical systems and appliances are in working order, and that the house is structurally sound. Negotiate who pays for any necessary inspections. There is no uniform custom in most areas. Many buyers prefer to pay for these inspections because they want to know that the inspector is conducting the service for them, not for the seller. (You can also purchase a warranty to back up the inspection, if you wish.)

● An agreement will be reached on how taxes, water and sewer charges, premiums on existing transferable insurance policies, utility bills, interest on mortgages, and rent (if there are tenants) are to be divided between buyer and seller as of the date of the settlement.

Before you sign the sales contract, make sure that it correctly expresses your agreement with the seller on such important details as the sales price of the home, method of payment, the time set for your taking possession, what fixtures, appliances, and personal property are to be sold with the home, and the other items described above.

The above list is not complete, but does illustrate the importance of the sales agreement and its terms. Before you sign a sales contract you may want to ask an attorney to review the proposed agreement and determine if it protects your interests, for once signed, the contract is binding on you and the seller. If you do not know of an attorney you may wish to consult the local bar association referral service or neighborhood legal service office.

Selecting an Attorney

If you seek the aid of an attorney, first ask what services will be performed for what fee. If the fee seems too high, shop for another lawyer. Does the attorney have substantial experience in real estate? The U.S. Supreme Court has said that it is illegal for bar associations to fix minimum fee schedules for attorneys, so do not be bashful about discussing and shopping for legal fees you can afford. Your attorney will understand.

Questions you may wish to ask the attorney include: What is the charge for reading documents and giving advice concerning them? For being present at settlement? Will the attorney represent any other party in the transaction in addition to you? In some areas attorneys act as closing agents handling the mechanical aspects of the settlement. A lawyer who does this may not fully represent your interests since, as closing agent, he would be representing the seller and other interests as well.

Selecting a Lender

Your choice of lender will influence not only your settlement costs, but also the monthly cost of your mortgage loan.

Lending institutions require certain settlement services, such as a new survey or title insurance, or they may charge you for other settlement-related services, such as the appraisal or credit report. You may find, in shopping for a lender, that other institutions may not have such requirements. Part Two of this booklet provides a description of the various kinds of services that may be required and fees that may be charged to you. You will also find a worksheet in Part Two, which you can use to compare requirements and cost estimates from different lenders.

Many lending institutions deal regularly with certain title companies, attorneys, appraisers, surveyors, and others in whom they have confidence. They may want to arrange for settlement services to be provided through these parties. This booklet discusses your rights in such a situation under the section below on Home Buyer's Rights.

If you choose a lending institution which allows you a choice of settlement service providers, you should shop and compare among the providers in your area, to find the best service for the best price. Where the lender designates the use of particular firms, check with other firms to see if the lender's stated charges are competitive.

Questions you may want to ask the lender should include these:

● Are you required to carry life or disability insurance? Must you obtain it from a particular company? (You may prefer no insurance or may wish to obtain it at a better premium rate elsewhere.)

● Is there a late payment charge? How much? How late may your payment be before the charge is imposed? You should be aware that late payments may harm your credit rating.

● If you wish to pay off the loan in advance of maturity (for example, if you move and sell the house), must you pay a prepayment penalty? How much? If so, for how long a period will it apply?

● Will the lender release you from personal liability if your loan is assumed by someone else when you sell your house?

● If you sell the house and the buyer assumes your loan, will the lender have the right to charge an assumption fee, raise the rate of interest, or require payment in full of the mortgage?

● If you have a financial emergency, will the terms of the loan include a future advances clause, permitting you to borrow additional money on the mortgage after you have paid off part of the original loan?

● Will you be required to pay monies into a special reserve (escrow or impound) account to cover taxes or insurance? If so, how large a deposit will be required at the closing of the sale? The amount of reserve deposits required is limited under RESPA. Some recent State laws have required that these accounts bear interest for the benefit of the borrower (buyer). If reserve requirements can be waived, you will be responsible for paying the particular charges for taxes or insurance directly to the tax collector or insurance company. Further information is in "Reserve Accounts" in Part Two of this booklet.

● In looking for the best mortgage to fit your particular financial needs, you may wish to check the terms and requirements of a private conventional loan versus a loan insured through the Federal Housing Administration or Farmers Home Administration or guaranteed by the Veterans Administration. The FHA, VA, and Farmers Home Administration loans involve Federal ceilings on permissible charges for some settlement services, which may be of interest to you. Ask lenders about these programs. Another source of information about the federally insured or guaranteed programs is from public documents, some of which are listed in the bibliography of this booklet.

● If you are dealing with the lender who holds the existing mortgage, you might be able to take over the prior loan, in a transaction called "assumption." Assumption usually saves money in settlement costs if the interest rate on the prior loan is lower than that being asked in the market. In times of inflation in the housing market, a higher downpayment might be required than if you had obtained a new loan. You may want to ask the seller whether he would be willing to "take back" a second mortgage to finance part of the difference between the assumed loan and the sales price.

Selecting a Settlement Agent

Settlement practices vary from locality to locality, and even within the same county or city. In various areas settlements are conducted by lending institutions, title insurance companies, escrow companies, real estate brokers, and attorneys for the buyer or seller. By investigating and comparing practices and rates, you may find that the first suggested settlement agent may not be the least expensive. You might save money by taking the initiative in arranging for settlement and selecting the firm and location which meets your needs.

Securing Title Services

A title search may take the form of an abstract, a compilation of pertinent legal documents which provides a condensed history of the property ownership and related matters. In many areas title searches are performed by extracting information from the public record without assembling abstracts. In either situation, an expert examination is necessary to determine the status of title and this is normally made by attorneys or title company employees. In areas where both title insurance companies and attorneys perform these and other settlement services, compare fees for services (such as title certification, document preparation, notary fee, closing fee, etc.), provided by each to determine the better source for these services.

In many jurisdictions a few days or weeks prior to settlement the title insurance company will issue a binder (sometimes called a Commitment to Insure) or preliminary report, a summary of findings based on the search or abstract. It is usually sent to the lender for use until the title insurance policy is issued after the settlement. The binder lists all the defects in and liens against the title identified by the search. You should arrange to have a copy sent to you (or to an attorney who represents you) so that you can raise an objection if there are matters affecting the title which you did not agree to accept when you signed the contract of sale.

Title insurance is often required to protect the lender against loss if a flaw in title is not found by the title search made when the house is purchased. You may also get an owner's title policy to protect yourself. In some States, attorneys provide bar-related title insurance as part of their services in examining title and providing a title opinion. In these States the attorney's fee may include the title insurance premium, although the total title-related charges in the transaction should be taken into account in determining whether you will realize any savings.

Bear in mind that a title insurance policy issued only to the lender does not protect you. Similarly, the policy issued to a prior owner, such as the person from whom you are buying the house, does not protect you. To protect yourself from loss because of a mistake made by the title searcher, or because of a legal defect of a type which does not appear on the public records, you will need an owner's policy. Such a mistake rarely occurs but, when it does, it can be financially devastating to the uninsured. If you buy an owner's policy it is usually much less expensive if purchased simultaneously with a lender's policy.

To reduce title insurance costs, be sure to compare rates among various title insurance companies, and ask what services and limitations on coverage are provided by each policy so that you can decide whether a higher rate is consistent with your needs.

Depending upon practice in your jurisdiction, there may be no need for a full historical title search each time title to a home is transferred. If you are buying a home which has changed hands within the last several years, inquire at the title company that issued the previous title insurance policy about a "reissue rate," which would be a lower charge than for a new policy. If the title insurance policy of the previous owner is available, take it to the title insurer or lawyer whom you have selected to do your search.

To mark the boundaries of the property as set out in the title, lenders may require a survey. A home buyer may be able to avoid the cost of a repetitive complete survey of the property if he can locate the surveyor who previously surveyed the project. He can update the existing survey. However, the requirements of investors who buy loans originated by your lender may limit the lender's discretion to negotiate this point. Check with the lender or title company on this.

HOME BUYER'S RIGHTS

Information Booklet

When you submit or the lender prepares your written application for a loan, the lender is legally required, under RESPA to give you a copy of this booklet. If the lender does not give it to you in person on the day of your loan application, he must put it in the mail to you no later than three business days after your application is filed.

Good Faith Estimates

When you file your application for a loan, the lender must also, under the terms of RESPA, provide you with good faith estimates of settlement services charges you will likely incur. If he does not give them to you, he has three business days in which to put them in the mail.

See Part Two of this booklet for a full item-by-item discussion of settlement services. On the form entitled "Settlement Statement," you will find Section L, which lists possible settlement services and charges you will encounter.

The lender is required to give you his good faith estimate, based upon his experience in the locality in which the property is located, for each settlement charge in Section L that he anticipates you will pay, except for paid-in-advance hazard insurance premium (line 903) and reserves deposited with the lender (all Section 1000 items). The estimate may be stated as either a dollar amount or range for each charge. Where the lender designates the use of a particular firm, the lender must make its good faith estimate based upon the lender's knowledge of the amounts charged by the firm. The form used for this good faith estimate must be concise and clear, and the estimates must bear a reasonable relationship to the costs you will likely incur. If the lender provides you good faith estimates in the form of ranges, ask the lender what the total settlement costs will most likely be. While the lender is not obligated to provide this information under RESPA, it is important for you to know as you evaluate the different mortgage packages being offered you.

Lenders were not required to give good faith estimates for reserves deposited with them or for the prepaid hazard insurance premium because these charges require information not normally known to the lender at time of loan application. It is important for you to make these calculations because they can represent a sizeable cash payment you may have to make at settlement. Calculation of the reserve items is presented later in this booklet under "Reserve Accounts." Ask the lender what his policies are in terms of reserve accounts, for what items the lender requires reserves and for what period of time. You may want to ask the lender to run through a hypothetical calculation for you based upon the date you will most likely close on the house. Other assumptions may be necessary, for example, the assessed value of the property for determining property taxes. The lender can probably be more specific on hazard insurance premiums, particularly for those coverages which a lender requires.

Once you have obtained these estimates from the lender be aware that they are only estimates. The final costs may not be the same. Estimates are subject to changing market conditions, and fees may change. Changes in the date of settlement may result in changes in escrow and proration requirements. In certain cases, it may not be possible for the lender to anticipate exactly the pricing policies of settlement firms. Moreover, your own careful choice of settlement firms might result in lower costs, just as hasty decisions might result in higher costs. Remember that the lender's estimate is not a guarantee.

Lender Designation of Settlement Service Providers

Some lending institutions follow the practice of designating specific settlement service providers to be used for legal services, title examination services, title insurance, or the conduct of settlement.

Where this occurs the lender, under RESPA, is required to provide you as part of the good faith estimates a statement in which the lender sets forth:

1. The name, address and telephone number of each provider he has designated. This must include a statement of the specific services each designated firm is to provide for you, as well as an estimate of the amount the lender anticipates you

will have to pay for the service, based on the lender's experience as to what the designated provider usually charges. If the services or charges are not clear to you, ask further questions.

2. Whether each designated firm has a business relationship with the lender.

While designated firms often provide the services needed, a conflict of interest may exist. Take, for example, the situation where the provider must choose between your interests and those of the lender. Where legal services are involved, it is wise to employ your own attorney to ensure that your interests are properly protected. It is wise for you to contact other firms to determine whether their costs are competitive and their services are comparable.

Disclosure of Settlement Costs One Day Before Closing and Delivery

One business day before settlement, you have the right to inspect the form, called the Uniform Settlement Statement, on which are itemized the services provided to you and fees charged to you. This form (developed by the U.S. Department of Housing and Urban Development) is filled out by the person who will conduct the settlement meeting. Be sure you have the name, address, and telephone number of the settlement agent if you wish to inspect this form or if you have any questions.

The settlement agent may not have all costs available the day before closing, but is obligated to show you, upon request, what is available.

The Uniform Settlement Statement must be delivered or mailed to you (while another statement goes to the seller) at or before settlement. If, however, you waive your right to delivery of the completed statement at settlement, it will then be mailed at the earliest practicable date.

In parts of the country where the settlement agent does not require a meeting, or in cases where you or your agent do not attend the settlement, the statement will be mailed as soon as practicable after settlement and no advance inspection is required.

The Uniform Settlement Statement is not used in situations where:

1. there are no settlement fees charged to the buyer (because the seller has assumed all settlement-related expenses), or

2. the total amount the borrower is required to pay for all charges imposed at settlement is determined by a fixed amount and the borrower is informed of this fixed amount at the time of loan application. In the latter case, the lender is required to provide the borrower, within three business days of application, an itemized list of services rendered.

Escrow Closing

Settlement practices differ from State to State. In some parts of the country, settlement may be conducted by an escrow agent, which may be a lender, real estate agent, title company representative, attorney, or an escrow company. After entering into a contract of sale, the parties sign an escrow agreement which requires them to deposit specified documents and funds with the agent. Unlike other types of closing, the parties do not meet around a table to sign and exchange documents. The agent may request a title report and policy; draft a deed or other documents; obtain rent statements; pay off existing loans; adjust taxes, rents, and insurance between the buyer and seller; compute interest on loans; and acquire hazard insurance. All this may be authorized in the escrow agreement. If all the papers and monies are deposited with the agent within the agreed time, the escrow is "closed."

The escrow agent then records the appropriate documents and gives each party the documents and money each is entitled to receive, including the completed uniform Settlement Statement. If one party has failed to fulfill his agreement, the escrow is not closed and legal complications may follow.

Truth-in-Lending

The lender is required to provide you a Truth-in-Lending statement by the time of loan consummation which discloses the annual percentage rate or effective interest rate which you will pay on your mortgage loan. This rate may be higher than the contract interest rate because the latter includes only interest, while the annual percentage rate includes discount points, fees, and financing charges and certain other charges besides, on the loan. The Truth-in-Lending statement will also disclose any additional charges for prepayment should you pay off the remaining balance of the mortgage before it is due.

Lenders are not required to provide you a Truth-in-Lending disclosure at the time of loan application, when the good faith estimate of settlement costs and this informational booklet are given to you. However, since the annual percentage rate the lender will be charging you is an important item of information which you can use as you shop for services, you may want to request its disclosure at time of loan application.

Protection Against Unfair Practices

A principal finding of Congress in the Real Estate Settlement Procedures Act of 1974 is that consumers need protection from ". . . unnecessarily high settlement charges caused by certain abusive practices that have developed in some areas of the country." The potential problems discussed below may not be applicable to most loan settlements, and the professionals in the settlement business will give you good service. Nevertheless, you may save yourself money and worry by keeping the following considerations in mind:

Kickbacks. Kickbacks and referrals of business for gain are often tied together. The law prohibits anyone from giving or taking a fee, kickback, or anything of value under an agreement that business will be referred to a specific person or organization. It is also illegal to charge or accept a fee or part of a fee where no service has actually been performed. This requirement does not prevent. agents for lenders and title companies, attorneys, or others actually performing a service in connection with the mortgage loan or settlement transaction, from receiving compensation for their work. It also does not prohibit payments pursuant to cooperative brokerage, such as a multiple listing service, and referral arrangements between real estate agents and brokers.

The prohibition is aimed primarily at eliminating the kind of arrangement in which one party agrees to return part of his fee in order to obtain business from the referring party. The danger is that some settlement fees can be inflated to cover payments to this additional party, resulting in a higher total cost to you. There are criminal penalties of both fine and imprisonment for any violation of these provisions of law. There are also provisions for you to recover three times the amount of the kickback, rebate, or referral fee involved, through a private lawsuit. In any successful action to enforce your right, the court may award you court costs together with a fee for your attorney.

Title Companies. Under the law, the seller may not require, as a' condition of sale, that title insurance be purchased by the buyer from any particular title company. A violation of this will make the seller liable to you in an amount equal to three times all charges made for the title insurance.

Fair Credit Reporting. There are credit reporting agencies around the Nation which are in the business of compiling credit reports on citizens, covering data such as how you pay your bills, if you have been sued, arrested, filed for bankruptcy, etc.. In addition, this file may include your neighbors' and friends' views of your character, general reputation, or manner of living. This latter information is referred to as an "investigative consumer report."

The Fair Credit Reporting Act does· not give the right to inspect or physically handle your actual report at the credit reporting agency, nor to receive an exact copy of the report. But you are entitled to a summary of the report, showing the nature, substance, and sources of the information it contains.

If the terms of your financing have been adversely affected by a credit report, you have the right to inspect the summary of that report free of charge (there may otherwise be a small fee). The accuracy of the report can also be challenged, and corrections required to be made. For more detailed information on your credit report rights, contact the Federal Trade Commission (FTC) in Washington, D.C. or the nearest FTC regional office. *The FTC Buyer's Guide No. 7: Fair Credit Reporting Act* is a good summary of this Act.

The Right to File Complaints

As with any consumer problems, the place to start if you have a complaint is back at the source of the problem (the lender, settlement agent, broker, etc.). If that initial effort brings no satisfaction and you think you have suffered damages through violations of the Real Estate Settlement Procedures Act of 1974, as amended, you may be entitled to bring a civil action in the U.S. District Court for the District in which the property involved is located, or in any other court of competent jurisdiction. This a matter best determined by your lawyer. Any suit you file under RESPA must be brought within one year from the date of the occurrence of the alleged violation. You may have legal remedies under other State or Federal laws in addition to RESPA.

You should note that RESPA provides for specific legal sanctions only under the provisions which prohibit kickbacks and unearned fees, and which prohibit the seller from requiring the buyer to use a particular title insurer. If you feel you should recover damages for violations of any provision of RESPA, you should consult your lawyer.

Most settlement service providers, particularly lenders, are supervised by some governmental agency at the local, State and/or Federal level. Others are subject to the control of self-policing associations. If you feel a provider of settlement services has violated RESPA, you can address your complaint to the agency or association which has supervisory responsibility over the provider. The supervisory agency for the lending institution is noted on the back cover of this booklet. If the lender has given you this information elsewhere, he is not required to provide it here. For the names of agencies supervising other providers, you will have to check with local and State consumer agencies. You are also encouraged to forward a copy of complaints regarding RESPA violations to the HUD Office of Consumer Affairs and Regulatory Functions, which has the primary responsibility for administering the RESPA program. Your complaints can lay the foundation for future legislative or administrative actions.

Send copies of complaints, and inquiries, to:

Assistant Secretary Consumer Affairs and Regulatory Functions
Attention: RESPA Office
U.S. Department of Housing and Urban Development
Room 4100 451 7th Street S.W. Washington, D.C. 20410

THE HOME BUYER'S OBLIGATIONS (REPAYMENT OF LOAN AND MAINTENANCE OF HOME)

At settlement you will sign papers legally obligating you to pay the mortgage loan financing the purchase of your home. You must pay according to the terms of the loan—interest rate, amount and due date of each monthly payment, repayment period—specified in the documents signed by you. You will probably sign at settlement a note or bond which is your promise to repay the loan for the unpaid balance of the purchase price. You will also sign a mortgage or deed of trust which pledges your home as security for repayment of the loan.

Failure to make monthly mortgage payments on time may lead to a late payment charge, if provided for in the documents. If you default on the loan by missing payments altogether and do not make them up within a period of time usually set by State law, the documents also specify certain actions which the lender may take to recover the amount owed. Ultimately, after required notice to you, a default could lead to foreclosure and sale of the home which secures your loan.

You should also be careful to maintain your home in a proper state of repair, both for your own satisfaction and comfort as the occupant and because the home is security for your loan. The mortgage or deed of trust may in fact specifically obligate you to keep the property in good repair and not allow deterioration.

Read the documents carefully at or before settlement, and be aware of your obligations as a homeowner.

PART II

This part of the booklet provides an item-by-item discussion of possible settlement services that may be required and for which you may be charged. It also provides a sample of the Uniform Settlement Statement form, and worksheets which you may find handy for comparing costs from different service providers.

Sections A through I of the Uniform Settlement Statement contain information concerning the loan and parties to the settlement. Sections J and K contain a summary of all funds transferred between the buyer, seller, lender, and providers of settlement services. The bottom line in the left-hand column shows the net cash to be paid by the borrower, while the bottom line in the right-hand column shows the cash due the seller.

Section L is a list of settlement services that may be required and for which you may be charged. Blank lines are provided for any additional settlement services.

HUD-1 Rev. 5/76

Form Approved
OMB NO. 63-R-1501

A.

U. S. DEPARTMENT OF HOUSING AND URBAN DEVELOPMENT

SETTLEMENT STATEMENT

B. TYPE OF LOAN
1. ☐ FHA 2. ☐ FmHA 3. ☐ CONV. UNINS.
4. ☐ VA 5. ☐ CONV. INS.
6. File Number:	7. Loan Number:
8. Mortgage Insurance Case Number:

C. NOTE: *This form is furnished to give you a statement of actual settlement costs. Amounts paid to and by the settlement agent are shown. Items marked "(p.o.c.)" were paid outside the closing; they are shown here for informational purposes and are not included in the totals.*

D. NAME OF BORROWER:	E. NAME OF SELLER:	F. NAME OF LENDER:

G. PROPERTY LOCATION:	H. SETTLEMENT AGENT:	I. SETTLEMENT DATE:
	PLACE OF SETTLEMENT:	

J. SUMMARY OF BORROWER'S TRANSACTION		K. SUMMARY OF SELLER'S TRANSACTION	
100. GROSS AMOUNT DUE FROM BORROWER:		400. GROSS AMOUNT DUE TO SELLER:	
101. Contract sales price		401. Contract sales price	
102. Personal property		402. Personal property	
103. Settlement charges to borrower (line 1400)		403.	
104.		404.	
105.		405.	
Adjustments for items paid by seller in advance		Adjustments for items paid by seller in advance	
106. City/town taxes	to	406. City/town taxes	to
107. County taxes	to	407. County taxes	to
108. Assessments	to	408. Assessments	to

(Form Continues on Next Page)

72

109.		
110.		
111.		
112.		
120.	**GROSS AMOUNT DUE FROM BORROWER**	
200. AMOUNTS PAID BY OR IN BEHALF OF BORROWER:		
201. Deposit or earnest money		
202. Principal amount of new loan(s)		
203. Existing loan(s) taken subject to		
204.		
205.		
206.		
207.		
208.		
209.		
Adjustments for items unpaid by seller		
210. City/town taxes	to	
211. County taxes	to	
212. Assessments	to	
213.		
214.		
215.		
216.		
217.		
218.		
219.		
220.	**TOTAL PAID BY/FOR BORROWER**	
300. CASH AT SETTLEMENT FROM/TO BORROWER		
301. Gross amount due from borrower (line 120)		
302. Less amounts paid by/for borrower (line 220)	(	)
303. CASH (☐ FROM) (☐ TO) BORROWER		

(Back of Form Continued on Next Page)

409.		
410.		
411.		
412.		
420.	**GROSS AMOUNT DUE TO SELLER**	
500. REDUCTIONS IN AMOUNT DUE TO SELLER:		
501. Excess deposit (see instructions)		
502. Settlement charges to seller (line 1400)		
503. Existing loan(s) taken subject to		
504. Payoff of first mortgage loan		
505. Payoff of second mortgage loan		
506.		
507.		
508.		
509.		
Adjustments for items unpaid by seller		
510. City/town taxes	to	
511. County taxes	to	
512. Assessments	to	
513.		
514.		
515.		
516.		
517.		
518.		
519.		
520.	**TOTAL REDUCTION AMOUNT DUE SELLER**	
600. CASH AT SETTLEMENT TO/FROM SELLER		
601. Gross amount due to seller (line 420)		
602. Less reductions in amount due seller (line 520)	(	)
603. CASH (☐ TO) (☐ FROM) SELLER		

L. SETTLEMENT CHARGES	PAID FROM BORROWER'S FUNDS AT SETTLEMENT	PAID FROM SELLER'S FUNDS AT SETTLEMENT
700. TOTAL SALES/BROKER'S COMMISSION based on price $ @ %=		
Division of Commission (line 700) as follows:		
701. $ to		
702. $ to		
703. Commission paid at Settlement		
704.		
800. ITEMS PAYABLE IN CONNECTION WITH LOAN		
801. Loan Origination Fee %		
802. Loan Discount %		
803. Appraisal Fee to		
804. Credit Report to		
805. Lender's Inspection Fee		
806. Mortgage Insurance Application Fee to		
807. Assumption Fee		
808.		
809.		
810.		
811.		
900. ITEMS REQUIRED BY LENDER TO BE PAID IN ADVANCE		
901. Interest from to @ $ /day		
902. Mortgage Insurance Premium for months to		
903. Hazard Insurance Premium for years to		
904. years to		
905.		
1000. RESERVES DEPOSITED WITH LENDER		
1001. Hazard insurance months @ $ per month		
1002. Mortgage insurance months @ $ per month		
1003. City property taxes months @ $ per month		
1004. County property taxes months @ $ per month		
1005. Annual assessments months @ $ per month		
1006. months @ $ per month		
1007. months @ $ per month		

(Form Continues on Next Page)

74

1008.		months @ $	per month		

1100. TITLE CHARGES

1101.	Settlement or closing fee	to			
1102.	Abstract or title search	to			
1103.	Title examination	to			
1104.	Title insurance binder	to			
1105.	Document preparation	to			
1106.	Notary fees	to			
1107.	Attorney's fees	to			
	(includes above items numbers:	)			
1108.	Title insurance	to			
	(includes above items numbers:	)			
1109.	Lender's coverage	$			
1110.	Owner's coverage	$			
1111.					
1112.					
1113.					

1200. GOVERNMENT RECORDING AND TRANSFER CHARGES

1201.	Recording fees: Deed $	; Mortgage $	; Releases $	
1202.	City/county tax/stamps: Deed $	; Mortgage $		
1203.	State tax/stamps: Deed $	; Mortgage $		
1204.				
1205.				

1300. ADDITIONAL SETTLEMENT CHARGES

1301.	Survey	to	
1302.	Pest inspection	to	
1303.			
1304.			
1305.			

1400. TOTAL SETTLEMENT CHARGES (enter on lines 103, Section J and 502, Section K)

SETTLEMENT COSTS WORK SHEET (Use this worksheet to compare the charges of various lenders and providers of settlement services.)

	PROVIDER 1	PROVIDER 2	PROVIDER 3
800. ITEMS PAYABLE IN CONNECTION WITH LOAN			
801. Loan Origination Fee %			
802. Loan Discount %			
803. Appraisal Fee to			
804. Credit Report to			
805. Lender's Inspection Fee			
806. Mortgage Insurance Application Fee to			
807. Assumption Fee			
808.			
809.			
810.			
811.			
900. ITEMS REQUIRED BY LENDER TO BE PAID IN ADVANCE			
901. Interest from to @ $ /day			
902. Mortgage Insurance Premium for months to			
903. Hazard Insurance Premium for years to			
904. years to			
905.			
1000. RESERVES DEPOSITED WITH LENDER			
1001. Hazard insurance months @ $ per month			
1002. Mortgage insurance months @ $ per month			
1003. City property taxes months @ $ per month			
1004. County property taxes months @ $ per month			
1005. Annual assessments months @ $ per month			
1006. months @ $ per month			
1007. months @ $ per month			
1008. months @ $ per month			

(Form Continues on Next Page)

76

1100. TITLE CHARGES

1101.	Settlement or closing fee	to		
1102.	Abstract or title search	to		
1103.	Title examination	to		
1104.	Title insurance binder	to		
1105.	Document preparation	to		
1106.	Notary fees	to		
1107.	Attorney's fees	to		
	(includes above items numbers;			
1108.	Title insurance	to		
	(includes above items numbers;			
1109.	Lender's coverage	$		
1110.	Owner's coverage	$		
1111.				
1112.				
1113.				

1200. GOVERNMENT RECORDING AND TRANSFER CHARGES

1201.	Recording fees: Deed $	; Mortgage $	; Releases $	
1202.	City/county tax/stamps: Deed $	; Mortgage $		
1203.	State tax/stamps:	Deed $	; Mortgage $	
1204.				
1205.				

1300. ADDITIONAL SETTLEMENT CHARGES

1301.	Survey	to		
1302.	Pest inspection	to		
1303.				
1304.				
1305.				

1400. TOTAL SETTLEMENT CHARGES (enter on lines 103, Section J and 502, Section K)

You would add up the costs entered on the lines of Section L, and carry them forward to Sections J and K, in order to arrive at the net cash figures on the bottom lines of the left and right columns.

Uses of This Form

1. **Settlement services comparisons.** As you shop for settlement services, you can use the Settlement Costs Worksheet as a handy guide, noting on it the different services required by different lenders and the different fees quoted by different service providers.

2. **Disclosure of actual settlement costs.** A copy of this form, or one with similar terminology, sequence and numbering of line items, must be filled out by the person conducting the settlement meeting. Your right to inspect the form one business day before settlement was discussed earlier in this booklet. The form will be completely filled in at the settlement meeting.

SPECIFIC SETTLEMENT SERVICES

The following defines and discusses each specific settlement service. The numbers correspond to the items listed in Section L of the Uniform Settlement Statement form.

700. Sales/Broker's Commission

This is the total dollar amount of sales commission, usually paid by the seller. Fees are usually a percentage of the selling price of the house, and are intended to compensate brokers or salesmen for their services. Custom and/or the negotiated agreement between the seller and the broker determine the amount of the commission.

701—702. Division of Commission

If several brokers or salesmen work together to sell the house, the commission may be split among them. If they are paid from funds collected for settlement, this is shown on lines 701-702.

703. Commission Paid at Settlement

Sometimes the broker will retain the earnest money deposit to apply towards his commission. In this case, line 703 will show only the remainder of the commission which will be paid at settlement.

800. Items Payable in Connection With Loan

These are the fees which lenders charge to process, approve and make the mortgage loan.

801. Loan Origination

This fee covers the lender's administrative costs in processing the loan. Often expressed as a percentage of the loan, the fee will vary among lenders and from locality to locality. Generally the buyer pays the fee unless another arrangement has been made with the seller and written into the sales contract.

802. Loan Discount

Often called "points," a loan discount is a one-time charge used to adjust the yield on the loan to what market conditions demand. It is used to offset constraints placed on the yield by State or Federal regulations. Each "point" is equal to one percent of the mortgage amount. For example, if a lender charges four points on a $30,000 loan this amounts to a charge of $1,200.

803. Appraisal Fee

This charge, which may vary significantly from transaction to transaction, pays for a statement of property value for the lender, made by an independent appraiser or by a member of the lender's staff. The lender needs to know if the value of the property is sufficient to secure the loan if you fail to repay the loan according to the provision of your mortgage contract, and the lender must foreclose and take title to the house. The appraiser inspects the house and the neighborhood, and considers sales prices of comparable houses and other factors in determining the value. The appraisal report may contain photos and other information of value to you. It will provide the factual data upon which the appraiser based the appraised value. Ask the lender for a copy of the appraisal report or review the original.

The appraisal fee may be paid by either the buyer or the seller, as agreed in the sales contract. In some cases this fee is included in the Mortgage Insurance Application Fee. See line **806**.

804. Credit Report Fee

This fee covers the cost of the credit report, which shows how you have handled other credit transactions. The lender uses this report in conjunction with information you submitted with the application regarding your income, outstanding bills, and employment, to determine whether you are an acceptable credit risk and to help determine how much money to lend you.

Where you encounter credit reporting problems you have protections under the Fair Credit laws as summarized under "Home Buyer's Rights" in this booklet.

805. Lender's Inspection Fee

This charge covers inspections, often of newly constructed housing, made by personnel of the lending institution or an outside inspector. (Pest or other inspections made by companies **other than the lender are discussed in connection with line 1302.**)

806. Mortgage Insurance Application Fee

This fee covers processing the application for private mortgage insurance which may be required on certain loans. It may cover both the appraisal and application fee.

807. Assumption Fee

This fee is charged for processing papers for cases in which the buyer takes over the payments on the prior loan of the seller.

900. Items Required by Lender to Be Paid in Advance

You may be required to prepay certain items, such as interest, mortgage insurance premium and hazard insurance premium, at the time of settlement.

901. Interest

Lenders usually require that borrowers pay at settlement the interest that accrues on the mortgage from the date of settlement to the beginning of the period covered by the first monthly payment. For example, suppose your settlement takes place on April 16, and your first regular monthly payment will be due June 1, to cover interest charges for the month of May. On the settlement date, the lender will collect interest for the

80

period from April 16 to May 1. If you borrowed $30,000 at 9 percent interest, the interest item would be $112.50. This amount will be entered on line 901.

902. Mortgage Insurance Premium

Mortgage insurance protects the lender from loss due to payment default by the homeowner. The lender may require you to pay your first premium in advance, on the day of settlement. The premium may cover a specific number of months or a year in advance. With this insurance protection, the lender is willing to make a larger loan, thus reducing your downpayment requirements. This type of insurance should not be confused with mortgage life, credit life, or disability insurance designed to pay off a mortgage in the event of physical disability or death of the borrower.

903. Hazard Insurance Premium

This premium prepayment is for insurance protection for you and the lender against loss due to fire, windstorm, and natural hazards. This coverage may be included in a Homeowners Policy which insures against additional risks which may include personal liability and theft. Lenders often require payment of the first year's premium at settlement.

A hazard insurance or homeowner's policy may not protect you against loss caused by flooding. In special flood-prone areas identified by HUD, you may be required by Federal law to carry flood insurance on your home. Such insurance may be purchased at low federally subsidized rates in participating communities under the National Flood Insurance Act.

1000. Reserves Deposited With Lenders

Reserves (sometimes called "escrow" or "impound" accounts) are funds held in an account by the lender to assure future payment for such recurring items as real estate taxes and hazard insurance.

You will probably have to pay an initial amount for each of these items to start the reserve account at the time of settlement. A portion of your regular monthly payments will be added to the reserve account. RESPA places limitations on the amount of reserve funds which may be required by the lender. Read "Reserve Accounts" in this booklet for reserve calculation procedures. Do not hesitate to ask the lender to explain any variance between your own calculations and the figure presented to you.

1001. Hazard Insurance

The lender determines the amount of money that must be placed in the reserve in order to pay the next insurance premium when due.

1002. Mortgage Insurance

The lender may require that part of the total annual premium be placed in the reserve account at settlement. The portion to be placed in reserve may be negotiable.

1003-1004. City/County Property Taxes

The lender may require a regular monthly payment to the reserve account for property taxes.

1005. Annual Assessments

This reserve item covers assessments that may be imposed by subdivisions or municipalities for special improvements (such as sidewalks, sewers or paving) or ,fees (such as homeowners association fees).

1100. Title Charges

Title charges may cover a variety of services performed by the lender or others for handling and supervising the settlement transaction and services related thereto. The specific charges discussed in connection with lines 1101 through 1109 are those most frequently incurred at settlement. Due to the great diversity in practice from area to area, your particular settlement may not include all these items or may include others not listed. Ask your settlement agent to explain how these fees relate to services performed on your behalf. An extended discussion is presented in "Securing Title Services" earlier in this booklet.

1101. Settlement or Closing Fee

This fee is paid to the settlement agent. Responsibility for payment of this fee should be negotiated between the seller and buyer, at the time the sales contract is signed.

1102-1104. Abstract or Title Search, Title Examination, Title Insurance Binder

These charges cover the costs of the search and examination of records of previous ownership, transfers, etc., to determine whether the seller can convey clear title to the property, and to disclose any matters on record that could adversely affect the buyer or the lender. Examples of title problems are unpaid mortgages, judgment or tax liens, conveyances of mineral rights, leases, and power line easements or road right-of-ways that could limit use and enjoyment of the real estate. In some areas, a title insurance binder is called a commitment to insure.

1105. Document Preparation

There may be a separate document fee that covers preparation of final legal papers, such as a mortgage, deed of trust, note, or deed. You should check to see that these services, if charged for, are not also covered under some other service fees. Ask the settlement agent.

1106. Notary Fee

This fee is charged for the cost of having a licensed person affix his or her name and seal to various documents authenticating the execution of these documents by the parties.

1107. Attorney's Fees

You may be required to pay for legal services provided to the lender in connection with the settlement, such as examination of the title binder or sales contract. Occasionally this fee can be shared with the seller, if so stipulated in the sales contract. If a lawyer's involvement is required by the lender, the fee will appear on this part of the form. The buyer and seller may each retain an attorney to check the various documents and to represent them at all stages of the transaction including settlement. Where this service is not required and is paid for outside of closing, the person conducting settlement is not obligated to record the fee on the settlement form.

1108. Title Insurance

The total cost of owner's and lender's title insurance is shown here. The borrower may pay all, a part or none of this cost depending on the terms of the sales contract or local custom.

1109. Lender's Title Insurance

A one-time premium may be charged at settlement for a lender's title policy which protects the lender against loss due to problems or defects in connection with the title. The insurance is usually written for the amount of the mortgage loan and covers losses due to defects or problems not identified by title search and examination. In most areas this is customarily paid by the borrower unless the seller agrees in the sales contract to pay part or all of it.

1110. Owner's Title Insurance

This charge is for owner's title insurance protection and protects you against losses due to title defects. In some areas it is customary for the seller to provide the buyer with an owner's policy and for the seller to pay for this policy. In other areas, if the buyer desires an owner's policy he must pay for it.

1200. Government Recording and Transfer Charges

These fees may be paid either by borrower or seller, depending upon your contract when you buy the house or accept the loan commitment. The borrower usually pays the fees for legally recording the new deed and mortgage (item 1201). These fees, collected when property changes hands or when a mortgage loan is made, may be quite large and are set by State and/or local governments. City, county and/or State tax stamps may have to be purchased as well (item 1201 and 1203).

1300. Additional Settlement Charges 1301. Survey

The lender or the title insurance company may require that a surveyor conduct a property survey to determine the exact location of the house and the lot line, as well as easements and rights of way. This is a protection to the buyer as well. Usually the buyer pays the surveyor's fees, but sometimes this may be handled by the seller.

1302. Pest and Other Inspections

This fee is to cover inspections for termite or other pest infestation of the house. This may be important if the sales contract included a promise by the seller to transfer the property free from pests or pest-caused damage. Be sure that the inspection shows that the property complies with the sales contract before you complete the settlement. If it does not you may wish to require a bond or other financial assurance that the work will be completed. This fee can be paid either by the borrower or seller depending upon the terms of the sales contract. Lenders vary in their requirements as to such an inspection.

Fees for other inspections, such as for structural soundness, are entered on line 1303.

1400. Total Settlement Charges

All the fees in the borrower's column entitled "Paid from Borrower's Funds at Settlement" are totaled here and transferred to line 103 of Section J, "Settlement charges to borrower" in the **Summary of Borrower's Transaction** on page 1 of the Uniform Settlement Statement. All the settlement fees paid by the seller are transferred to line 502 of Section K, **Summary of Seller's Transaction** on page 1 of the Uniform Settlement Statement.

Comparing Lender Costs

If a lender is willing to reduce his fees for such items as loan origination, discount points and other one-time settlement charges, he may gain it back if he charges a higher mortgage interest rate.

Here is one rule of thumb which you can use to calculate the combined effect of the interest rate on your loan and the one-time settlement charges (paid by you) such as "points." While not perfectly accurate, it is usually close enough for meaningful comparisons between lenders. The rule is, that one-time settlement charges equaling one percent of the loan amount increase the interest charge by one-eighth (1/8) of one percent. The 1/8 factor corresponds to a pay back period of approximately 15 years. If you intend instead to hold the property for only five years and pay off the loan at that time, the factor increases to 1/4.

Here is an example of the rule. Consider only those charges that differ between lenders. Suppose you wish to borrow $30,000. Lender A will make the loan at 8.5 percent interest, but charges a two percent origination fee, a $150.00 application fee, and requires that you use a lawyer, for title work, selected by the lender at a fee of $300.

Lender B will make the loan at 9 percent interest, but has no additional requirements or charges. As part of that nine

CALCULATING THE BORROWER'S TRANSACTIONS

A Sample Worksheet

This page is a sample worksheet for a family purchasing a $35,000 house and getting a new $30,000 loan. Line 103 assumes that their total settlement charges are $1,000. (This figure is the sum of all the individual settlement charges, which will be listed in detail in Section L, of their Uniform Settlement Statement.) The $1,000 figure is merely illustrative. The amount may be higher in some areas and for some types of transactions, and lower for others.

J. SUMMARY OF BORROWER'S TRANSACTION	
100. GROSS AMOUNT DUE FROM BORROWER:	
101. Contract sales price	35,000.00
102. Personal property	200.00
103. Settlement charges to borrower (line 1400)	1,000.00
104.	
105.	
Adjustments for items paid by seller in advance	
106. City/town taxes to	
107. County taxes to	
108. Assessments 6/30 to 7/31 (owners assn)	20.00
109. Fuel oil 25 to gal. @.50/gal	12.50
110.	
111.	
112.	
120. GROSS AMOUNT DUE FROM BORROWER	36,232.50
200. AMOUNTS PAID BY OR IN BEHALF OF BORROWER:	
201. Deposit or earnest money	1,000.00
202. Principal amount of new loan(s)	30,000.00
203. Existing loan(s) taken subject to	
204.	
205.	
206.	
207.	
208.	
209.	
Adjustments for items unpaid by seller	
210. City/town taxes to	
211. County taxes 1-1 to 6-30 @$600/yr	300.00
212. Assessments 1-1 to 6-30 @100/yr	50.00
213.	
214.	
215.	
216.	
217.	
218.	
219.	
220. TOTAL PAID BY/FOR BORROWER	31,350.00
300. CASH AT SETTLEMENT FROM/TO BORROWER	
301. Gross amount due from borrower (line 120)	36,232.50
302. Less amounts paid by/for borrower (line 220)	(31,350.00)
303. CASH (☐ FROM) (☒ TO) BORROWER	4,882.50

Your Financial Worksheet

Once you have decided which providers you wish to use for your settlement services and have selected the lender who will make your loan, you can calculate the total estimated cash you will need to complete the purchase. The form below, which is a part of the Uniform Settlement Statement, can be used as a worksheet for this purpose.

J. SUMMARY OF BORROWER'S TRANSACTION	
100. GROSS AMOUNT DUE FROM BORROWER:	
101. Contract sales price	
102. Personal property	
103. Settlement charges to borrower (line 1400)	
104.	
105.	
Adjustments for items paid by seller in advance	
106. City/town taxes to	
107. County taxes to	
108. Assessments to	
109.	
110.	
111.	
112.	
120. GROSS AMOUNT DUE FROM BORROWER	
200. AMOUNTS PAID BY OR IN BEHALF OF BORROWER:	
201. Deposit or earnest money	
202. Principal amount of new loan(s)	
203. Existing loan(s) taken subject to	
204.	
205.	
206.	
207.	
208.	
209.	
Adjustments for items unpaid by seller	
210. City/town taxes to	
211. County taxes to	
212. Assessments to	
213.	
214.	
215.	
216.	
217.	
218.	
219.	
220. TOTAL PAID BY/FOR BORROWER	
300. CASH AT SETTLEMENT FROM/TO BORROWER	
301. Gross amount due from borrower (line 120)	
302. Less amounts paid by/for borrower (line 220)	( )
303. CASH (☐ FROM) (☐ TO) BORROWER	

percent interest, though, Lender B will not charge an application fee and will absorb the lawyer's fee. What are the actual charges for each case?

Begin by relating all of Lender A's one-time charges to percentages of the $30,000 loan amount:

2 percent origination fee	=	2 percent of loan amount
$150 application fee	=	0.5 percent of loan amount
$300 lawyer's fee	=	1 percent of loan amount
Total		3.5 percent of loan amount

Since each 1 percent of the loan amount in charges is the equivalent of 1/8 percent increase in interest, the effective interest rate from Lender A is the quoted or "contract" interest rate, 8.5 percent plus .44 percent (3.5 times 1/8), or a total of 8.94 percent interest. Since Lender B has offered a nine percent interest rate, Lender A has made a more attractive offer. Of course, it is more attractive only if you have sufficient cash to pay Lender A's one-time charges and still cover your downpayment, moving expenses, and other settlement costs. This is simply a method to compare diverse costs on an equal basis. In the above illustration, Lender A does not receive the $300 lawyer fee.

The calculation is sensitive to your assumption about the period of time you plan to own the house before paying off the mortgage. As indicated above, the factor increases to 1/4 if you expect to pay off the mortgage in five years. Applying this new factor to the above illustration, the effective interest rate for Lender A would be 8.5 percent plus .87 (3.5 x 1/4) for a total of 9.37 percent interest. Lender A's offer is no longer more attractive than Lender B's which was 9.0 percent.

In doing these calculations you should also be careful as to which one-time fees you place into the calculation. For example, if Lender B in the above illustration did not include in his charge a legal fee but told you that you had to secure legal services in order to obtain the loan from him, you would have to add to Lender B's interest rate the legal fee that you had to incur.

You can use this method to compare the effective interest rates of any number of lenders as you shop for a loan. If the lenders have provided Truth-in-Lending disclosures, these are an even better comparative tool. You should question lenders carefully to make sure you have learned of all the charges they intend to make. The good faith estimate you receive when you make a loan application is a good checklist for this information, but it is not precise. Thus, you should ask the lender how the charges and fees are computed.

100. Gross Amount Due From Borrower

Page 1 of the Uniform Settlement Statement summarizes all

actual costs and adjustments for the borrower and seller, including total settlement fees and charges found on line 1400 of Section L.

101. Contract Sales Price

This is the price of the home agreed to in the sales contract between the buyer and seller.

102. Personal Property

If, at the time the sales contract was made, you and the seller agreed that some items were to be transferred with the house, the price of those items is entered here. If it was agreed to include these items in the price of the home, their cost will be part of the sales price recorded on line 101. Personal property could include items such as carpets, drapes, stove, refrigerator, etc.

103. Settlement Charges to Borrower

The total charges detailed in Section L and totaled on line 1400, are recorded here. This figure includes all of the items payable in connection with the loan, items required by the lender to be paid in advance, reserves deposited with the lender, title charges, government recording and transfer charges, and any additional related charges.

104-105. Additional Costs

This space is for listing any additional amounts owed the seller, such as reserve funds if the buyer is assuming the seller's loan. This may not be applicable to your settlement.

106-112. Adjustments

These include taxes, front footage charges, insurance, rent, fuel and other items that the seller has previously paid for covering a period which runs beyond the settlement date. The costs are usually divided on a proportional basis with the seller being reimbursed for charges accruing after the date of transfer of title.

120. Gross Amount Due

This is the total of lines 101 through 112.

200. Amounts Paid By Or On Behalf Of Borrower

(See items 201-220)

201. Deposit or Earnest Money

This is the amount which you paid against the sales price when the sales contract was signed. It is credited to the purchase.

202. Principal Amount of New Loan

This is the amount of the new mortgage which you will repay to the lender in the future.

203. Existing Loan(s)

If you are taking over the seller's mortgage(s) instead of obtaining a new loan or paying all cash, the amount still owed on those prior loans will be shown here.

210-219. Adjustments

This includes taxes or assessments which become due after settlement, but which the seller pays because they cover a period of time prior to settlement. See "Reserve Accounts" for a further discussion of these matters.

220. Total Amounts Paid By/For Borrower

This is the sum of lines 201 through 219.

300. Cash At Settlement From/To Buyer

Remaining are the summary lines which are 301-303 for the borrower (and 601-603 for the seller). Subtracting line 302 (gross amount paid by or for the borrower) from line 301 (gross amount due from the borrower) results in the net cash the borrower must pay at settlement.

RESERVE ACCOUNTS

In most instances, a monthly mortgage payment is made up of a payment on the principal amount of the mortgage debt which reduces the balance due on the loan, an interest payment which is the charge for use of the borrowed funds, and a reserve payment (also known as an escrow or impound payment) which represents approximately one-twelfth of the estimated annual insurance premiums, property taxes, assessments and other recurring charges.

When settlement occurs you may need to make an initial deposit into the reserve account; otherwise, your regular monthly deposits to it will not accumulate enough to pay the taxes, insurance or other charges when they fall due. Under RESPA, the maximum amount the lender can require borrowers or prospective borrowers to deposit into a reserve account at settlement is a total gross amount not to exceed the sum of: (a) an amount that would have been sufficient to pay taxes, insurance premiums, or other charges which would have been paid under normal lending practices, and **ending** on the **due date** of the first full monthly mortgage installment payment; plus (b) an additional amount not in excess of one-sixth (2 months) of the estimated total amount of taxes, insurance premiums and other charges to be paid on the dates indicated above during any twelve month period to follow.

An illustration will help clarify this calculation. Assume the following set of facts on a loan, and that taxes are paid at the end of the period against which taxes are assessed.

Example:
Settlement date · April 30, 1977

Due Date of first
mortgage loan repay-
ment · June 1, 1977

89

Taxes due yearly	$360.00
Monthly tax accrual	$ 30.00
Due date for taxes	December 1st for the calendar year

The reserve amount for category (a) is $180.00. This represents the amount of taxes accruing between December 1, 1976 (the last tax due date) and May 30, 1977 ($30.00 x 6 months). Reserve amounts chargeable under category (b) could be up to two months advance payment times $30.00 or a total of $60.00. Therefore, total reserve deposits for taxes at settlement would be a maximum of $240.00. Changing the due date for taxes and/or the first mortgage payment results in a different reserve amount for the same illustration.

The same procedure is used to determine the maximum amounts that can be collected by the lender for insurance premiums or other charges. You need to know the charges and due dates in order to compute the amounts.

Once you begin your monthly mortgage payments, you cannot be required to pay more than one-twelfth of the annual taxes and other charges each month, unless a larger payment is necessary to make up for a deficit in your account or to maintain the cushion of the one-sixth of annual charges mentioned in (b) above. A deficit may be caused, for example, if your taxes or insurance premiums are raised.

You should note that the above monthly mortgage payments reserve limitations apply to all RESPA covered mortgage loans whether they were originated before or after the implementation of RESPA.

Adjustments Between Buyer and Seller

The previous section dealt with setting up and maintaining your reserve account with the lender. At settlement it is also usually necessary to make an adjustment between buyer and seller for property taxes and other charges. This is an entirely separate matter from the initial deposit which the borrower makes into the new reserve account.

The adjustments between buyer and seller are shown in Sections J and K of the Uniform Settlement Statement. In the example given in the foregoing section, the taxes, which are payable annually, had not yet been paid when the settlement occurs on April 30. The home buyer will have to pay a whole year's taxes on the following December 1. However, the seller lived in the house for the first four months of the year. Thus, one-third of the year's taxes are to be paid by the seller. Accordingly, lines 208 and 508 on the Uniform Settlement

Statement would read as follows:

County taxes
1/1/77 to 4/30/77
$120.00

The buyer would be given credit for this amount in the settlement and the seller would have to pay this amount or count it as a deduction from sums payable to the seller.

In some areas taxes are paid at the beginning of the taxable year. If, in our example, the taxes were paid by the seller on January 1, 1977 for the following tax year ending December 31, 1977, the buyer will have to compensate the seller for the taxes paid by the seller for those months that the buyer will be in possession of the property (April 30–December 31). This adjustment will be shown on lines 107 and 407 of the Uniform Settlement Statement. With settlement occurring on April 30, those lines will read as follows:

County taxes
4/30/77 to 12/31/77
$240.00

This amount would be credited to the seller in the settlement.

Similar adjustments are made for insurance (if the policy is being kept in effect), special assessments, fuel and other utilities, although the billing periods for these may not always be on an annual basis. Be sure you work out these prorations with the seller prior to settlement. It is wise for you to notify utility companies of the change in ownership and ask for a special reading on the day of settlement, with the bill for pre-settlement charges to be mailed to the seller at his new address. This will eliminate much confusion that can result if you are billed for utilities which cover the time when the seller owned the unit.

Equal Credit Opportunity Notice

The lender may provide the applicant the Equal Credit Opportunity Notice on this page. (Federal Reserve Board Regulation B, 12 CFR 202.4(d)) The Equal Credit Opportunity Act, 15 U.S.C. 1691 et. seq., prohibits discrimination against credit applicants on the basis of sex and marital status. Beginning March 23, 1977, the Act extends this protection to race, color, religion, national origin, age, whether all or part of the applicant's income is derived from any public assistance program, or if the applicant has in good faith exercised any right under the Consumer Credit Protection Act. The applicant should note that the lender must either provide the notice here, on an application form, or on some other separate sheet of paper. This notice provides the name of the lender's supervising agency.

APPENDIX

Consumer Literature on Home Purchasing, Maintenance, Protection, and other Topics

U.S. Department of Housing and Urban Development

Appraisals

Questions and Answers on Home Property Appraisals	HUD-38-F

Condominiums

Financing Condominium Housing	HUD-77-F
HUD/FHA Non-Assisted Program for Condominium Housing	HUD-227-F
Questions About Condominiums	HUD-365-F
HUD/FHA Comparison of Condominium and Cooperative Housing	HUD-321-F

Cooperatives

Let's Consider Cooperatives	HUD-17-F
HUD/FHA Program for Unsubsidized Cooperative Housing	HUD-256-F

Home Mortgage Insurance

Home Mortgage Insurance	HUD-43-F
Programs for Home Mortgage Insurance	HUD-97-F

Home Ownership

The Home Buying Serviceman	HUD-121-F
HUD's Home Ownership Subsidy Program	HUD-419-HPMC

Miscellaneous

Protecting Your Home Against Theft	HUD-315-F
Termites	HUD-323-F
Be An Energy Miser in Your Home	HUD-324-PA

Mobile Homes

Buying and Financing a Mobile Home	HUD-243-F
Mobile Home Financing Through HUD	HUD-265-F

General Interest

Wise Home Buying	HUD-267-F
Should You Buy or Rent a Home	HUD-328-F
Protecting Your Housing Investment	HUD-346-PA
Home Owners Glossary of Building Terms	HUD-369-F
Home Buyers Vocabulary	HUD-383-HM
Your Housing Rights	HUD-177-EO

Contact: U.S. Department of Housing & Urban Development, 451 Seventh Street, S.W., Washington, D.C. 20410, Room B-258 or HUD Regional, Area and Insuring Offices throughout the country.

U.S. Veterans Administration

Pointers for the Veteran Homeowner

Questions and Answers on Guaranteed and Direct Loans for Veterans

To the Home-Buying Veteran

Contact: Your Nearest VA Regional Office

U.S. Department of Agriculture

Selecting and Financing a Home

Contact: Office of Communications, U.S. Department of Agriculture, Washington, D.C. 20250

U.S. Department of Labor

Rent or Buy? (No. 178D)

Contact: Consumer Information, Public Documents Distribution Center, Pueblo, Colorado 81009

General Services Administration

Consumer Information: A Catalog of Selected Federal Publications

Contact: Consumer Information Center, Pueblo, Colorado 81009

PART II

Laws Every Homeowner and Tenant Should Know

Chapter 27

LEGAL RIGHTS AND OBLIGATIONS OF THE BUYER

No one has ever been able to explain satisfactorily why millions of people who would never dare pretend to be expert in any other area of human endeavor are so convinced of their extraordinary talent as real estate appraisers or brokers.

If you are smart you will realize that real estate is a highly complex and technical field and that you probably are not quite the expert in this specialized area that you imagine yourself to be.

Most people simply must rely on the advice and help of professional trained attorneys, appraisers, mortgage bankers and brokers. Unfortunately, few seem to understand this, and the great majority of buyers place all of their dependence on only the real estate broker—whose integrity they have not carefully checked—or, still, attempt to go it alone.

You need seasoned brokers of unquestionable integrity to guide you on location, condition, best terms available and financing. In any locality, bank mortgage officers, bank conveyancers and attorneys can best steer you to the worthiest brokers.

Remember, you pay nothing for all the information and education you get from these seasoned and experienced brokers. If you do buy through one of them, the seller pays his fee; and no one pays all the other brokers who helped you immeasurably.

It has always been a mystery to me why so many buyers prefer to shortchange themselves by restricting their use of brokers or omitting them altogether. Others foolishly allow the same broker who is perhaps well qualified to serve them in one locality to escort them into distant towns which are just as strange to the broker as they are to the buyer. This seems to me like a case of the blind leading the blind. I wonder why the buyer does not more often think to rely on a thoroughly experienced broker in each separate locality.

In case you yourself as a buyer fear brokers, or simply do not know how to use them wisely, the following list of tips should be helpful:

1. Never set foot into a broker's office before you have carefully checked his integrity. Remember, perhaps only one out of ten brokers belongs to their trade association, and many who do belong unfortunately do not observe their association's excellent code of ethics. The trade association does not expel known rascals and rogues because it likes their dues, and it prefers to lull the public into believing that they can sleep well nights because their "Realtor" is awake. Just as there are good and bad members of the Realtor association, there are also good and bad nonmembers among the 90 percent of licensed brokers who prefer not to be association members.

2. Innocent victims of unscrupulous brokers who have come to me as an attorney-at-law specializing in real estate all seem to have made one common mistake: not consulting their lawyer *before signing anything or turning over any money.*

3. Now, honestly, does it make sense to rush into a strange broker's office with a cash deposit of hundreds, or even thousands of dollars, and sign anything he puts before you, when he owes all of his legal duty to act in the best interests of his principal, the seller, and not in your best interests? The law holds that the broker is in an arm's-length transaction with you. As you push this self-serving broker into perhaps a three-thousand dollar commission or more, why do you hold back a possible couple of hundred dollars' fee from your own lawyer, whose plain legal duty it is to act in *your* best interests?

If you do not think a real estate contract is an important enough reason to use a lawyer, then why do you suppose "contracts" is a basic subject in the freshman year of law school? Do you really know of any more important or more complex type of contract? Actually, a real estate contract is one of the very few types of contracts entitled to the extraordinary remedy of "Specific Performance" in a court of equity. This means that while you are restricted to suing for actual money damages for the breach of most contracts, either the buyer or the seller is entitled to force the party in breach of a real estate sales contract to specifically perform his part of the purchase and sale agreement.

Certainly, it is a case of fools treading where angels fear to go for unwary buyers to sign a real estate sales contract without prior review by their attorneys.

These broker contract forms are printed up for sale to brokers, sometimes by the Realtor trade association itself. They are heavily weighted in favor of the broker, falling far short of adequate protection for either the buyer or the seller. All you have to do is to compare one of these one-sided, unfair contract forms with the lists of minimal protection every buyer and seller should get as outlined below and in Chapter 28.

4. *Minimal protection for a buyer in a purchase and sale agreement would include the following provisions:*

    a. A financing clause making the agreement subject to the specific financing needed for buyer to be able to perform on closing day, "failing which deposit is to be promptly returned." (This financing clause should take into consideration the amount of mortgage money needed by the buyer, the highest interest rate he can afford to pay, the number of years over which he will need to spread his payments and the maximum amount of "points" or bonus money, if any, he will be required to pay the bank in order to secure the mortgage.

    b. Subject to insurance protection by the seller in an amount at least 80% of the sale price. Also, an escrow clause should be put in the contract, such as: "In the event of fire or casualty damage exceeding $3,000, the buyer shall have the option of cancelling this contract and receiving his deposit back, without recourse to either party."

    c. Subject to seller's delivering a deed of good and clear record and a marketable title, except for those encumbrances which are specifically spelled out in the agreement and assented to by the buyer.

    d. Subject to property conforming to zoning ordinances and building codes.

    e. Subject to actual delineations of boundary lines conforming to the present apparent boundaries.

    f. Subject to buyer's having the right to a reasonable extension of time for performance, if necessary. The following language, part of the fine print in many contracts, would effectively bar this right and cause a loss of buyer's deposit for nonperformance, no matter how unfairly: "Time is of the essence of this contract."

    g. Where the contract is subject to V.A. or F.H.A. approval, the escape clause permitting withdrawal by the buyer in case of appraisal falling below the sale price must specifically spell out the "prompt refund of deposit to the buyer." Otherwise the public law allows the deposit to be handled "in accordance with the terms of the contract." I regret to warn my readers that more and more "Brokers" are using their own tailor-made contract forms which deliberately deprive these buyers of a refund of their deposit when the property fails to meet approval by the government appraiser. In other words, the V.A. or F.H.A. buyer who always thinks he can get his deposit back if the government appraisal is less than the price, sadly finds out—too late—that he is "locked in" and "married" to the contract, so that he can't get out.

Apparently due to overcrowding and intense competition among the brokers more and more brokers who used to be good guys are turning bad. Meanwhile, the State Bar Associations stand idly by while these bandit brokers draw up their unfair contracts, even though they completely lack the legal competency to prepare them properly and fairly. Too often, the broker associations, far from protecting the public, actually aid, and abet, and shield, and protect these brokers—as long as they keep paying their dues.

h. Since the buyer buys a used house "as is," some protection in addition to the aforementioned conformance to zoning ordinances and building codes may be in order, particularly if there is doubt as to the condition of the roof, basement, plumbing, wiring, etc.

i. All appliances should be guaranteed to be in working order, at least at the time the buyer is to take possession.

j. Only the V.A. requires a "termite certificate." Every buyer should require this protection from a seller or obtain one himself. The usual cost is only fifteen or twenty dollars. There is a famous Massachusetts case about a buyer who found his newly purchased home ruined by termites. The unfortunate purchaser was denied any remedy by the court because the seller never specifically told him the house was free of termites.

k. Certainly there have been enough cases of hardship due to uncompleted or improperly completed new houses to justify a requirement that either the builder furnish a "performance bond" or the buyer obtain one himself. However, the problem has become so widespread and notorious that the insurance companies are now issuing these performance bonds only on big developments, and not for a single custombuilt house.

l. The buyer's deposit should be held in escrow by a stake-holder until closing day. It should never be permitted to be used by a seller before it becomes a certainty that the transaction will actually be able to become consummated.

m. If personal property is included in the sale the amount paid by the buyer should be separate from the price paid for the real estate. Subsequent tax assessments and bills to the buyer could reflect a significant tax saving.

n. Due and unpaid betterments should be the responsibility of the seller.

o. In case of an estate sale be sure the seller has a court license to sell.

p. The buyer should be certain he will actually have occupancy on closing day. If the seller is to be allowed to remain on the premises beyond closing day, a sufficient holdback of funds should be enforced by the buyer to make it worthwhile for the seller to get out when he promised to. Also, the buyer should be paid at least enough to repay him for all out of pocket expenses he will suffer while the seller stays on after closing day, and the seller should agree in writing that he is remaining on the premises for use and occupancy only, and not with the rights of a tenant.

q. The amount of cash to be paid by the buyer must be specific; otherwise, according to a Connecticut case, oral evidence is inadmissible and the contract is unenforceable.

Note: The above suggested provisions constitute *minimal* protection only to a buyer, and under normal conditions. They are not to be used as a substitute for your own lawyer's Contract of Sale especially drafted by him to satisfy your particular needs. If you still prefer to omit your lawyer and let a strange broker who has a fiduciary duty to the seller, and a natural and human inclination to look out for himself, draft your contract to buy— you are on your own. Just remember that your lawyer is trained for this task a whale of a lot better than any broker. In any event, the oversimplified standard form most brokers use cannot possibly protect your interest adequately.

5. Remember, you can revoke your offer any time before notice of acceptance has been communicated back to you. It is the "acceptance" that creates the formation of a contract.

6. If the seller once rejects your offer, he cannot later accept it and bind you. The rejection kills the offer forever. His subsequent acceptance is merely a counter offer which you now have the right to accept or reject.

7. A contract attempted on a Sunday or legal holiday is illegal. It constitutes a nullity in the law. The parties have no standing in a court of law. A Massachusetts case holds that a Sunday deposit is not returnable. On the other hand, if the contract started on a Sunday is really completed in its entirety on a subsequent weekday, then the courts will enforce it. Remember, it does no legal good to date the contract for a subsequent weekday. If you actually signed it on Sunday, it is still a mere nullity.

8. Ask questions of the seller and his agent the broker. Make them answer your questions. Don't permit them to evade you. Remember, they are liable to you for misrepresentations of such material facts as the tax bill, heating bill, dry basement, etc. They are not liable for personal opinion or seller's puffs such as "this is the best buy in town." Likewise, they have no legal duty to volunteer any information to you. Don't let them remain silent about things that are important to you. If they deliberately deceive you about a material fact, they are liable in tort for deceit for *all* of your damages. According to a recent landmark Massachusetts case, if they even *innocently* misrepresent a material fact you are entitled to rescind the contract and be made whole.

9. Always offer less than you are prepared to pay. After all, the seller normally starts high in price. Make the broker do as good a selling job on the seller as he did on you.

10. Remember, when you make your first offer you may not really be ready to be bound completely and irrevocably. If you are only on a fishing expedition—looking for the seller's rockbottom price—use an "offer and acceptance" form only, not a formal and final contract of sale. The big legal difference is this: "specific performance" will not be granted when the parties have indicated that they have not yet made their final agreement. Most "offer" forms spell out in black and white that the parties intend to enter into a full purchase and sale agreement later. So the worst that can happen to you as a buyer when you have signed only an "offer" form is to lose your deposit. And you can protect yourself even against this loss by inserting an escape clause or out, in case you need it.

Chapter 28

LEGAL RIGHTS AND OBLIGATIONS OF THE SELLER

BEWARE OF OVERPRICING

You are always better off pricing your house at or near fair market value. Brokers simply will not advertise and sell your house as hard if they know it is overpriced. Instead, they will stretch you out until you have to be more reasonable in your demands, or they will bring in low offers anyway. Once you accept an unexpectedly low offer you become liable for a full commission to the broker—usually 6 percent of the sale price. Meanwhile you have succeeded in keeping away many qualified buyers who would have been making good offers if your price were right.

If you are trying to sell your overpriced house yourself, even if you succeed in landing a sucker you may be sure that the bank, the F.H.A. or the V.A. will not go along with you on their appraisal. They will only torpedo your sale anyway with an appraisal so far under your price that the buyer will be lost. So you wind up gaining nothing and losing a lot by putting your house on the market at more than five percent over its fair value.

You can get a Veterans Administration "preappraisal" for about $50. Any seller can do this. You do not have to be a veteran. Likewise, any seller can get an F.H.A. "conditional commitment" for about $50. (The final commitment is given only after F.H.A. approves the buyer.) In any event, an independent fee appraisal is readily obtained for a fee of about $50 to $100.

In this case it would be advisable to tell the appraiser that you are more interested in the fair market value figure than you are in an impressive formal report full of boiler plate and window dressing. Tell him a plain one-page letter will suffice. After all, you already have the legal description of your property in measurements and boundaries on your copy of your deed or mortgage, so there is no need for him to copy that into your report. You may also tell him to omit a lengthy description of your county, city, neighborhood and site.

He might just as well omit consideration of a "cost approach" as an indication of value, expecially if your house is over fifteen years old. And "income approach" to value for a single-family dwelling often borders on the ridiculous. Tell the appraiser you will settle for a "comparable sales approach" as an indication of fair market value. Actually, most appraisers agree that this approach is the only valid reliable and dependable approach to the appraisal of a single-family dwelling. The "cost" and "income" approaches are used at best as guidelines and at worst as boiler plate (window dressing or filler material).

Remember, any appraisal is better than no appraisal. You must not rely entirely on your own emotionally inflated idea of the value of your house.

It would be well for you to keep in mind the following tips:

1. Just because one or a group of listing brokers go along with your high starting price does not mean that they are *appraising* your house this high. They are simply trying to get your listing and a chance to make a commission when are finally able to secure a low offer. So it would be less than accurate for you to claim now that your house has been *appraised* for the price these brokers went along with.

2. Good broker-appraisers will either appraise your house at the *right price* for a fee, or take the listing at *your price* for a chance at the commission. They usually know better than to try to do both at the same time. They know that too often when they try to give a truthful, accurate appraisal simultaneously with taking a listing, they lose both an appraisal fee and the listing.

3. One of the problems in trying to arrive at fair market value is that real estate appraisal is an art, not a science.

4. Another problem is the complete absence of any governmental control, regulation or licensing of appraisal activity. Every brand-new rookie real estate broker prints signs, ads, stationery and business cards describing himself as an appraiser. He even offers to appraise residential, commercial, industrial or investment property and land for all comers.

5. Modern appraisal technique has been put on a professional basis by the American Institute of Real Estate Appraisers only within the past generation. This trade association (one of the many divisions of the National Association of Real Estate Boards) has the usual lofty code of ethics of such associations. It has been trying hard to raise and make uniform the standards of appraisal practice. However, its present small membership is trying even harder to keep its membership extremely restricted and selective. Consequently, even though other splinter appraisal societies exist, the number of trained professionals is extremely limited and not nearly enough to meet the demand for appraisal work. This is why it is so important for you to obtain a V.A., F.H.A. or properly qualified independent fee appraiser. Your bank mortgage officer should be able to help you select a worthy appraiser.

If you advertise, remember that Sunday is the best day; second best day for results is Wednesday. It always helps to indicate clearly in your ad that a bargain is available due to "an estate that must be settled" or "transferred owner who must sacrifice," or "priced to sell without a broker's commission." Avoid extravagant verbosity in your ad. Always ask yourself, "Is this word necessary?" However, your ad must be long enough to attract attention, create interest, stimulate desire and ask for action.

EXCLUSIVE RIGHT TO SELL LISTING

Most broker and broker associations go all out to wrest from the seller the right to sell his own house. Far too often the seller relinquishes control over the sale of his house for too long a period of time to a do-nothing broker in abysmal ignorance of the bitter consequences.

The usual hardship case results from the seller's thinking he is appointing only an exclusive agent, when in reality he is giving some strange, fast-talking broker the "exclusive right to sell" his house—meaning that he can no longer sell it himself without paying that broker a full commission.

The next most frequent seller gripe is that he did not read the fine print in the "exclusive" contract requiring him to give written notice of revocation of the exclusive listing to the broker at least thirty days in advance of its termination, otherwise the exclusive is to continue for another ninety days, etc. Some states bar these automatic continuations; most states allow them. This is one way an unwary seller can be hurt bad, especially if the exclusive broker is not even trying to help him.

Too often the seller thinks he is getting exposure with, and help from, a large number of cooperating brokers while still retaining the right to sell his own house. He does not realize that the "multiple listing" is based first upon some broker's obtaining an "exclusive right" to sell the house, which he shares or "co-brokes" with other cooperating brokers on his multiple listing circuit.

Before giving a multiple listing exclusive listing to a broker, be sure to take these precautions:

1. Make sure you read *all* the fine print and fully understand it.

2. Call your lawyer when in doubt.

3. Make the broker specify a *minimum* amount of advertising you are going to get in a newspaper of sufficiently wide distribution to do the job.

4. Make the broker agree in writing that he will conduct a preview showing of your house to all the cooperating brokers on his circuit who

are allegedly going to be vigorously selling your house. After all, if they never see it themselves, how are they going to be able to sell it effectively? I would like to have a quarter for every seller I have met who has complained about being under multiple listing for two or three months with a hundred or so brokers, only to have his house shown no more than two or three times and never receiving one single offer.

5. Make sure the broker belongs to a multiple listing circuit that requires its member brokers to place *all* their exclusive listings on multiple listing. Otherwise the practice in your area may be for the brokers to keep good salable exclusives to themselves while placing only hard-to-sell "dogs" on multiple. If this is so, all the brokers and many of the buyers in your locality will know this. As a result, you will not be helping the sale of your house very much by going on multiple listing. Analysis shows that member brokerage offices average about one and a half multiple listing sales a year, when the option exists. On the other hand, when the brokers must place all their exclusives on multiple listing their offices usually average about one multiple listing sale a month.

6. Always remember that no broker really wants to see his salesmen make more than 15 percent of his sales on a split-commission basis. The broker needs full commissions on the few occasions when he actually completes sales in order to pay expenses. Most brokers just don't like to work for half a commission. Most salesmen fail to get excited about working for half of a half commission.

7. Be sure your listing broker is not putting you on multiple listing because he does not really believe he can sell your house readily, and feels he would like to make a part commission in case lightning strikes and some other broker accidentally sells your house. Sometimes no broker in your town is a member of multiple listing. You may lose too much by giving up local broker coverage just to get listed by a circuit of out-of-town brokers.

8. If your house actually is overpriced, a white elephant, or a dog on the market, you might just as well go on multiple listing in any event. However, if you have a problem-free house priced at fair market value, it will probably sell almost automatically. Therefore you should not normally relinquish your right to sell it yourself. Either an "exclusive right to sell listing" or a "multiple listing" always deprives you of this right.

OPEN LISTING

Many times after you have favored one broker with an "exclusive right to sell" your house and he has failed to get you any action at all, he will still stubbornly refuse to share the listing and commission with another broker who has a red hot buyer for your house. You may never be aware of this, and even if you knew about it the "exclusive" broker would not have to accommodate you by sharing the listing.

One way to be sure *all* the worthy brokers in your area who really want to work hard to help you will be able to sell your house is to list with brokers *you* choose on an "open listing" basis. This also means you retain the right to sell your own house yourself. Most listings everywhere are on this "open" basis, meaning that the owner is open to do business with any broker or any direct buyer who was not introduced by a broker who had the listing. In fact, under the modern view some states have legislated the right of the seller to sell directly to a buyer who was originally produced by an "open listing" broker. This new legal theory is that the broker in order to earn a commission must be more than just a contributing cause of the sale; he must be the efficient procuring cause of the sale. The modern view, according to New Jersey law, is that the sale must go through in order for the broker to enforce a commission claim. For example: producing an "offer" which does not meet all the terms of the listing does not entitle the broker to a commission.

For the seller who lists his house on an "open" basis, a few tips follow:

1. Be sure to give your listing only to worthy brokers. Local lawyers and bank mortgage officers can advise you about a broker's competence and integrity.

2. Get some brokers from surrounding towns helping you. Most buyers consider a group of adjacent towns.

3. Be certain that you are reserving the right to accept or reject any offer at *your* pleasure. Get this in writing. This way you cannot be sued for a commission by a broker who claims he produced a buyer ready, willing and able to buy, if you do not wish to accept the buyer.

4. If you want to take your house off the market, send each listing broker a written revocation of his listing. A recent Massachusetts case held that a broker could not enforce a commission claim against a seller who put his house back on the market and sold it to a customer of that broker a few months after the broker had received a revocation of his listing in writing.

5. Remember, if you have not hired the broker he cannot enforce a commission claim against you even if he did send the buyer to you.

6. In all fifty states a broker must be licensed in order to enforce a commission claim, even if you did hire him.

7. No real estate "salesman" can enforce a commission claim against

you if he is working independently. A real estate *salesman* by law must be working for one, and only one, licensed broker.

8. In order to avoid a commission claim by more than one broker, as where a second broker claims that the same buyer was really procured through *his* efforts, simply insert the following clause in your contract to sell: "Broker agrees that he is the only broker entitled to a commission in this sale, and he will indemnify the seller and save him harmless from any commission claim by any other broker."

9. Never let a "hungry" broker bluff you and force you to accept his buyer when the buyer's offer is not as much as the price you gave to the broker at the time of the listing. There are only two ways you can become legally liable to a broker for a commission. One way is if a licensed broker produces a buyer on the terms of the listing you gave him. The only other way you must pay a commission is when you *accept* a written offer by a buyer *on any terms* through a licensed broker.

NET LISTING

In this type of listing the broker is entitled to all of the sale price above a "guaranteed, net amount to the seller." Obviously, it is best to have a "net" listing in writing. In Texas *no* listing can be enforced unless it is in writing.

Some states have outlawed the "net" listing because some brokers abuse its use by overreaching a seller who is ignorant of the true value of his house. Examples of the seller victims in these cases are elderly widows, and young wives and mothers emotionally anxious to reunite with their husbands who have been suddenly transferred across country.

A good broker does not want one cent over the regular customary commission rate in his area (usually 6 percent of the actual selling price). Likewise, one of the hallmarks of a good broker is that he will insist on a full commission—except where, in needy cases, like a good doctor or lawyer, he voluntarily cuts his fee as an act of charity to avoid undue hardship to his client.

Most brokers would rather forgo the rare case where they may make a killing on a "net" listing to insure their customary six percent commission in the usual case where the seller accepts an offer significantly lower than the listing price. The rare, excessive commission would only stick like a lump in the seller's throat anyway, and would probably cause bad public relations for the broker as well.

MINIMAL PROTECTION FOR THE SELLER IN A CONTRACT TO SELL

1. Don't make a move without your lawyer! Any seller would be foolish to remove his property from the market and marry himself to an unknown buyer just because some broker hungry for a commission recommends it. This is the time when the seller needs a friend with no personal ax to grind. Only an experienced real estate attorney can help the seller at this point. The seller must consult his attorney *before* signing any acceptance to an offer. A binding contract is formed the moment the seller's acceptance is communicated to the buyer. If the seller accepts a complete, formal and final purchase and sale agreement he becomes subject to "specific performance" in an equity court. This rare extraordinary remedy is not accorded to ordinary contracts. It means that the buyer can force the seller to go through with the deal petitioning the court to order the seller to execute a deed in conformance to his contract to sell. Even a well-intentioned broker would hardly know enough law to protect the seller completely in such a legally complex contract as an agreement to sell real estate. Certainly if any seller ever needed a lawyer to draft his contract of sale, it is the seller of real estate.

2. The seller should know for a fact that the sales price is fair, as by an appraisal.

3. The seller should always have the option to quit the deal with no penalty if the buyer does not have written bank committal for his financing within a reasonable time—normally a couple of weeks. This clause saves the seller from bitter disappointment sixty or ninety days later on a closing day that never happens. This clause, so necessary to the seller's protection, is rarely used in actual practice.

4. The seller should be sure the contract specifically spells out that all deposits are to be forfeited *to him* in the event of default by the buyer. The seller always basically has the right to the deposit unless and until he contracts this right away, as by agreeing in the fine print to share the defaulted deposit with the broker.

5. The seller should insist that an independent stake-holder hold all deposit money in escrow.

6. The seller should insist on a large enough deposit by the buyer to insure against his default.

7. The seller should insist that all deposit money be in *cash*, or bank check.

8. If the seller gets stuck because the buyer defaulted when the broker held a deposit in the form of a post-dated check or a promissory

note, and cash deposit was specified, then the seller has the legal right to sue the broker for his damages.

9. The seller should use an insurance clause as follows: "Seller agrees to keep the property insured until closing day *as presently insured.*"

10. The seller should be required to pay a broker commission only "when, as and if the sale is consummated pursuant to the terms of this agreement." The exact amount of the commission should be spelled out in the agreement.

11. As previously stated, the seller should require the broker to defend him and save him harmless from any other brokerage commission claim. Likewise, a similar protective clause should be used in a contract of sale with a direct buyer.

12. The seller should be certain that all buyers have the legal capacity to bind themselves in a contract. Buyers may not be minors under twenty-one years of age, insane, senile, under undue influence or drunk at the time of contracting to buy.

13. The agreement, of course, must be in writing; otherwise it would be barred from enforcement by the statute of frauds.

14. All prior oral agreements are washed out by the subsequent written contract of sale.

15. The buyer's credit rating and ability to pay according to bank or V.A. or F.H.A. standards should be ascertained and evaluated as carefully as possible *before* the seller signs the contract to sell.

16. The seller should see to it that the price of any personal property passing with the sale is not included in the sale price of the real estate. This will save him money on deed excise stamps and various taxes which may be involved.

17. If the sale is subject to buyer's taking over seller's mortgage, the seller should be sure of the following:

   a. That there is not an "alienation" clause in seller's present mortgage barring such a sale. If there is the bank may have the right to call in the whole balance of the mortgage due at once upon the mere attempt by the seller to assign his mortgage.

   b. That in the agreement, "the buyer specially agrees to assume and pay the seller's present balance due on his mortgage to . . . (specify seller's mortgagee bank)." Otherwise the seller's bank would have no legal right to collect mortgage payments from the buyer in those states which bar third party beneficiaries from suing on contracts between two other parties.

   c. That he (the seller) understands that the bank will usually never release him from his original mortgage note.

d. That if he is assigning a G.I. or F.H.A. mortgage he promptly applies to the V.A. or the F.H.A. for a release from liability for any loss caused by a subsequent mortgage breach or forfeiture by the buyer. Some good banks will also grant a release to the seller on his note if the V.A. or F.H.A. grants a release.

18. If the seller is agreeing to sell his house within a few years after he took out his mortgage, he should check his mortgage for a possible prepayment penalty clause. If he is liable for such a penalty he may be able to avoid paying it by requiring the buyer in the agreement of sale to take out his mortgage in the same bank. The F.H.A. may legally charge up to one percent of the face amount of the mortgage for prepayment before ten years to a non-F.H.A. buyer. Once again the F.H.A. seller could avoid payment of this penalty by requiring his buyer in the contract of sale to finance through the F.H.A.

19. The seller should bear in mind in agreeing to the sale price that he is liable for the following charges in addition to the broker's commission.

a. On all G.I. and F.H.A. mortgages obtained by buyers the buyers may legally pay only one point (one percent of the face amount of the mortgage). In case the bank charges more than one point as a bonus for granting a low-interest-rate mortgage, the sellers or brokers must pay all points over one.

b. If the V.A. or F.H.A. require repairs to be made on the property before approval will issue, this expense is primarily the responsibility of the seller.

c. The seller cannot legally sell his house to a "G.I. buyer" for one cent more than the V.A. appraisal, when this is lower than his contract price, unless the buyer signs and certifies as follows: that he knows he is paying more than the appraised value and that he is not borrowing the additional amount involved.

d. The seller may legally sell his house to an F.H.A. buyer when the F.H.A. appraisal is lower than his contract price, but the buyer usually exacts a price concession in return for his performance, since he has the option to be released—that is, when the contract is properly drawn with an honest escape clause.

e. There may be unpaid betterments or special assessments due the town tax collector. The seller will have to pay these by closing day unless he has a clause in the contract of sale requiring the buyer to assume them.

f. The seller faces certain expenses at the closing:

1. Lawyer's charge for drafting the contract of sale, drafting his deed to the buyer, and possibly an escrow agreement.
2. Payment of state excise stamps (in Massachusetts, currently $2.28 per thousand of sales price, or of equity transferred in sales subject to mortgage).
3. If it is the custom in the area, the seller may bear the cost of title insurance, or an abstract of title, or possible state or county sales taxes. Be sure to refer to new Federal R.E.S.P.A. closing guide in supplement at end of Part I of this book.

20. If a furnished house, apartment house or commercial building is being sold, how are personal property taxes to be adjusted?

21. The seller's usual responsibility to give the buyer "a good and clear record and marketable title" on closing day should be limited by the following clause, "except for restrictions and easements of record." After all, these restrictions on the full use of the property run with the land and the seller would be unable to lift them. The Massachusetts Supreme Court has decided that a "restriction" on the record is no such encumbrance as gives the buyer the right to refuse acceptance of a deed.

22. If the seller will need to remain on the premises for a time after the closing date, provision must be made in the agreement to allow him this privilege legally. A few days is usually allowed as a matter of courtesy. However, for any longer stay by the seller the buyer should be reimbursed on a per diem basis for his out-of-pocket expenses for his bank payment, etc. In this case an appropriate sum, such as $500 or $1,000, is normally held in escrow by a stake-holder to guarantee that the seller will actually vacate the premises by the extended date.

23. If the seller is to take back a second mortgage from the buyer in order to facilitate the sale, it is important that this mortgage instrument be drawn and recorded by a lawyer, not a broker.

TAX CONSEQUENCES OF SALE

1. You may postpone the income tax on your profit from the sale of your principal residence by paying as much as your net sale proceeds for a new residence within 18 months before or 18 months after the sale (2 years after if you build instead of buy). You may reinvest a lesser amount and increase your mortgage loan. You are not required to reinvest all the funds made available by the sale of the old house.

2. To avoid a large tax on the whole profit payable that year you may create an "installment sale" and spread the tax over a period of years.

This is particularly advantageous if you expect your income and tax rate to decline in the future. To accomplish this you must not take over 30 percent of the sale price in the year of the sale.

3. A tax expert should be consulted to take full advantage of gift tax and estate tax laws available to you.

4. If you have rented your property for a year prior to the sale, you may deduct all your expenses of maintaining the house during the rental period.

5. You may wish to postpone the sale if you have a profit and that year you have other tax losses.

6. If you are selling at a profit within six months of buying, you may be losing a "capital gain" income tax advantage.

7. If you or your wife are over sixty-five and you have used the house as your residence for at least five of the last eight years, your profit on the sale is tax exempt up to $20,000, partially tax exempt for the amount over $20,000.

FIDUCIARY DUTY OF BROKER

Never forget if you use a broker to sell your house that you are the principal and the broker is *your agent*. Many brokers illegally act as if they are the principal and the seller is their agent to gurantee them a full commission in case the house gets sold on terms dictated by the broker.

The plain legal fact is that the law imposes a "fiduciary duty" upon the broker to at all times, and in all circumstances, act *in the best interests of his principal, the seller*. This means that as long as you have not contracted away most or all of your rights to the control of the sale of your house—as through a harshly drawn "exclusive right to sell" listing contract—the law keeps you in the driver's seat.

WHAT GOES WITH THE HOUSE

Real estate is usually defined as the land and everything that is attached to it, such as buildings, trees, shrubs, etc. Actually everything under the land, in the absence of especially separated mineral rights, also is part of the real estate, as is everything over the land up to the highest heavens, except for public laws permitting the passage of aircraft.

The buyer gets *all* the real estate but none of the owner's personal property. The problem arises when personal property has become part of the real estate and meets the legal tests of a fixture which does pass with the real estate.

The usual court tests are three:

1. Has the personal property been *permanently* annexed to the real estate?
2. Is it the *intention* of the parties that this annexed personal property become part of the real estate?
3. What is the custom in the locality?

PERMANENT ANNEXATION

Usual fixtures might include: shades, venetian blinds, shutters and awnings, furnaces, heaters, stoves, ranges, oil and gas burners, hot water heaters, air conditioners, screens, storm windows and doors, lighting fixtures and hardy shrubs. Some of these articles are not very permanently annexed to the property and could easily be removed. However, if the intention of the parties and local custom declare them to be *fixtures*, then they are part of the real estate and automatically pass to the buyer. On the other hand, sometimes an article like a furnace or machinery is very securely annexed yet does not belong to the seller and so does not pass to the buyer as part of the realty.

It is important that the seller should spell out specifically in his contract to sell exactly what he intends to give to the buyer as part of the real estate. This will save misunderstanding at the closing, and sometimes save the sale.

Chapter 29

HOW TO AVOID PROBLEMS WITH YOUR BROKER

The broker is the legal agent of the seller to whom he owes the fiduciary duty to act in his best interests. This being the case, buyers are just kidding themselves when they expect that the broker is going to look out for their interests.

The relationship between the broker and the buyer is considered an "arm's-length" transaction in the eyes of the law.

The usual ways in which problems arise between a buyer or seller and the broker involve deposit money, defaulting on agreements, attempts by the seller or buyer to deprive the broker of his commission, and the broker's looking out for his *own* best interests.

The buyer must remember that in the law a real estate broker is the classical example of a *special* agent with limited powers or authorization from his principal, the seller. Normally his authority is restricted to finding a buyer. In the absence of a power of attorney he has no authority to sign a sale contract for the seller, and, of course, no power to sign a deed from the seller to the buyer. In fact, as many cases have attested, the buyer could be stuck with a total loss by turning over any funds to a broker in excess of a normal deposit, if the broker should happen to abscond with the buyer's purchase money.

The broker, as the agent of the seller, is under no more duty than the seller is to volunteer any information to the buyer. He is liable only for positive misstatements of material fact. So now you know why he suddenly acts as if he is hard of hearing when you try to pin him down for facts like the tax bill, fuel bill, where the boundary lines are, or if water leaks through the roof or into the basement. The broker knows that he is safe as long as he sticks to seller's puff or personal opinion, such as your daughter's matrimonial opportunities with the wealthy next door neighbor, etc.

For an intentional misstatement of a material fact the broker and his principal, the seller, could be liable for *all* consequential damages to you. Even for an innocent misstatement of a material fact you are entitled to "recision"—meaning release from the contract. Never forget that the broker is entitled to his commission just for bringing the parties together. The Massachusetts Supreme Court has held that, "It is no part of the broker's duty to produce a legally enforceable contract." Therefore, it makes a great deal of sense to me that both the seller and the buyer should be careful to be represented—all the way—by a lawyer.

The following tips should be helpful:

1. Don't give a long-term "exclusive right to sell" to a broker without written and signed protection to you for advertising, promotion, showings and release by you in two or three weeks in the absence of any action by your broker or his multiple listing organization. Check carefully *all* brokers you deal with for education, training, background and record of honest results. Check the *man*. Do not be misled by false fronts or labels.

2. Make sure that all deposit money is held "in escrow" by a third party stake-holder to be turned over to the aggrieved victim in the event of default or damage by the other party to the sale contract. Be sure to spell out clearly in the "offer and acceptance" form, or in the fully

completed "purchase and sale agreement," the exact conditions upon which the deposit will be either returned or lost. Sunday or holiday deposits are not returnable unless the agreement is actually completed on a subsequent weekday.

3. Remember that for any broker to be *entitled* to a legally enforceable commission he must meet these three tests:

    a. He is licensed, with an up-to-date renewal and bond.

    b. He is hired by the seller (his principal).

    c. He is the primary or efficient procuring cause of the sale.

In many states for the broker to be the primary cause of the sale he does not need to complete the sale. However, the modern view is like the New Jersey rule which states that it is illegal to collect a real estate broker's commission unless the sale goes through; or the Massachusetts rule which will not enforce a broker' commission in a purchase and sale agreement unless the sale goes through.

4. Make the buyer or broker sign a clause in the sale agreement guaranteeing that no other broker is entitled to a commission.

5. Remember that the broker is hired merely to find a buyer acceptable to you on your terms in the listing agreement. The broker is entitled to his commission whether the sale goes through or not, in many states, once you have accepted the broker's buyer. Make the broker sign a clause that you will pay him "only when, as and if the sale is consummated pursuant to the terms of the agreement."

6. The amount of the broker's commission is not legally fixed in any other manner than by agreement between the seller and the broker.

7. The amount of deposit or down payment money is not legally fixed in any other manner than by agreement between the buyer and the seller. Don't let a broker or a seller bluff you, if you are a buyer. Place a small deposit at first, as a binder, at least until you know if your offer is accepted by the seller in writing (the only way in which your sale contract can become binding). As a seller, never sign "accepted" to an offer until you know for sure that an actual real live bona fide buyer has placed a deposit in escrow of at least $500 *in cash*. Make sure that this alleged buyer has a bank committal in writing for his financing within a period of a couple of weeks or you have the option of putting your house back on the market.

8. Remember that as soon as your offer is accepted in writing you stand to lose your deposit if you do not go through with the deal, unless you have specifically provided an appropriate escape clause as part of your offer. On the other hand, if all you have signed is a preliminary "offer and acceptance" form the only thing at stake is the deposit, or, at most, a suit for money damages for breach of contract.

9. Never forget that once the seller signs accepted to a full, complete and final purchase and sale agreement, *both* parties are entitled to "specific performance." This means that a buyer can be forced to buy and a seller can be forced to sell. They are not restricted to only money damages in a law court, as is the case in an ordinary contract suit. When the seller keeps the deposit as liquidated damages due to buyer's default, he cannot also sue for damages due to loss in resale.

10. Remember that under the "statute of frauds" which every state has, no action is legally enforceable by the buyer or seller in a real estate sale unless the transaction is in *writing* and signed by the party to be charged.

11. Beware of "fine print" in an exclusive right to sell listing contract which calls for *automatic continuation* of the contract. Some progressive states have outlawed these harsh continuation clauses and bar the brokers who attempt to use them from enforcing a commission claim.

12. Make the broker understand that if he induces a prospective buyer to believe that the house can be purchased for less than the price you are asking he will then be violating his fiduciary duty to act in your best interests. The law says that you are then excused from paying the broker his commission.

13. Remember, you do not have to accept different terms, but if you close the deal on terms different from those offered by your broker you are still liable for a commission to the broker, because he was the "procuring cause" of the sale.

14. The courts recognize that a time must necessarily arrive after an interested buyer has failed to purchase when the seller may begin an entirely new solicitation independent of the broker. Some state courts have held as little as three months' inactivity by the broker with a prospective purchaser to constitute abandonment of effort by the broker, and clear the way for the seller to sell directly to the same buyer without obligation to pay the broker a commission.

15. In many states, as in Massachusetts and New Jersey you can close a deal either directly or through a second broker with a buyer who was shown your house first by another broker. The first broker would not be entitled to a commission. So if you do not want to pay the commission twice, be sure to consult your attorney. Perhaps, your state requires a "first" broker to be more than a mere contributory cause of the sale, or requires that a sale must go through in order for a broker to earn a commission.

16. In an "open" listing where your house is listed with several brokers to be sold to the first buyer produced on your terms, all other brokers are automatically discharged as soon as one broker makes a sale.

It is not necessary for you to inform the other brokers of the sale. However, considering the number of sorehead and hungry brokers about, it would be best to inform them, to stave off groundless commission suits, and out of common courtesy.

17. Even if the broker gets your price for you, if his *terms* vary from those you required and you reject the buyer, you need not pay him a commission.

18. If you had direct dealings with the buyer prior to employment of the broker now demanding a commission from sale to the same buyer, you need not pay the commission. Under these circumstances the broker was not the procuring cause.

19. In a broker's claim for commission when the broker has knowledge of his buyer's financial inability to finance the purchase, the broker is duty bound to make this disclosure and is not entitled to a commission just because he induced his principal, the seller, to sign an acceptance of his worthless offer.

20. A buyer may withdraw his offer any time before acceptance by the seller.

21. If the seller once rejects the buyer's offer, he cannot later accept it. Any new acceptance now by the seller is a counter offer which the buyer is free to accept or reject.

22. A broker's suit for commission is governed by the law of the state where his employment took place, not the state where the property is located.

23. A seller cannot escape his liability to a broker for a commission by removing his house from the market, then selling direct to a buyer who was originally procured by the broker. However, if the broker received a *written letter of revocation of his "open" listing*, the seller may subsequently deal directly, in good faith, with a buyer who was originally a customer of the broker, without liability for a commission.

24. In the usual oral listing contract made between the seller and the broker nothing is said about the broker's being required to produce a binding written contract with the purchaser, one capable of enforcement by a suit for specific performance. In the absence of this specific requirement, unless your state adopts the modern New Jersey rule and requires that the sale must go through for a broker to earn a commission, the broker earns a legally enforceable commission in one of two very simple ways:

    a. Producing a buyer ready, willing and able to buy on all the terms of the listing.

    b. Producing a buyer with whom the seller is satisfied and a contract is made. In this event the agent is not concerned as to the ability of the purchaser to buy; the seller relieves him of that duty when he accepts the buyer.

25. The listing contract is for personal services of the broker and is not subject to the statute of frauds. Most states allow oral listing contracts. Most listings are oral, informal, "open" type listings, whereby the seller is free to list with any broker he pleases or to sell the house himself.

26. Whoever hires the broker must pay him for personal services rendered, whether or not the hirer owns the property.

27. If the seller reserves the right of acceptance of a buyer, he cannot be forced to pay a commission against his will. This right of the seller to accept a buyer may be conditioned upon the seller's having found another place to live—or any other specific reservation, either written or oral.

28. To earn his commission the broker has the duty of an agent to follow the instructions of his principal, the seller. The broker must report all offers to the seller. Only the seller can judge the worthiness of an offer. If the seller sells directly to a customer of the broker after the broker had failed to submit an offer from that buyer, then the broker cannot collect his commission.

29. A broker may purchase property he has listed if full disclosure of his dual role is made to the seller. The broker is not entitled to *secret* profits. However, once the seller agrees to sell to the broker their agency is ended, and the broker is under no obligation to furnish his former principal, the seller, with information concerning subsequent events, including a quick resale at a big profit.

30. When you buy or sell directly without the aid of a broker be sure you use an experienced real estate attorney. There is *no substitute* for this much needed protection *before* you sign anything or transfer money.

31. If *you buy or sell through a broker* be absolutely certain that your interest is being protected by an experienced real estate attorney. There is *no substitute* for this protection *before* you sign anything or transfer money.

32. Never forget that no other contract in all the law involves more legal technicalities than a real estate contract of sale. The foisting upon an unsuspecting, unknowledgeable and unwary public of so-called "short form" uniform real estate contract forms prepared and executed by non-lawyers is a national disgrace. Incalculable millions of dollars are irretrievably lost, and untold misery is wreaked annually in this country upon thousands of buyers and sellers who walk naked and unprotected

into real estate transactions governed by inadequate terms and provisions drafted hurriedly by self-serving brokers untrained in the law.

Chapter 30

MORTGAGE FINANCING YOU SHOULD KNOW

There are only three ways you can finance a house: 1. Conventional financing—the normal case where you simply get the mortgage money from the bank, credit union or other qualified lending institution. The bank is not protected from loss by the government. 2. F.H.A. financing—the bank requests an appraisal approval of the house and an income analysis approval of you from the Federal Housing Administration before they advance the funds to you. If the F.H.A. approves of the deal the bank is insured against loss by the insurance fund created by F.H.A. buyers who pay an extra one-half of one percent interest for this purpose. 3. G.I. financing—as always, the bank gives the mortgage money, but only after the Veterans Administration appraises the house for the full amount of the sale price and guarantees the bank against loss.

CONVENTIONAL FINANCING

The mortgage problem is the buyer's problem, not the seller's or the broker's. The buyer would be well advised to check several banks for the best financing to suit his needs. Mortgage policies vary significantly from bank to bank. These are the things to compare:

1. The interest rate.

2. The number of years over which the bank is willing to permit you to spread the payments. Of course, the shorter the years, the lower your total interest bill will be. However, most buyers need to spread out the years to bring the monthly payments within their budget reach. This is further aggravated by today's ever-increasing interest rates, house prices and local property taxes. Actually the buyer of a modest house

priced about $40,000 is actually destined to spend about one quarter million dollars on a long term mortgage when you consider the following costs: a. ultimately paying 2½ or 3 times the face amount of the mortgage, including interest over the years; b. taxes over the years; c. insurance over the years; d. water and sewer charges over the years; e. maintenance over the years; and f. utilities over the years.

Another thing to watch out for is the new practice of many banks to write the mortgage for only 5 years while the payments are based on 25 years.

3. Will the bank permit you to sell your house "subject to the mortgage"? Most banks have "alienation" clauses in their mortgages prohibiting this. If this is the case, the mere attempt by you to have your buyer take over your mortgage could cause the bank to "call" your mortgage and demand full payment at once. The bank always has the power to assign your mortgage. You should have the same right in case you need it.

4. Does the bank have an escalation clause in the mortgage? If so, the bank could raise your interest rate at will or "at periodic intervals" stated in the mortgage. During the "credit crunch" of 1966 many mortgagors were surprised to find their interest rates suddenly increased.

5. Closing costs can vary appreciably from bank to bank.

6. How liberal is the bank about waiting for you to pay before starting foreclosure proceedings? What kind of credit rating will they give about you to inquiring would-be creditors, especially if you do not always pay right on time?

7. What is the policy of the bank about charging "prepayment penalties," as when you sell your house and have to pay off your mortgage ahead of time? Some states as in Massachusetts have recently enacted statutes severely limiting the bank's right to charge prepayment penalties. However, these laws are not retroactive.

8. How much consideration will the bank give you for your other borrowing needs in consideration for your placing your mortgage there?

Never, never sign an "offer" form or a sales contract without specifying the mortgage funds to which the offer or contract is subject, including the terms you need. Always add the clause, "failing which the deposit is to be returned promptly to the buyer."

F.H.A. FINANCING

The Federal Housing Administration deals only with lending institutions. You must go to your bank first—directly, or through a real estate

118

broker. For about $50 you get a bargain-price appraisal of the house you intend to buy. In addition, you get the right to withdraw from the deal if the appraised value comes in lower than the price you are asked to pay. That is, you may withdraw if you signed a fairly drawn contract of sale. Regrettably, I must warn you that more and more realtors and other brokers are using harsh, one-sided contract forms which give you no "out"—even when the appraisal comes in lower than the price. The tricky language, in fine print, that these reprehensible brokers use reads like the following: "If the V.A. *or* F.H.A. appraisal is lower than the sale price but is acceptable to the seller then *both parties* agree to become bound by the terms of this agreement."

Since these appraisals are primarily based on past comparable sales, in a rapidly rising market—as now—they tend to come in lower than the prices buyers are willing to pay. This tends to give the buyer an excellent opportunity to demand a price concession. It also tends to put the squeeze on the seller and the broker. The F.H.A. buyer is allowed to pay a higher price than the appraised value if he desires.

The F.H.A. is allowed to charge their mortgagors a penalty of one percent of the face amount of the mortgage for prepayment within ten years when selling to a non-F.H.A. buyer. However, the buyer may pay up to 10 percent of principal in any one year penalty free.

The big advantage of F.H.A. home financing is the low down payment-maximum amount of mortgage feature.

On houses up to $15,000 in price, only 3 percent down payment money is required and the lending bank will be insured against loss on a maximum mortgage of 97 percent. That part of the sale price between $15,000 and $20,000 requires 10 percent down payment. All of the sale price above $20,000 requires 20 percent cash down. Thus, a $15,000 house would require only $450 down; a $20,000 house only $950 down, and a $25,000 house would require a buyer to pay $1,950 cash down.

Watch out for the maximum amounts of F.H.A. mortgage money available for a single family, or two- or three- or four-family house.

Where the dwelling will not be lived in by the buyer, only 85 percent of the maximum allowable mortgage would be available. This 85 percent rule would also apply to a borrower refinancing his present home or an income property he does not live in. The home financing part of F.H.A. financing is limited to structures with a maximum number of four dwelling units. The F.H.A. also makes an income analysis of the buyer to determine his ability to pay before issuing a firm commitment.

A seller may pay the fee, through a bank, to request an F.H.A. appraisal of the house he is about to put on the market. F.H.A. appraisals are made within five days of their request.

Many banks, but not all, will accept F.H.A. mortgage applications from buyers. Cooperating banks must use the F.H.A.'s mortgage form and note. The percentage of cooperating banks varies with the spread between the interest rate to the bank allowed by the F.H.A. compared with current interest charges for "conventional" mortgage loans in your area; and the number of banks willing to comply with new F.H.A. guarantee requirements.

Never, never sign an "offer" form or sales contract without specifying your dependence upon your required amount of F.H.A. approved mortgage. Always add the clause, "failing which, deposit is to be returned promptly to the buyer."

The F.H.A. buyer may buy jointly with another in order to obtain approval of ability to pay, or for any other reason.

Income from a working wife, where this is a characteristic of that particular family's life, is allowable. Likewise overtime pay where it is normal and expected to continue. Income from a second job is also allowable.

There are no fixed rules with the F.H.A. Local directors are allowed to increase appraisals three percent without review. Reappraisals are freely granted where three comparable sales are first submitted to the requesting bank for their review. All the F.H.A. is trying to do is to decide if under all the circumstances the applicant can "swing the deal."

G.I. FINANCING

The Veterans Administration normally requires the veteran to apply through a bank for a V.A.-guaranteed mortgage. The lending bank is guaranteed against loss by the V.A. out of public funds. Hence, G.I. mortgages cost veterans one-half of one percent less than F.H.A. borrowers must pay, since the F.H.A. insurance charge is one-half of one percent—paid by the borrower. Currently the lowest interest rate anywhere for mortgage money is on G.I. mortgages, except the "prime" conventional rate on mortgages where the borrower pays 30 percent or more cash down. It is regrettable that many veterans entitled to this benefit have never taken advantage of it. Also, a large number of veterans are still entitled to a second G.I. mortgage if they had to sell due to a transfer or sickness, provided they have applied to the V.A. for release from liability on their first mortgage, and their bank has released them as well.

Like the F.H.A., the V.A. public law appraises the buyer's ability to pay as well as appraising the house and limits its home financing plan for individuals to dwellings of one to four units. However, in the V.A., each additional G.I. joining the first one in common ownership entitles one more dwelling unit over the four. In other words, two G.I.'s could buy five units; three veterans together could buy six units.

If the veteran does not earn enough to be approved for the mortgage he is seeking, he may bring in a parent or other family member to help him qualify as to ability to pay, however, many banks expect the buyer to stand on his own two feet.

Like the F.H.A., the G.I. buyer must attest to the fact that he has the intention of residing in the property. Only the V.A. requires the seller to furnish the buyer a satisfactory termite report.

Under a new 1968 public law the G.I. buyer may now pay a higher price than the V.A. appraisal. However, he must sign and attest to the facts that he understands the price to be greater than the appraisal, and that he will pay the excess amount in cash before the closing so that no debt for this excess will remain after the closing.

POINTS (BONUSES PAID TO BANKS FOR MORTGAGES)

In normal times, many banks pay brokers a finder's fee of one percent of the face amount of the mortgage for placing mortgages with them.

However, nowadays, when the banks can get 9 percent and more for conventional mortgages all over the country, the lower percent return to them on F.H.A. or V.A. mortgages does not appear to justify the payment of a finder's fee on these types of mortgages.

Most of the banks which will indeed accept V.A. or F.H.A. mortgages at all now want to be reimbursed for their interest loss by a one-time origination fee payable at the closing as a bonus to them. This bonus charge is generally called "points." It is computed in this manner. The bank knows the *average* mortgage will last six years. If they lend a G.I. or F.H.A. borrower funds at 7½ percent when they could get 9 or more percent on a conventional loan of the same money, they then assume that they are losing one-half of one percent a year for six years, or a total of 3 percent. Consequently, they expect to be paid a discounted bonus of this 3 percent, in advance, at the time of the closing. This 3 percent charge would be called "three points." Each "point" represents one percent of the face amount of the mortgage. The actual number of points charged varies with the local spread between the existing free market interest rate on conventional loans and the percent ceiling rate on G.I. and F.H.A. mortgages permitted to the banks by the public law setting up those agencies.

When the banks can get enough interest on G.I. and F.H.A. loans to satisfy them, they will make this type of loan—and without charging the extra bonus points. The result is that more buyers with little cash down payment money are able to benefit by the low-money-down G.I. or F.H.A. government-backed mortgage loans.

It is well to remember that both the V.A. and F.H.A. public laws permit the buyer to pay only *one* point to get a mortgage from the bank. The sellers and brokers must arrange to pay all points over the legal limit of one for the buyer.

When the buyer buys an existing house the V.A., F.H.A. and the bank all proceed on the assumption that the buyer buys "as is," except that recent F.H.A. law requires the seller to guarantee the buyer against major defects in the house for one year.

Both the V.A. and the F.H.A. insist on "escape clauses" in their buyers' contracts of sale permitting release to the buyer in the event of disapproval by them. It is interesting that a recent Massachusetts case held that the *seller* could not use this escape clause for release from the sale contract if the buyer could produce the full contract sale price from *any* financing source. In other words, this escape clause is for the buyer's benefit only. Warning! Never let a con-artist broker get your signature on an unfair V.A. or F.H.A. sales contract form (printed to order for his exclusive use) which robs you of the usual buyer's escape clause in the event of failure of the government's approval of the sale price.

Chapter 31

LANDLORD AND TENANT LAW

TENANCY AT WILL

A lease is not necessary to establish a landlord-tenant relationship. A tenancy at will may be created by oral agreement, or an implied agreement arising out of the conduct of the parties, or under a written agreement where there is no fixed or determinable time.

Most tenancies are verbal and run from week to week, month to month, or even year to year. They terminate when one of the parties gives the other written notice, in advance, at least as much as the interval of the rent period. The notice usually does not need to be signed personally by either the tenant or the landlord. Before modern statutes, a tenancy at will could be terminated at the will of either party.

To be a tenant one must not only have the consent of the landlord to possess or occupy the premises, but he must also have the *exclusive* possession against all the world, including the owner. If he cannot exclude the owner he is merely a bare licensee and could be evicted without notice by the landlord. And this is so even if the licensee were relying upon a written lease for the protection of a valuable commercial enterprise. Lodgings and concessions are typical examples of mere licenses as distinguished from tenancies. The severely limited rights of the licensee are discussed more fully in Chapter 32.

The notice to vacate given under the tenancy at will must be consistent to be effective. If the tenant continues to pay the rent, and the landlord continues to accept the rent, the notice of vacating is no longer enforceable, unless rights were expressly reserved. The exact time of vacating must be stated or determinable in order for the notice to be sufficient.

If a tenant at will quits the premises without giving the proper statutory notice, the tenancy will continue, as will the tenant's liability for rent under the ordinary principles of contract.

It has been held that a city housing authority may terminate a month-to-month lease without giving reason and this would not constitute abuse of process.

The various states have statutes providing for termination of a tenancy at will for nonpayment of rent. Massachusetts General Laws, Chapter 86, Section 12, reads: "In case of neglect to pay the rent due from a tenant at will, fourteen days' notice to quit given by the landlord to the tenant shall be sufficient to determine the tenancy; provided that the tenancy of a tenant who has not received a similar notice from the landlord within twelve months next preceding the receipt of such notice shall not be determined if, within five days after the receipt thereof, he pays or tenders to the landlord the full amount of rent due."

Other ways in which the tenancy at will may be terminated besides the giving of legal notice or nonpayment of rent are: by agreement of the parties and the landlord's acceptance of the tenant's surrender of the premises. Automatic termination by statute is generally caused by the tenant's attempt to assign his tenancy, or his illegal use of the premises.

When the tenancy has been terminated *without the fault of the tenant,* by the act of the landlord, or by operation of law, the court may grant a discretionary stay of judgment and execution upon request by the tenant for a limited period of time as the court may deem just and reasonable. However, when the tenancy has been terminated *due to the fault of the tenant,* as by a fourteen day notice for nonpayment of rent, the court lacks the discretionary power to aid the tenant by granting a delay in the judgment and execution.

WRITTEN LEASES

Louisiana permits oral leases. However, four-fifths of the states require a lease for more than a year to be in writing. Maine has a writing requirement for leases running for more than two years. A lease for more than three years must be in writing in Indiana, Maryland, New Jersey, New Mexico, North Carolina, Ohio and Pennsylvania. Under its statute of frauds, Massachusetts requires every lease to be in writing.

In Connecticut a lease for more than one year is unenforceable unless recorded in the registry of deeds. Recording of the lease is necessary in Maryland, Massachusetts and New Hampshire for leases which may run for more than seven years. This includes leases for less than seven years with a right of renewal carrying them beyond seven years.

If the lease is not in writing in Massachusetts it creates a tenancy at will. The same statute requires delivery of the lease in order for it to be effective.

If a lease has no indication of the duration of its term it is ineffective as a lease and creates a tenancy at will. However if the lease is definite as to its term, but leaves out the time for its commencement, then the term begins to run from the time of the delivery of the lease.

ASSIGNMENT VS. SUBLETTING

The printed lease forms invariably prohibit the tenant from either assigning or subleasing the premises. However, subletting is permissible if the lease prohibits only assignment. On the other hand, assignment is a breach of the prohibition to sublet. When a tenant's entire interest is transferred, this is an assignment of his lease. A transfer of less than the entire interest of the tenant results in a sublease.

In an assignment the new tenant, as assignee of the original lessee becomes liable to the original landlord. The same lease is still in effect; it has merely been assigned. A sublease creates a new tenancy between the parties to it. The original tenant becomes landlord to the new tenant. Consequently, the lessee and not the sublessee is liable to the lessor for any breach of the lease.

RENT

Rent may be payable in anything of value. It does not have to be paid in money. It is payable up to midnight on the due date.

By law, rent is payable at the end of the term. This is why every lease expressly calls for payment in advance.

LANDLORD'S LIABILITY

There is no obligation on the part of a landlord to repair the leased premises. The tenant takes the premises as they are. Likewise, the tenant must maintain the premises and return them to the landlord at the end of the term in the same condition except for reasonable wear and tear.

Generally the landlord is not liable to the tenant, members of the tenant's family or his guests for injuries sustained on that part of the premises under the control of the tenant.

Even when injuries are caused by a defect on that part of the premises under the control of the landlord, the landlord may still be free from liability under the following circumstances:

1. The injured party takes the premises in the same condition as they were at the time of the letting. So if the defective condition existed at the time of the letting to the tenant, then no recovery may be had against the landlord. The law says that a guest, employee or member of the family of the tenant has no greater rights against the landlord than the tenant has.

2. Sometimes, injured persons not contemplated by the parties to be using the premises, and those who come upon the premises merely for their own convenience, may sue the landlord only for reckless, wanton or willful misconduct. However, some modern statutes are placing a duty of ordinary care upon the landlord with respect to all types of guests and do away with the distinction between social guests and business invitees.

3. Where the tenant and not the landlord negligently created the cause of the injury.

4. Landlord may win directed verdict, unless plaintiff shows that landlord knew of unsafe conditions.

TENANT'S LIABILITY TO PARTY INJURED
ON PREMISES UNDER HIS CONTROL

1. The tenant has a duty of ordinary care and is liable for ordinary negligence to a business invitee.
2. The tenant owes a duty of slight care and is liable for gross negligence to a social guest.
3. The tenant is liable only for reckless, wanton, or willful misconduct to a licensee or trespasser.
4. However, modern statutes are beginning to hold the tenant liable for ordinary care to all types of guests.

WHAT SMART LANDLORDS PUT IN THEIR LEASES

1. Require sufficient advance payment of rent.
2. Require an adequate security deposit.
3. Prohibit assignment or subletting without permission.
4. Have lease run over one year to a termination date at a time of the year good for finding a new tenant, in case tenant fails to renew.
5. Use automatic renewal clause, except for timely notice of termination, if your state law does not ban this, as Connecticut does.
6. Retain permission to enter premises for inspection at reasonable times.
7. Secure permission to show premises to new prospective tenants at reasonable times for sixty days prior to termination date.
8. Use tax escalation clause to enable automatic rent increase to offset increased property taxes.
9. Use automatic "cost of living" rent increase tied to some known index.
10. Limit the number of persons permitted to use the apartment regularly.
11. Use a "percentage lease" on commercial property to permit participation in excess profits of tenant.
12. Require tenant to keep up maintenance and repair of the premises.
13. Have regulations or house rules for the benefit of *all* the tenants.
14. Do not allow first tenants in the building to insist on "exclusion clauses" which will limit landlord's right to lease remainder of units.
15. Prohibit children, where not barred by anti-discrimination laws.
16. Prohibit animals.

WHAT TENANTS SHOULD REMEMBER

1. Printed lease forms favor the landlord.

2. No tenant should ever sign a lease without consulting his lawyer first.

3. Question of whether a writing is a lease or merely a license; test is whether exclusive possession of the premises is given, or merely possession to use. A bare licensee may be evicted forthwith.

4. If your right to renew lease is only "for a further period," landlord can terminate at end of original term.

5. Assigning the lease to a corporation does not relieve the tenant from rent.

6. Mailing of key to lessor does not constitute a surrender of the lease.

7. New owners must honor your lease, including any advance rent payments. Purchaser is bound by tenant's payment in advance for full term.

8. Where lease prohibits animals on premises, manager of apartment building has no authority to waive requirement.

9. Injunctive relief against landlord is available for zoning law violation.

10. If you are leasing a one-story building, owner has no right to erect a second-story addition. This would constitute a breach of the lease for infringement upon your right to erect advertising signs.

11. Landlord's failure to respond to your letter giving up premises does not constitute a surrender.

12. Where lease contains option to purchase by a certain date, exercise of option by a letter mailed on that date is too late.

13. When tenant abandons premises, landlord may remove personal property. Landlord must store for reasonable period, usually three months.

14. Lease for no other purpose than specified prohibits use of premises for any different purpose.

15. Landlord may not prevent tenant from moving his personal property out of premises, even if tenant owes back rent. Landlord is limited to his rights as a creditor.

16. Landlord may not stand idly by making no effort to relet premises when tenant breaks lease. Landlord has duty to mitigate damages.

Chapter 32

RIGHTS TO DEPOSITS

Basically, the deposit in a real estate transaction belongs to the seller, and if the buyer defaults the seller may declare a forfeiture and keep the deposit as liquidated damages rather than sue the buyer for damages. The seller must be careful that the broker is not keeping a deposit from a defaulting buyer when it should be turned over to the seller. However, there are many situations which provide for all or part of the deposit to be paid to the broker, or back to the buyer.

WHEN THE BUYER IS ENTITLED TO GET BACK HIS DEPOSIT

1. In the case of a mutual mistake in the contract by both the buyer and the seller the contract would be voided and the buyer is entitled to the return of his deposit. The parties need not be entirely mistaken. A *substantial difference* between the true facts and the facts as believed by both buyer and seller would permit recovery of the deposit by the buyer. However, if the buyer makes a unilateral mistake he cannot recover the deposit. The buyer is held accountable to know that the broker has only the limited powers of a special agent to receive initial deposit money only and not substantial additional payments. The buyer would stand the loss for these if the broker absconded.

2. If the seller or his agent, the broker, is guilty of misrepresentation of a material fact, even though innocently made, the buyer may have rescission and is entitled to be made whole—including getting back his deposit money.

3. If the seller cannot perform without fault on his part and the agreement calls for deposit return and release of the seller.

4. If the seller defaults and the contract calls for the deposit return to the buyer.

5. If the buyer provided an "escape clause" in his agreement calling for the return of his deposit.

WHEN THE BROKER IS ENTITLED TO ALL OR PART OF THE DEPOSIT

1. If the agreement of sale provides for the deposit to be divided between the seller and the broker as liquidated damages in the event of default by the buyer.

2. Where the seller has already signed over the deposit to the broker as part of his commission, the broker may keep the deposit even though the buyer should subsequently default.

3. Where the seller has agreed for the broker to hold the deposit in escrow until the closing, then at closing day the broker merely collects whatever commission amount is due him over and above the deposit amount which he already has.

WHEN THE TENANT IS ENTITLED TO GET BACK HIS DEPOSIT

1. Leases frequently call for "security" deposits. This is money paid in advance—usually one, two or three months' rent as protection to the landlord against damage to his property at the time of the expiration of the lease. If there is no damage, or, in any event, that part of the security deposit in excess of actual damage must be returned to the tenant upon the expiration of the lease. The tenant is not allowed to apply the deposit toward his last rent payment due.

2. When a prospective tenant has made a deposit on an apartment he has the legal right to revoke his offer to rent the apartment and his deposit must be returned at any time before the landlord has fully accepted him. This is so even if the rental application (which is subject to final approval and acceptance by the landlord) specifically states that the deposit will be forfeited upon default by the tenant.

Chapter 33

INSURANCE LAW YOU SHOULD KNOW

It would be beyond the resources of the average homeowner to absorb, himself, the losses which may result from home ownership. Besides, most owners have mortgages and their mortgagee banks insist on a *fire insurance* policy in an amount at least equal to the *size of the mortgage*.

In some states real estate conveyances are not permitted to take place without the protection of a *title insurance* policy. Most housewives with children to raise and educate would not dare to be without *mortgage insurance* protection. And few homeowners could personally sustain the losses which may result from their liability to other persons and their property.

Insurance companies and their brokers and agents are licensed, regulated and controlled by the states in which they operate. While it is usually safe to rely on your broker or agent for guidance in routine purchases and coverages, when it comes to claims, suits and settlements you need your lawyer.

Most homeowners can afford to buy insurance only against the major risks and must run the risk of paying their own bills from improbable or petty losses. Investment property owners frequently halve their insurance costs by using a $250 deductible clause.

MULTIPLE LINE POLICIES (THE HOMEOWNERS PACKAGE)

A multiple line policy provides both fire and casualty coverages—two of the four coverages mentioned above which homeowners need. There are five homeowner policies, known as 1, 2, 3, 4 and 5. All insure against fire, extended coverage (damage caused by windstorm, explosion, smoke from faulty heating or cooking units, hail, riot, automobile and aircraft damage), vandalism, breakage of building glass, residence theft and comprehensive personal liability. Policy 2 adds the perils of falling objects, weight of ice or snow, collapse of building, short circuit, leakage from or freezing of plumbing or heating system and rupture of steam or hot water system. Policy 4 adapts policy 2 to the needs of tenants. The building protection in policy 2 is extended to "all risks" by combining policies 3 and 4. Policy 5 insures buildings and contents against "all risks."

Homeowner policies cover owner-occupied dwellings, up to four-family multiple structures. Only fixed percentages of the dwelling value are covered. These policies cover private structures, personal property and additional living expense caused when the dwelling is vacated due to an insured loss. Office occupancy is allowed, but farming must be incidental.

Building losses are paid on a replacement basis if the dwelling is insured for at least 80 percent of replacement cost. If the policy-holder insures his property for less than the required 80 percent, then the insured shares the loss in proportion to the deficiency of insurance.

All homeowner policies have a $50 deductible for wind and hail. Policies 1, 2, 3 and 4 may have a similar deductible for all perils except fire. Policies 2, 3 and 4 offer an optional modified deductible applying to perils except fire, extended coverage, rupture of heating system, vandalism and theft. Policy 5 has a $100 deductible to all losses except fire, which may be reduced to $50 for 10 percent of the basic premium.

These deductible amounts are said to be "disappearing" because, as the loss exceeds the amount of the deductible proportionately less of the $50 or $100 deduction applies. Finally, at loss of $500 or more, deductible completely disappears.

The following restrictive provisions apply to the various perils in the extended coverage endorsement:

Windstorm—Damage by wind-driven rain or snow to the interior of a building is covered only if the wind first causes a break in the walls or roof.

Explosion—Loss caused by steam boiler is not covered. Special steam boiler insurance would be required.

Vehicle damage—No liability for loss caused by vehicles owned or operated by insured or tenant. No liability for damage to fences, driveways, sidewalks or lawns.

Smoke—Only smoke from sudden, unusual and faulty operation of any heating or cooking unit connected to chimney while on the described premises. Smoke from fireplace is excluded.

Dwellings up to four families are allowed unlimited vacancy. Any person who would suffer a pecuniary loss if damage occurred has an insurable interest and may take out and collect the proceeds from a fire insurance policy.

The insured must report a fire loss at once (which means within a "reasonable time"). The company has sixty days after notice to pay a claim. Proof of loss must be submitted by the insured within that time.

The following conditions would *void* a fire policy:

1. If any material fact or circumstance is concealed or misrepresented by the insured.

2. In case of fraud or false swearing by the insured.

A fire policy is *suspended* while:

1. The hazard is increased within the control or knowledge of the insured.

2. The premises are vacant or unoccupied beyond a period of 30 consecutive days. Vacancy exists when both the property is unused and the contents are removed.

The rate is the cost for each $100 of fire insurance. The premium is determined by multiplying the amount of insurance by the rate.

To collect on a fire policy there must be an actual flame or burning. Damage from heat alone is not covered. The fire must be a "hostile" fire—one which takes place outside its proper confines. In the standard fire policy there is no payoff for damage from a "friendly" fire—one confined to the place where it is supposed to be, as in a stove or fireplace. Fire insurance protects against loss by fire or lightning plus the attendant damage by smoke, water and efforts to put out the fire.

The company is not liable when the damage or destruction of the property is intentionally caused by the insured. However, the fact that the insured negligently caused the fire, or did so while insane, does not relieve the company of liability on a fire insurance policy.

The comprehensive personal liability protection covered by all types of homeowner policies protects individuals and their families against legal liability for their acts or negligence which cause injury or damage to others. All injuries caused by the insured or his family, and their animals, are covered except injuries *intentionally* caused by the insured, injuries to employees eligible for workmen's compensation or injuries arising out of the ownership or use of automobiles, aircraft, inboard motor boats exceeding fifty horsepower, sailboats exceeding twenty-six feet in length, or from the conduct of a profession or business.

The premium is considerably less for homeowners insurance compared with that of the individual policies which it includes in a package deal.

Added charges may be needed for increased limits for contents and liability, as well as special charges for certain boats and extended theft. The extended theft endorsement (at extra cost) includes mysterious disappearance and theft from an unlocked car.

MORTGAGE CANCELLATION INSURANCE

Many first-time homebuyers mistakenly believe that the premiums they pay to the bank for Federal Housing Administration insurance, or hazard insurance, include the protection of an automatic mortgage balance payoff in the event of the death of the breadwinner. For this kind of highly desirable protection a special type of "term" life insurance is required. A *life* insurance policy for the amount of the mortgage debt for a term of years equal to the mortgage payment period is what is needed. The premium is relatively low because it is computed on the basis that as your mortgage balance decreases, the insurance protection decreases until the policy terminates when the mortgage is finally paid off. This type of insurance protection is especially helpful to young, newly formed households faced with low beginning income and the high expenses of raising a family. It is also necessary in the absence of other savings or assets in the family.

Until now one minor problem with this type of policy has been that the remaining years on the mortgage sometimes come to an odd number like seventeen, whereas the policies have been available only in even blocks of ten, fifteen, twenty, twenty-five or thirty years. However, currently a number of top-flight insurance companies competing for this market are cooperating with lending banks to offer flexible policies to fit the exact amount of the mortgage balance and the exact remaining years of the mortgage payments. This new merchandising plan also makes it easier for the homeowner to make his premium payment as part of his regular monthly bank payment.

The usual terminology used by the banks and insurance companies to promote this new merchandising scheme for mortgage cancellation insurance is "Home Protector Plan." The cooperating banks are those other than savings banks, since the savings banks already have "savings bank life insurance."

TITLE INSURANCE

Title insurance is a contract to indemnify the owner or mortgagee of real estate against loss arising from defective titles, liens or encumbrances. This type of title protection is used in nearly all large cities in the United States. Premiums and rates vary with each locality.

The policy is taken in the amount of the price the buyer pays for the property. When the property is bought subject to an existing mortgage the amount of this mortgage is specifically exempted from the liability of the title-guaranty company. Before the sale transaction is closed, the buyer makes application to the title-guaranty company for a title policy. If the preliminary report furnished to the buyer by the title company before the closing indicates rejection by the company, the buyer then knows that the seller cannot give him good title.

It is well for the buyer to remember that even though he pays the mortgagee bank's conveyancer for a title search, or pays for a title insurance policy protecting the mortgagee, only the buyer's *own* title policy protects him when he is trying to sell or refinance and finds his title attacked.

Remember, title insurance is not blanket or total protection. All recorded claims against the title, such as: mortgages, liens, attachments, etc. are excepted from protection by the policy. Also, typically there are numerous other exceptions from protection by the policy such as violations of zoning ordinances and building codes, etc.

As always there is no substitute for an experienced real estate attorney if the buyer is to achieve substantial protection. He never gets 100% protection from all risks and eventualities.

Chapter 34

TAX LAWS, EXEMPTIONS AND DEDUCTIONS

LOCAL REAL ESTATE TAXES

Your tax bill is determined by multiplying the assessment on your house by the tax rate. The amount of *your assessment*, therefore, is the key to your tax bill.

Most complaints about assessments are that they are too high, or unequally levied compared to similar properties in the same city. In an effort to arrive at some semblance of uniform, fair assessment, more and more states have passed laws requiring all assessments to be at full market value. This in turn requires more and more reassessments of whole towns. Again, aiming at uniformity and fair treatment to all taxpayers alike, the towns are typically hiring large out-of-state appraisal firms who specialize in this type of appraisal work. These firms are geared for these mass appraisal assignments and have standardized procedures to achieve minimum cost to the city per appraisal report. Naturally, the city likes this aspect, plus the feeling that if any mistakes are being made by the appraisal company they will at least be uniform mistakes, and minimize complaints by neighboring homeowners about obviously unequal assessments.

Regrettably, these reassessment undertakings just do not work out satisfactorily at all by way of minimizing complaints. In town after town hundreds of irate taxpayers have stormed their town halls in protest meetings. Frequently groups of taxpayers are forced to go into court to seek relief from alleged irregularities in their assessments.

The three main reasons for all this misunderstanding and commotion are:

1. Frequently present assessments are unequal, measured by actual current market value. This is caused by unequal changes in value to different properties over the many years since the last assessments were levied.

2. Many times the present assessments were levied unequally in the first place due to primitive appraisal techniques, bias, prejudice and favoritism.

3. Even a single independent appraisal of *one* property where the appraiser is given all the time in the world and has all the modern tools, techniques, methods, and procedures at his disposal could easily be significantly erroneous due to unreliability or insufficiency of the necessary basic data used, or the inexperience or poor judgment of the appraiser. Imagine what can happen in a mass appraisal process, performed in a hurry, at a price which nearly denies any profit at all. Even in those states which require assessments to be at full market value, as a matter of actual practice the assessments are in fact at rates less than full value, such as 90 percent or 80 percent of the fair market value of the properties. This practice tends to please the taxpayers and make them feel that they are getting a bargain in their tax bill. However, their property may still be *unequally* assessed or *overassessed* in comparison to other similar properties in town. Such inequality would be grounds for legal proceedings.

Homeowner tax bills are usually paid by the bank which in turn collects on a monthly basis from the owner along with his mortgage payment. It has long been a bone of contention in many quarters that the bank collects their mortgagors' tax money in advance without paying any interest for its use. Politicians have even made an issue of this practice in their state campaigns for high political office, contending that taxpayers were being illegally deprived of interest due on their advance tax payments. However, the banks do have the excuses that: 1. They are technically holding the money as a stake-holder in escrow for the town tax collector and so are not profiting from any use of the funds (actually, of course, they frequently do use the money and earn profit from it). 2. They are performing a service to the mortgagor at their own expense just to keep him from falling behind in his tax payments and breaching his mortgage contract, which would leave him liable for foreclosure. 3. In any event, the mortgagor agreed in writing for the bank to do this when he signed his mortgage contract.

My own personal feeling is that it is well the bank does perform this service and makes it part of its mortgage contract. I am certain that there would be more tax liens and tax sales if tax payments were left entirely up to the homeowner to meet in a lump sum once a year. The fact is that town tax collectors are not as liberal about waiting around for their money as one might imagine. After all, the banks do not have a crystal ball and they never know in advance which individual mortgagor they might be saving from a forced tax sale or mortgage foreclosure. Quite understandably, they strongly desire their mortgages to remain in force and consider that they have somehow personally failed their depositors every time a mortgagor fails to keep up his mortgage commitments. I think it is a good and healthy thing that they take this much interest. For all of this they deserve any little profit they make from their tax escrow funds.

However, under new consumer legislation the States have been enacting new laws requiring the banks to pay interest on these advance tax collections to the homeowners. These new laws have caused many banks to allow mortgagors who have placed substantial down payments such as 30%, or 40%, or 50% to pay their own taxes. Remember, banks still generally insist on collecting advance monthly tax payments on all commercial mortgages, and consumer laws do not require them to pay interest on them.

SPECIAL ASSESSMENTS—BETTERMENTS

Unlike your regular real estate tax which is tax deductible, a special tax assessment is considered a capital outlay, not an expense, and hence not deductible for federal income tax purposes. The reason for this is that a betterment tax is imposed for an improvement to your property such as a sidewalk, curb, sewer, street, street light, etc. Since your property is considered increased in value by this improvement, payment for it is classified as a capital outlay rather than an expense.

Your share of a local improvement may be based on any system which would be fair under the circumstances, such as the value of your assessment, your front footage, or the total square footage of your land.

Frequently the betterment tax is spread over a period of years. Also the actual imposition of the tax may be delayed until after the improvement is completed. For these reasons it is important for the buyer of real estate to inquire carefully about these matters at the town assessor's office. Then the buyer should provide in the contract of sale for the "seller to pay for all betterments levied before the actual closing date."

REAL ESTATE TAX EXEMPTIONS—ABATEMENTS

Disabled veterans (in some states, all veterans), persons over age seventy, widows and other special groups of people enjoy permanent partial exemptions from real estate taxes in many states. In addition to this permanent type of exemption there is a widespread use of tax abatements which are temporary partial exemptions from local real estate taxes.

The Soldiers and Sailors Relief Act also offers temporary relief from real estate tax enforcement. If a homeowner who enters military service loses his house on a tax sale, he is given the right to redeem his property within six months of discharge from the service. Of course, most states have "equity or redemption" laws whereby *all* homeowners who lose their property on tax sales can redeem it back within periods of one, two or three years, after the payment of all unpaid taxes and costs (see Chapter 33).

The flagrant misuse of tax abatements by local politicians for personal gain has caused some cities to suffer needlessly from serious depletions in tax revenue. The result is that the tax *rate* all homeowners pay must be greatly and constantly increased. Of course, some abatements are justifiable and deserved. However, the "tax chiseler" who connives directly or indirectly with a local politician to win an unjustified abatement must be careful how much he pays for a "temporary" one. For unless he gets a permanent abatement he may find his tax bill sharply increased the very next year, or at least after the next change of political administration. In any event, honest taxpayers should openly scorn this type of property owner and politician alike. They should never be considered lucky or clever, but rather as the common cheats that they are.

Buyers of houses should be particularly careful to check not only the local tax rate but also assessing practices, and especially compare what tax rates would be if the towns were all on a 100 percent assessment basis. This way you are comparing actual tax bills for similar property and not just rates which, standing alone, are meaningless.

When undertaking a new purchase of a house the buyer should always be aware that tax money goes down the drain and can never be recouped. A high tax bill on a house is a serious impairment to its ready salability and depresses its fair market value.

FEDERAL INCOME TAX DEDUCTIONS FOR HOME EXPENSES

Local property taxes seem to be reaching for the sky with a widespread increase, this year alone, of upward of 10 percent. The total cost of home ownership is so high that the "little fellow" is virtually being driven out of the single-house market. Throughout the country there are twice as many new units being built in multiunit structures as there are single-family units. This current reverse trend of what has been going on over the last fifty years is threatening once again to place the majority of our population in rented housing. Even though the federal income tax law allows real estate taxes and certain other home expenses as direct deductions from taxable income, average big city total housing cost is still running 15 percent higher for owners than for renters. In the face of present high costs of land, new housing construction, mortgage interest and real estate taxes, the homeowner needs all the tax advantages and shelter he can get, if single-family housing is to survive.

Real Estate Tax Deductions are allowed for all types of state and local real estate taxes except special assessments for improvements which increase the value of your house. Service charges imposed by a governmental agency like the town water department are considered personal living expenses rather than taxes, and are not deductible. This deduction is allowed only to the owner of the property. A nonowner cannot take this deduction even if he actually pays the tax.

Interest on Your Mortgage is the second principal deduction allowed. This deduction is available as well to the condominium apartment owner, and to the proportionate share of interest paid by a cooperative apartment owner on the mortgage for the building.

Penalty Payments for Prepayment of a Mortgage are deductible, but "points" (discounts paid by a buyer or seller in order to obtain a new mortgage from the bank) are not deductible.

Part of Your House for Business Purposes constitutes a deduction as business expenses for that portion of the house expenses used for business. The proportionate square foot floor space used for business is the fractional amount of deduction allowed.

Tax Exemptions on the Sale of Your House (see Chapter 28).

FEDERAL ESTATE TAX EXEMPTION

All modest estates escape federal estate taxes under the $60,000 standard exemption on the net amount of the estate, which eliminates the need even to file a return. The net estate is the gross estate less total expenses and debts, a marital deduction up to 50 percent and charitable gifts.

If an estate is above $60,000 it should be discussed with your attorney as to the advisability of trusts. Your estate includes your equity in your house (the value you own over your mortgage debt); your life insurance, if you control the right to the proceeds; property transferred within three years prior to your death; property transfers which take effect at your death; furniture, cash, investments and all other personal possessions.

The estate is liable for the federal estate tax, payable by your executor when your property is transferred to your beneficiaries.

A state inheritance tax is imposed on each beneficiary of the estate depending upon his relationship and the amount of the inheritance.

Some states, as in Massachusetts effective January 1, 1976, are currently changing their inheritance tax laws to State Estate tax laws which operate similarly to the federal estate tax laws.

SOCIAL SECURITY TAXES FOR HOUSEHOLD EMPLOYEES

An obligation is imposed on the employer of household help to remit taxes due on wages paid to all employees eligible for social security. Household employees are included in the social security law. If you fail to pay these taxes and your former household employee applies for benefits, you could be liable not only for back payments but for interest and penalties as well.

You must pay this social security tax for a household employee who earns at least $50 in a calendar quarter. All cash payments must be included.

For detailed information on compliance procedure obtain from the local district office of the Internal Revenue Service a copy of "Household Employer's Social Security Tax Guide," and Form 942 with instructions. Quarterly returns are due by April 30, July 31, October 31 and January 31.

TAX ESCALATION CLAUSES IN LEASES

So-called "net, net" leases require the tenant to pay even the real estate taxes of the landlord in certain commercial, industrial and investment property. In leases for houses or apartments it is common for the landlord to reserve the right to increase the rent as his own taxes may be increased. This is known as a tax escalation clause.

Chapter 35

CONTRACT LAWS FOR PROPERTY OWNERS

A. WORKERS HIRED TO PERFORM SERVICES OR REPAIRS

The question arises here as to whether the property owner or his insurance company is liable for accidents or injuries caused by the workers employed by the owner. If the owner is furnishing the tools and materials and supervising the details of the work, then the workers are classified legally as servants of the owner, who is now their master and liable for accidents caused by them within the scope of their employment. As for accidents among the workers, the doctrine of assumption of the risk relieves all employers of liability except those guilty of contributing to the cause of the injury, and except as state workmen compensation laws may apply.

If, on the other hand, the property owner is looking for the results of the work only and the tools, materials and supervision of the details of the job are left to the workers, then they are classified legally as *independent* contractors. Now the owner is not liable for their accidents or injuries.

The fact that the workers may provide some merchandise and material incidental to their work or services performed does not subject their contract with the owner to the Uniform Commercial Code Governing Sales of Goods. Hence, a contract for $500 or more would not have to be in writing to be enforceable under the statute of frauds, as in a sale of goods.

B. BUILDERS

Good builders are ready to admit that every owner who builds a house or buys an unfinished house from a builder should have the protection of a performance bond. They advise the owner to spend the modest fee involved and get one himself if the builder refuses.

The plain fact is that builders are invariably late in finishing a house. So much so, in fact, that typically they will balk at agreeing to a penalty charge for lateness that would not even take effect until several months after they swear the house will be all finished.

140

The percentage of builder bankruptcies is almost unbelievable. And many of those who manage to avoid bankruptcy have so many attachments from subcontractors and suppliers that they continue to be unable to give clear title to the buyer, whose "closing" day becomes incredibly delayed or even impossible.

When the builder remains solvent and is able to keep building, the town building laws, plus inspections from your mortgagee bank, tend to keep him pretty well in line. Usually state statute laws require the builder to guarantee the new house against major defects for a period of one year after completion of construction.

Other forces working for you as an owner are the readiness of the Veterans Administration, or the Federal Housing Administration, or the bank supplying conventional financing to apply the pressure of censure, or even withhold future mortgage approvals if the builder fails to stand behind his work.

All of this is a great advantage over the plight of the poor used house buyer who must purchase "as is," without any comeback or help from anyone.

However, the builder does not have to be an insurer or guarantor to the buyer against any and all disappointment, frustration or loss. In the end only a well-drafted construction agreement by a competent and experienced real estate attorney will provide the necessary basic protection that the buyer will need. Some suggested clauses that the buyer needs in this contract follow:

1. The contractor at his cost shall erect, build and completely finish in a faithful and workmanlike manner a house upon a piece of land belonging to the owner _____ according to a plan and specifications submitted to the owner by the contractor.

2. The contractor is to supply all good and substantial material and labor and becomes completely responsible for said work, which is to commence on _____ (date) _____ and be completed on or before _____ (date) _____ and delivered to the owner free from mechanics or other liens.

3. The contractor shall, upon completion of such work, at his own expense remove and clear away any unnecessary and unused materials and rubbish from same and leave the whole of the work in a clean and proper manner.

4. The contractor guarantees all material and construction from all defects, hidden and apparent, for a period of one year.

The bank supplying the construction mortgage searches the title or requires title insurance, and advances the construction money to the builder only as the work progresses. The bank always holds back at least

10 percent of the builder's money for at least thirty days after completion as a safety measure and to provide leverage and insurance that the builder will stand behind the defects that normally show up during the breaking-in period of the house.

A few helpful hints gleaned from actual experience follow:

1. Do not move into a builder's house and start spending money fixing it up before he "closes" with you and gives you good and marketable title. You may wind up losing not only your own down payment of, say, $5,000 but perhaps an additional $5,000 of improvements to a house for which the builder may *never* be able to give you good and marketable title.

2. Never permit a real estate broker or the builder's lawyer to induce you to sign a contract of sale which has not been drafted or reviewed by your own lawyer. Never forget that the real estate broker has a plain legal duty to look out for the best interests of his principal, the seller.

3. Never give a builder a large cash deposit to secure a bargain price for a house which may never be built on a lot to which you may never be able to obtain a clear title. Have your lawyer check everything out *first*. If necessary, place a small binder and agree to tender the remainder of the deposit required after your lawyer has given his approval.

4. Remember that any *prior oral* understandings or promises you may have had from the builder all become merged into—or washed out by—the subsequent written contract. Therefore you must read and understand this written contract thoroughly.

5. However, most states permit the parties to a written contract—especially in contractor cases—to get together and agree to cancel a written agreement and set up a whole new agreement *verbally*. And this without any new consideration at all. The court skirts around this by contending that the real consideration is your obtaining a finished job rather than a mere right to sue for damages.

In view of this, you must be sure that your builder is not bidding low only to jack up the price later, or leave you in the lurch.

C. CONTRACTORS AND REMODELERS

Beware of overimproving your house. Most homeowners make the mistake of thinking that they can get back on a sale all the money they pay to improve their house. Unfortunately experience does not bear this out, except in a few restricted instances, such as updating of kitchens and baths.

Remember a buyer is entitled to and expects to get a roof, a heating system, siding, a painted house, etc. For these improvements as well as most others that you may make, buyers simply will not reimburse you.

Consequently you must always consider moving to a new house whenever you are faced with the prospect of substantial and expensive remodeling, addition or alterations.

Your next consideration must be a careful check of your local zoning ordinances and building codes (see Chapter 36-E). Remember, it is possible for you to seek and obtain a "variance" if the general zoning in force on your land creates a special hardship for you, and your abutters and neighbors will not oppose your request. For this type of help you should hire the lawyer who "fits" with the local Board of Appeals.

In any event, be prepared for the shock of an immediate reassessment of your property with a sharp increase in your tax bill. Your next tax bill will not only reflect the added value of your improvement, but may well increase by bringing up to date an old-fashioned low assessment that had been slipping past unnoticed for years.

You must be especially careful if you sell your house soon after remodeling that you don't misquote the old tax bill to the buyer when a new assessment may already be in the records. Under the law until recently, the buyer would be stuck under the doctrine of *caveat emptor*. However, under a recent landmark Massachusetts case, the buyer who had already moved in was allowed to be released and receive his money back because the seller *innocently* misrepresented the tax bill. Actually, the court was satisfied that the seller did not know himself that a new assessment had been made following recent remodeling. Nevertheless, the court would not permit even an *innocent* misrepresentation of a material fact, such as a significantly higher tax bill, to become binding upon a buyer who had a right to expect that the seller knew his true tax bill.

If you are still game about going ahead with your remodeling, you must get at least three bids from every different type of contractor involved, such as plumber, carpenter, electrician, mason, etc. You will be amazed at the variance in the prices asked. Frequently it is safer to take the middle rather than the lowest bid.

Remember, the low bidder may never finish the job. If you have to obtain a replacement contractor a new inspection and permit will be necessary from the appropriate town building inspection department.

Accordingly, it is wise for you not to have these contractors all paid up until they actually finish their work. At least where they have money due, you have some leverage to keep them from getting too busy elsewhere to come back and finish installing your bathtub or toilet, etc.

When it comes to payment, remember that as a rule payments arranged by the contractor are much more expensive than a loan you could get yourself at a bank. Beware of second mortgage loans granted by a contractor. It may seem painless merely to sign your name, but too often the pain comes later in the form of high interest rates and immediate foreclosure if you are late in your payments.

Home improvement company salesmen are frequently notorious "dynamiters." Remember, once you sign up you are "it." There is usually no way out without suffering substantial damages. They just don't let you change your mind. It is bad enough for the wife to sign. But at least her interest in the co-ownership of your home, as in a tenancy by the entireties, is not attachable in some states such as Massachusetts. Before you, the husband, sign, be sure to consult your lawyer and have him review the contract.

You can always make a better deal by contracting out the work on competitive bids with money you raised yourself on a secured bank loan, an unsecured personal loan or an F.H.A. home improvement loan. If your alterations are extensive and costly, you may wish to refinance your mortgage. You may need the advantage of the lower monthly payment this way, even though the eventual cost may be greater. After all, today banks find that the average life of a first mortgage is only six years anyway. In other words, homeowners either sell or refinance in that period of time.

Of course, new consumer legislation gives you 3 days to change your mind and revoke this type of contract.

D. DOMESTIC EMPLOYEES

As already indicated in Chapter 34, domestic employees are covered by social security and payroll deductions are required by the federal government. The contract upon which this relationship is based is subject to all the principles applicable to contracts generally. Also, the law of employment is largely the same as the law of agency.

Some helpful reminders follow:

1. The contract of employment may be *implied* as well as expressed, as when the employer accepts services which, as a reasonable man, he knows are rendered with the expectation of receiving compensation. For example, an interesting Maine case held that a niece who left her home (in the South) to "take care of the house" for her elderly sick aunt on the promise in a letter to her of remembering her in the aunt's will was able to collect from the aunt's estate the fair value of her services rendered. It

144

goes without saying that you must be careful that a free-loading visiting relative or friend does not wind up suing you for back wages, and applying for social security benefits which would bring the federal government down on your head on top of everything else.

2. While the employment contract is in effect the master is usually liable for injuries caused by the wrongful conduct of his servants while they are acting "within the scope of their employment." Acts within the scope of employment include activity generally related to those acts which are authorized and those acts which are incidental to the main authorization. Even intentional wrongs or criminal action by the employee may fall within the servant's scope of employment. For example, if your employee breaks the law while carrying out an errand for you, he is still within the scope of his employment and could make you responsible for the consequences of an injury to a third person. The doctrine of respondent superior governs this situation; that is, "let the master answer for the acts of his servant."

3. You may terminate the employment contract with your servant at the expiration date specified in your contract, by mutual agreement at any time, or by notice at the will of either party. Death of the employee or his inability to perform his duties also terminates the employment. Likewise, the employment relationship would normally be terminated at your own death. You may stipulate in the employment contract that termination will result from your dissatisfaction with the employee's services. If you act in good faith, you would be the sole judge of your reason for exercising this right. If there is no contract and the employment is at will, then you may discharge your servant at will for any reason, or for no reason.

If there is an employment contract that bars you from terminating at will, then you need justification to avoid liability for damages. The following employee behavior constitutes justifiable grounds for discharge:

a. Fraudulent misrepresentation of experience in order to obtain the job.
b. Refusal to work at times specified in the contract.
c. Inability or incompetency to perform his duties in a reasonably efficient manner.
d. Willful disobedience of a proper order reasonably expected to be followed.
e. Disloyalty to the best interest of the employer.

An employee wrongfully discharged may bring the following court actions:

a. Breach of contract for the unexpired term.

b. Claim for wages for the expired term.

c. Claim for value of services already rendered. (This election would bar a subsequent suit for breach of contract.)

Under the following circumstances, an employee may justifiably abandon his employment:

a. Nonpayment of wages. However, the employee is not entitled to anticipate nonpayment before the wages are actually due.

b. Requirement of illegal or immoral services. Mere exposure to immoral influences would be enough.

c. Harmful conditions likely to result in injury to the employee's health, safety or reputation.

d. Employee prohibited from performing duties for which he was hired.

e. Employee required to perform services not contemplated. The employer must demand, not merely request, this extra work. The employee may not complain of mere unpleasantness or difficulty per se.

If the employee wrongfully abandons his employment, the employer would not normally profit, as a practical matter, from a legal action for damages for breach of contract against the employee. However, the employer may sue a third person who maliciously induces his employee to breach his contract of employment.

E. SALES OF MERCHANDISE

Sales are governed by the law of contracts, except where this law has been expanded and liberalized to facilitate commerce, as by the Uniform Commercial Code now adopted by forty-seven states. Two states (Arizona and Idaho) still have the antecedent of the "code," the Uniform Sales Act. Louisiana is the only state left following the common-law rules of contract law. Before we consider extra rights under the Uniform Code let's review some basic conditions which must be met to constitute a valid and enforceable contract for the sale of goods.

1. If the goods amount to $500 or over the contract must be in writing to satisfy the statute of frauds. However, either part payment or part delivery of the goods could satisfy this statute in the absence of a writing.

2. The buyer and seller must have the legal capacity to contract. This

means that a minor may treat the contract as void or valid at his election, all the way up to a "reasonable time" after he attains his majority. To be safe you must think of a legal infant as being a two-year-old baby. Likewise one who is insane, intoxicated, under duress or under undue influence would be legally incapacitated from entering into an enforceable sales contract.

3. There must be some "consideration" passing from the buyer to the seller, called the "price." The price may be in goods or services as well as money. The price may be determined at a later date. If it is left out of the contract, then a reasonable price or the market price will be used.

4. There must be mutual consent to a *present* passing of title. Remember, often a transaction completed by a salesman is not a present sale but merely a contract to make a sale in the future. The fact that title has not yet passed makes a big difference when the respective rights of the parties become litigated, for example to determine who should bear the risk of loss to the goods.

5. There must be an offer. Preliminary dickering or invitations to do business do not constitute a valid offer. On the other hand, a written offer signed by a merchant expressing an intention to keep the offer open cannot be revoked during an expressed period up to three months. This irrevocability would continue for a reasonable period of time in the absence of any expressed period mentioned.

6. There must be an acceptance of the offer. It is the acceptance that creates the binding contract. The acceptance of a sales contract may be in any manner and by any medium which is reasonable under the circumstances, in the absence of a specific manner or medium expressly required in the offer or by the circumstances of the sale. If the offer has been accepted by shipment the buyer must be notified of this within a reasonable time.

7. The sale must be legal. Many states prohibit sales on Sunday. In this case the parties would have no enforceable rights, even to get their money back. However, if any essential is left to be done on a weekday, then the contract would still be enforced.

Under the Uniform Commercial Code, modern court decisions have been wearing away the old harsh rule of *caveat emptor* (let the buyer beware). Under this ancient maxim the buyer had to rely on his own judgment unless the seller made an express warranty to him. The big difference now is that the law implies various warranties for the protection of the buyer. However, buyers must remember that *caveat emptor* still applies when they have ample opportunity to make sufficient examination of the goods to reveal any defect. In this case only fraud by the seller could protect the buyer from loss.

Implied Warranties that Protect the Buyer

In addition to the usual warranties of title and express warranties, today there are two kinds of implied warranties important to the buyer: 1. warranty of fitness for a particular purpose, and 2. warranty of merchantability.

1. Whenever the buyer makes known to the seller the particular use to which he intends to put the goods and relies on the seller's judgment to select suitable goods, then the seller makes an implied warranty that the goods will be fit for that special purpose.

2. Whenever the seller is a merchant (a person who normally deals in the type of goods sold) he makes an implied warranty that the goods are merchantable (fit for the usual purpose for which goods of that type are used). Food and beverages come under this implied warranty of merchantability. However, there is no breach of warranty when a harmful object found in food is to be expected or would be naturally found, such as a chicken bone in chicken, etc. The warranty of merchantability extends to second-hand goods by a merchant seller.

Implied warranties may be waived by an express writing, or modified by custom of the trade, or course of past dealings.

Difference between Product Liability for Breach of Warranty and Liability for Negligence

Today, a suit for breach of warranty may be brought against the seller by the buyer, members of his household, or his guests for personal injury sustained by them. In many states the buyer may sue the remote distributor or manufacturer for breach of warranty.

Most states give the buyer a choice of suing the seller for breach of warranty or for negligence. To prevail in the contract action for breach of warranty the buyer need only prove that there was a sale, there was a warranty, that the goods did not conform to that warranty, and that he was injured as a result of the breach. On the other hand, proving negligence is much more difficult. The buyer would have to be familiar with the manufacturer's methods and prove that he was negligent. By the time the manufacturer proves his costs and methods for quality control and inspection, negligence becomes extremely difficult to prove. It is modern recognition by the courts of this precise difficulty of proving negligence that has brought about the recent expansion of sellers' warranty liabilities under the Uniform Commercial Code.

Buyer's Rights and Remedies

1. You must notify the seller of a breach of warranty within a reasonable time.

2. The measure of damages is the difference in value of the goods between the value on acceptance and their value as warranted.

3. The buyer is entitled to all incidental and consequential damages.

4. The buyer may deduct the amount of the damages from any unpaid balance owed, provided he gives notice of this intention to the seller.

5. The buyer may cancel the contract and still sue the seller for breach of contract.

6. The buyer may recover any payment made as well as damages for breach of contract.

7. The buyer may sue for fraud independent of his remedy for breach of warranty.

8. If the seller neglects to, or refuses to, deliver the goods, the buyer may sue for damages. Normal damages would be the difference between the contract price and the market price.

9. Under the Uniform Commercial Code, the buyer may be entitled to *specific performance* of the contract in an equity proceeding. Under this remedy the court may require the seller to deliver the goods. Prior to the code this remedy was available only for unique goods. Now it is available for other hardship cases as well.

10. The buyer may maintain an action for *replevin* to recover possession of the goods from the seller, if the seller is wrongfully withholding the goods.

11. The buyer may *rescind* the contract and sue for any part of the price paid.

12. If the buyer breaches the contract, the seller is permitted to retain only so much of any payment as will compensate him for actual damages. In the absence of a reasonable liquidated damages clause, the seller's damages are computed at 20 percent of the purchase price or $500, whichever is smaller. Any payment made by the buyer in excess of this amount must be returned to the buyer.

13. The exclusion of damages for personal injuries caused by defective merchandise is illegal when the goods are sold for the buyer's consumption.

Chapter 36

PROPERTY RIGHTS AND OBLIGATIONS

A. COOPERATIVES AND CONDOMINIUMS

The condominium method of ownership is new in the United States, although it has been used extensively for many years in Europe and Latin America.

In a condominium, an individual owns separately one or more single-dwelling units in a multiunit project. Each apartment owner actually has his own deed and his own mortgage, unless he bought for cash. In addition, he and the owners of the other units have an undivided interest in the common areas and facilities that serve the project.

The common areas include such elements as land, roofs, floors, main walls, stairways, lobbies, halls, parking space and community and commercial facilities. Some of these may be restricted areas; that is, they may be limited to a certain family unit or to a certain number of family units.

The extent of interest that the owner of a living unit has in the common areas and facilities is governed by the ratio of value of his unit to the total value of all the units. This ratio also represents his voting interest in the condominium owners' association. Along with the owners of other units in the project, he has the right to use the common areas and facilities and the obligation to maintain them. The owners make monthly contributions of their proportionate share of the cost of maintaining these common areas and facilities.

Condominiums as Distinct from Cooperatives

Condominium housing differs somewhat from cooperative housing. For instance:

1. In condominiums, individuals take title to their units. In cooperatives, each one has a stock ownership in the cooperative and the right to live in one of the units.

2. In condominiums, individuals vote on a proportionate basis. In cooperatives, each person has one vote no matter what the size of his unit.

3. In condominiums, individuals are taxed separately on their units.

In cooperatives, they pay their share of taxes on the project in their monthly carrying charges.

4. In condominiums, individuals may or may not have mortgages on their units, depending on their own wishes and their ability to finance the purchase of their units. In cooperatives, the cooperative mortgage covers all the units and the members are not free to exclude their units from the cooperative mortgage or to obtain mortgages on different terms.

Often in high rise or high-rent complexes, cooperative and condominium apartments have been plagued by such a high vacancy rate that the units had to be rented out in order to secure occupancy.

One reason why condominium ownerships have become more popular than cooperative ownerships is that during a period of recession or depression, many co-op apartment owners may not be able to make their monthly payments and the corporation could be foreclosed for failure to pay its mortgage or tax payments, thus the co-op apartment owner's interest could be wiped out.

B. MINORITY GROUPS—HOW THEY GET IN, HOW THEY ARE KEPT OUT

The U.S. Department of Housing and Urban Development plans vigorous enforcement of the requirement for open occupancy in housing, which is now the law of the land as part of the Civil Rights Act of 1968, and the U.S. Supreme Court decision upholding an old 1866 law giving a Negro the right to buy *any* home he can afford. Even prior to this brand-new bombshell Supreme Court ruling, open housing was to become effective in three stages. By January 1, 1970, about 80 percent of the nation's 65 million dwelling units were to be covered. The 1968 bill immediately covers apartments financed with the help of government agencies such as the Federal Housing Administration. Starting in 1969, coverage was to be extended to apartment buildings, however financed, and to newly built single-family homes in tract developments and elsewhere (provided the builder is in the business of selling more than two houses a year).

After January 1, 1970, all single-family, owner-occupied homes were to be covered if sold through a real estate broker. By this time the bill would prohibit racial discrimination in an estimated 80 percent of the nation's housing.

Broad as this new Federal Open Housing Law is, many states are already enforcing more far-reaching legislation. Leader among the states in progressive housing laws is Massachusetts, where since 1958 all but owner-occupied two-family houses must be sold without discrimination.

The biggest loophole in the new 1968 federal law is that an individual homeowner even after 1970 may discriminate if he sells his house himself rather than through a broker. The owner must be careful not to discriminate in his lawn sign, or in his newspaper advertisement, or he would lose his exemption. In this situation (about 20 percent of all housing sales), if a Negro makes an offer he could be turned down for racial reasons, and he would have no recourse.

To plug this loophole—and all loopholes—the U.S. Supreme Court has just upheld an 1866 law providing that a Negro has the right to buy *any* home he can afford. *All* real property comes under this new Supreme Court decision upholding the 1866 law.

Even though the owner is now absolutely prohibited from discriminating, nothing can ever stop him from taking his house off the market at will.

However, minority group members will always be able to move in as nominee buyers at the closing whenever an advance agent buys under a "nominee clause" which states that either he *or his nominee* will close on the appointed closing date.

Property owners are protected against harassment by a requirement that offers to buy or rent must be "bona fide" offers—in other words, a person must be ready and capable of going through with a transaction rather than just testing the owner.

A person with a complaint of discrimination may seek confidential conciliation by local, state or federal officials, or file suit in court for an injunction or for damages. However, he must first check to see if there is a state or local open housing law. That machinery must be tried first, unless the coverage and remedy is substantially weaker than the federal law. You start the federal machinery by complaining formally to the Department of Housing and Urban Development, which gives a copy of the complaint to the alleged discriminator. Department officials will verify your story and, if they think you have a case, they'll try to talk the homeowner into selling you the house. They can't embarrass the homeowner by publishing his name, and what he says can't be used in any subsequent court action without his permission.

If this effort fails, you can sue the homeowner in court. It's up to you, the buyer, to prove that his refusal to sell was racially motivated. If you do, the court can order the owner to sell you the house if it's still available, pay whatever actual damages you suffered from the incident and pay you up to $1,000 in punitive damages.

If you are an alleged discriminator, while the minority group member's complaint is being processed at the Housing Department or in the courts you could sell your house to another buyer. That is, you could sell to another if the would-be minority group buyer has not requested and been granted from a judge a temporary restraining order. The new law authorizes this. If granted, it would freeze your house until your suit was disposed of. In the absence of this injunction, if you nail down a sale to another buyer, the judge can't undo the sale and throw out the new occupant even if the minority group member ultimately proves you discriminated. The minority group member wouldn't get your house, but he could get your money in the form of cash damages. For every person filing a complaint of discrimination there are ten others who fail to file a complaint.

C. (1) RESTRICTIONS

The courts permit property owners to put in deeds to buyers reasonable restrictions on the use of the real estate transferred. However, courts will not enforce impractical restrictions. If the character of a whole neighborhood has changed an ancient restrictive covenant would not be enforced. For example, in Park Square, Boston, a highly developed and commercially valuable business section today, the Massachusetts court refused to enforce an ancient restrictive covenant in a deed limiting the use of the property to residential purposes.

Well-drawn seller's purchase and sale agreements usually include the following clause after the language requiring the seller to give the buyer a good and clear record and marketable title: "except for restrictions of record." This clause is needed to protect a seller, since courts have held that a contract to sell property free and clear from encumbrances is breached if a title search reveals restrictive covenants on the record.

From the point of view of the buyer, however, it is preferable that the agreement either omit any reference to restrictions or require their enumeration.

C. (2) EASEMENTS

An easement is any right, privilege or benefit that one enjoys in the land of another.

There are easements "by deed," as where one landowner has purchased and recorded some right of use in another's land. Easements may also be gained "by prescription" (adverse possession or squatter's

153

rights), as where an abutter uses the land of his neighbor for the required statutory period of years. All of the legal elements required for "adverse possession" must be satisfied. These are spelled out later in this chapter under "adverse possession." In addition, some states like Massachusetts allow easements "by necessity," as where a landlocked owner is permitted a necessary access to the nearest street over the shortest, most practical route through the land of his neighbor.

Examples of easements are common driveways, overhead utility wires, underground drainage lines installed and maintained by the town public works or water department, etc.

Many contracts of sale include a printed clause stating that the property is to be conveyed "subject to easements of record." As in the case of the clause "subject to restrictions of record," this is fine for the seller. However, these clauses are always dangerous for the buyer to sign, since he deprives himself of the right to reject the conveyance if subsequent title examination reveals objectionable easements on the land he is buying. To protect the buyer these clauses should be omitted. If there is any mention about easements at all in the agreement of sale, they should be described in detail.

If the buyer is planning on benefiting by an easement over adjacent land, the agreement of sale should spell out this right.

C. (3) ENCROACHMENTS

Any invasion or intrusion into another's land is an encroachment. The encroachment is typically a hedge, wall, fence, auxiliary building such as a detached garage, or an overhang of a building such as a bay window or fire escape.

Considering the importance of conformance to zoning ordinances and building codes, as well as visual appeal to the salability of your property, the slightest encroachment could amount to a severe depreciation of the value of your land and even affect the marketability of your title. As we have just seen under "easements by prescription," if the encroachment continues for a sufficient number of years to satisfy your state statutory period for adverse possession you could completely lose that part of your property encroached upon.

Proper protection for a buyer in a sale agreement should provide against encroachment encumbrances. A clause should call for all buildings on the land to be conveyed to conform to applicable building codes, zoning ordinances, restrictions and easements.

It is of great importance to act against an encroachment in time to prevent losing your land by adverse possession. You must be particularly vigilant about building overhangs and fences erected by your neighbor, since these are permanent encroachments.

Remember, your neighbor's trees belong to him. You may cut off roots and branches which encroach upon your property, but you may not interfere with the trunks of those trees if they are wholly or partially on your neighbor's land.

You are not liable to your neighbor for damages to him from your trees which fall on his land, unless you have been negligent.

Your legal remedies for encroachments are:

1. For compensation satisfactory to you, grant an easement by deed to your neighbor.

2. If the encroachment is minor and unobjectionable you may grant a temporary license, reserving power to revoke it. It would be safe to record this temporary license.

3. Apply for an equity court injunction against the encroachment.

4. Money damages for the encroachment will not always satisfy you in that this does not give you your property back.

5. Try personal persuasion to get your neighbor to remove the encroachment.

6. If all else fails, and it is practical to do so, you may physically remove the encroachment. Your lawyer can advise you how to act under the circumstances of your case so that you will not become liable in damages to your neighbor. After all, he started your trouble in the first place.

In addition to protection from encroachments, the law protects you against your neighbor's using his land to injure your property in the following ways:

1. You are entitled to the surface support of your land. If your neighbor excavates his soil in a manner which causes the surface of your land to cave in he is liable to you for damages.

2. If your neighbor changes the surface grade of his land, he must build a retaining wall, at his expense, to prevent earth or spillage of drainage water from piling up on your land.

3. "Spite" fences over six feet high are universally prohibited by local ordinance.

4. Your neighbor may not remove or destroy in whole or in part a party wall, unless necessary for safety, and then only upon notice to you.

As a general rule "easements by necessity" are not granted for light, air and view, so your neighbor may block your right to these amenities with impunity. However, you are frequently protected in this regard by local zoning ordinances and building codes.

C. (4) ADVERSE POSSESSION

Title to land may be acquired by holding or using the land adversely to the true owner for a period of years specified by state statute. The time requirement varies by state, usually between ten and twenty years' duration. To acquire title in this manner the claimant must take actual and exclusive possession in an open, visible and notorious manner, hostile to the true owner (meaning not with permission) for a continuous period of years necessary to satisfy the statute. If twenty years is required, as in Massachusetts, the total period of time may be built up through successive owners. This is called "tacking."

The theory and purpose of adverse possession is not to reward a wrongdoer, but rather to stabilize and quiet titles to land. Thus, the law bars claims by those who may originally have held title but are guilty of sleeping on their rights for too many years.

As previously stated, an easement may be acquired by adverse possession. This would be called an "easement by prescription" (discussed earlier in this chapter under "easements"). In the case of the easement by adverse possession, the use need not be literally continuous through all times of the year, nor must it be "exclusive" use.

You must always be vigilant that part of your land is not lost by adverse possession to a greedy neighbor who implants fences, hedges, trees, shubbery, flowers or lawn on your side of the actual boundary line.

All buyers would be wise to insist in their contract to buy that a clause requires "the actual delineations of boundary lines to extend to present fences."

D. EMINENT DOMAIN—HOW YOUR HOUSE IS APPRAISED

The federal and all state constitutions empower the government to take private property for public use upon the payment of "just compensation." Just compensation has been interpreted by the courts to mean "fair market value." Fair market value is the highest price a buyer will pay and the lowest price a seller will accept when both are negotiating freely and not under compulsion, with a full knowledge of all the facts, and the property has been exposed on the market for a reasonable period of time. This governmental power is called the power of "eminent domain" or "condemnation."

Your land is "taken" even though you are not physically deprived of it.

It is a taking if you are simply deprived of the normal use of your property.

The growing trend of urban renewal, along with the constantly increasing need for highways, schools, etc., has brought condemnation proceedings home to a very substantial percentage of homeowners.

Condemnation power is frequently delegated by a local, state or federal agency to privately owned facilities for the public use.

Only the amount of your property which is *necessary* for the intended public use may be taken away from you.

Some state laws provide you with compensation for a decrease in value of your property even when your land is not taken, as where a highway is built right next to your house.

If all of your property is taken you are entitled to fair market value. If there is only a partial taking you are entitled to the difference between the fair market value of your whole property before the partial taking and the fair market value of the remaining part of your land after the taking.

The government appraisers as well as independent fee appraisers employed by them, or by you, all use the same generally accepted three approaches to arrive at an "appraisal." An appraisal is only an estimate (or educated guess) of the fair market value of your property as of a given date. The three recognized approaches to fair market value are:

1. *Comparable sales approach*—in which three or more comparable houses which have recently sold in the same locality within an adjustable range in price are compared feature for feature with your subject property for an indication of its fair market value.

2. *Cost approach*—in which the starting point is always replacement cost new, derived from a cost manual or from local contractor cost estimates. From this replacement cost new is subtracted all types of depreciation to arrive at the sound, "as is" value of your house. The three types of depreciation always considered are:

   a. *Physical depreciation*—such as wear and tear. Some is curable—for instance, the need for a paint job. Some is incurable—i.e., inherent bone structure depreciation.

   b. *Functional depreciation or obsolescence*—outmoded or poor design, layout or fixtures. Some is curable—i.e., an old-fashioned kitchen or bathroom. Some is incurable—inefficient room layout, inadequate space or hallways.

   c. *Economic depreciation or obsolescence*—caused by factors outside the house itself, such as a declining neighborhood. Always incurable.

To the sound value of your house is added the value of your lot. The total is an indication of the fair market value of your house. Your land value is estimated usually from recent comparable land sales in the area by the square foot or front foot method.

3. *Income approach*—in which the gross monthly rental value of your house is estimated. Then this amount is multiplied by a factor called a "gross rent multiplier" to arrive at an indication of the fair market value of your house. The gross rent multiplier used is the number arrived at by averaging how many times more houses sell for in your area than their gross monthly rental value.

Many states now provide that you may take whatever money is offered to you by the government and still sue the agency involved for the additional amount to which you believe you are entitled. Your lawyer hires an expert appraiser as a witness to substantiate the higher value you are seeking. Experience shows that you usually win a verdict for a somewhat higher amount than what you had been asked to settle for out of court. The lawyer usually receives one-third of the additional award.

E. BUILDING CODES AND ZONING LAWS

Building codes regulate the construction of your house and represent basic protection for the average house buyer unable to distinguish between good and bad construction. Obviously, the higher the standards are in the town the more protection and better quality housing the buyer gets. Building codes protect the homeowner and occupants against fire, water, settlement, the weather, noise, crowding and lack of light, air and view. This is accomplished by the establishment of front, rear and side setback lines, and minimum standards for construction materials and workmanship.

Building codes regulate not only new construction but also additions, alterations and remodeling. Before any major work on the house is started a permit must be obtained. Your application for a permit must include a copy of your plans and specifications. Your plans must comply with all applicable building codes and zoning ordinances.

The town building department issues the permit and makes periodic inspections until they give final approval.

Owners should insure that clauses in their agreements require the builder or remodeler to conform to the local building codes. Final payment should not be made until the owner or builder receives an occupancy certificate from the building inspector.

If a building inspector issues a permit based upon his incorrect interpretation of the zoning law, the landowner is not protected. Therefore the buyer's attorney should personally check the local zoning laws.

Ordinarily you may expect to receive a higher tax bill as a result of increased assessment after improving your property. The reason for this is that the assessing department follows up new building permits issued. Any reassessment that is unequal or unfair compared to other similar properties in town is challengeable by you. To accomplish this successfully, as well as trying to extricate yourself from building code violations, always hire the local lawyer who fits well with the town officials involved.

Zoning ordinances regulate the character and use of your property. They are imposed under the police power of the state. In this way the government restricts or deprives your full use of your own property without having to compensate you. The theory is that the zoning laws are imposed for your protection. By statute they must be reasonable and uniform. Zoning laws are never allowed to be retroactive. An existing building at the time the zoning is adopted cannot be declared illegal.

Most homeowners are unaware that an "in-law apartment" in a house subjects the property to all the conditions required for a two-family house. Normally, in-law apartments constitute substantial violations of the local zoning laws or building codes.

An alarming number of "converted" two-family houses are "bootleg two families" in that they are in violation of zoning laws or building codes.

"Variances" are frequently granted where the application of the general zoning law creates an undue hardship to a particular homeowner. The procedure to follow in applying for a variance is as follows: First, you must apply to the building inspector for a building permit; then, after he turns you down, you petition to the Board of Appeals for the variance. Local lawyers usually charge $100 to $150 to assist you in your appeal.

The real key to success in a reasonable application for a variance is the degree of cooperation or lack of opposition you receive from your abutters and neighbors, who are publicly invited to attend your hearing before the Board of Appeals.

You may appeal a rejection into the courts. However, you must strictly follow statutory requirements. You have no legal right to rely upon appeal by others. Your failure to exhaust all administrative remedies is fatal to your court action. The judicial review power of the court is limited to determining whether the zoning board's order is illegal, arbitrary or unreasonable; the public interest must be weighed against the individual's hardship. Yet courts have seen fit to declare some zoning ordinances unreasonable, confiscatory and invalid.

A recent government-commissioned study reports that local zoning ordinances intended to maintain property values or preserve the character of a community usually act effectively to keep poor people from living in the suburbs. "Large lot zoning has become the symbol of a community anti-Negro policy." High priced large-lot, single-dwelling zoning could dilute the impact of the new national open housing law. The report said that it is not economically possible for everyone to have "upper middle class" houses, and a large volume of new housing is needed. There must be a point of compromise of standards at which it will be possible to supply housing within the financial reach of those who need it.

Courts have held that a zoning ordinance does not constitute an encumbrance which would justify a purchaser in refusing to accept title. Many buyers have suffered severe losses by discovering too late that their property is not zoned for their needs, or that they cannot qualify for some business permit or license that they will need. This is still another reason for the need to consult a real estate attorney before "signing up" for a parcel of real estate.

F. WATERFRONT PROPERTY

With the recent addition in this country of millions of new vacation homes and pleasure boats, waterfront property rights and responsibilities have become much more important in our law.

Navigable Waterfront Rights

Navigable waters include the seashore, rivers and lakes. The waterfront owner here owns and controls in an absolute sense to high-water mark, and in a qualified sense to low-water mark. That is, between the high-water line and the low-water line the owner's rights are subject to the right of the public to navigate.

Riparian (River or Stream) Rights

1. In most states you are entitled to the continued flow of the water in its natural course, subject to reasonable use by upstream owners.
2. If a governmental agency acts upstream in such a way as to deprive

downstream owners of their riparian rights, the downstream owners are entitled to just compensation for their loss in eminent domain proceedings.

3. You may acquire or lose title to land that is added or taken away by the action of the water upon your property.

4. If the stream is unnavigable, opposite riparian owners own up to the middle of the stream.

5. Each riparian owner has an equal right to reasonable use of the body of water, for such purposes as swimming, boating and fishing.

G. TYPES OF OWNERSHIP

1. Fee Simple Estate

The highest quality of ownership one may possess in real estate is called a *fee simple estate* or just plain fee.

This type of estate in land is held by *one person* all to himself, *forever*, including all the rights of ownership, even the right to dispose of the land upon his death.

2. Life Estate

When one person has all the ownership rights to himself, but only during his lifetime, he is said to hold a *life estate*. The same instrument which creates the life estate normally spells out who the *remaindermen* will be to take the estate after the death of the life estate holder. For example, the grantor deeds to Jones for life and upon Jones' death remainder goes to Jones' son George in fee simple.

If no remainder estate is set forth in the deed to the life tenant, then, upon the death of the holder of the estate for life, the estate in fee reverts back to the original grantor or, if he has died, to his estate.

The life estate holder can never grant out more than he actually owns. For example, he would not have the power to deed to another in fee simple. Accordingly, the buyer or long-term lessee from a life estate holder must be sure that the remaindermen who follow the life tenant have also signed off to him.

3. Joint Tenants

Two or more persons who own equal, undivided interests in the whole of a parcel of real estate with automatic rights of survivorship constitute the ownership estate known as a joint tenancy. The terminology here is misleading to a layman, who thinks of tenants only in the sense of a landlord-tenant relationship, where the tenant's rights, of course, fall short of outright ownership.

The whole essence of a joint tenancy is the feature usually stated and always implied—"with automatic right of survivorship." This means that when one joint tenant dies his share goes to the surviving joint tenant, who takes the whole property.

This type of estate fits the needs of family situations, as where a husband and father grants in his will all of his real estate to his wife for life and then to his children as *joint tenants with automatic rights of survivorship*.

Under modern statutes one joint tenant may sell his share of the real estate to an outsider. However, the new owner takes his share only as a tenant-in-common, the same way a creditor of a joint tenant exercises his claim.

Until the joint tenancy is severed, each tenant has an absolute right to possession and use of the entire property.

As a result of statutes specifying that conveyances or devises of land to two or more persons shall be construed as a tenancy-in-common unless automatic survivorship is explicitly stated or manifested from the tenor of the instrument, it is important to add the following clause when setting up a joint tenancy: "as joint tenants and not as tenants-in-common."

The automatic survivorship feature of the joint tenancy is an effective avoidance of probate.

4. Tenants-in-Common

This estate is especially designed to meet the nonrelative business situation, such as a group of men pooling their resources to buy a large investment property.

The tenants-in-common may own unequal shares of the property. The whole essence of this estate is that when one tenant dies his share passes to his *own estate* for the benefit of his own family or his heirs. Of course, there must be probate proceedings, with or without a will, upon the death of a tenant-in-common, since the distinguishing feature of this tenancy is the lack of any provision for automatic survivorship.

As in the joint tenancy, each tenant-in-common owns an undivided interest in the whole property and consequently is entitled to the possession and use of all the property. This also means that where one

162

tenant-in-common buys his foreclosed property at an auction sale he must hold it for his other tenants-in-common.

The rights of a tenant-in-common are fully subject to creditor's claims, as is a joint tenancy.

5. Tenants by the Entireties

This form of ownership can exist only between husband and wife. It is very similar to the joint tenancy discussed above except that certain additional important features are added to suit the marital situation. In fact, a Massachusetts statute holds that a declared joint tenancy when held by husband and wife will be treated as a tenancy by the entireties unless there is a specific expression of intention to the contrary. On the other hand, a deed to just a husband and wife creates a tenancy-in-common unless a different intention is expressed.

When divorce occurs the tenancy by the entireties dissolves into a tenancy-in-common.

Of course, the whole essence of this tenancy is that the surviving spouse automatically becomes the sole owner of the entire estate and thus probate is avoided.

A deed by either the husband or wife alone cannot defeat the right of the surviving spouse to the entire estate. One spouse may convey directly to the other.

While the husband is alive he alone is entitled to the complete control and possession of the property and to all the income and benefits. However, an award from a taking by eminent domain would belong to both the husband and wife as tenants by the entireties.

While probate is avoided by the use of the above joint estates, it is no longer possible to avoid death taxes this way. When one joint owner dies, his estate is taxed according to his proportionate share of the original cost of the property. A contribution of the original cost by a surviving owner must be clearly proved; otherwise the entire estate tax will apply upon the death of the first joint owner.

Prior to Jan. 1, 1976 in Massachusetts, all single-family dwellings actually occupied by the husband and wife as their residence were completely exempt from the state inheritance tax in cases of a tenancy by the entireties or joint tenancy. The first $25,000 in the value of a multiple-unit structure was also exempt for the husband and wife who occupied as tenants by the entireties. However, effective January 1, 1976 the State Inheritance Tax is abolished for all deaths after that date and a State Estate Tax based on the Federal Estate Tax is now imposed.

6. Community Property

In community property states all property acquired through the joint effort of husband and wife during their marriage belongs equally to both of them. This theory found its way into our laws in some of our states through Spanish or French influence such as was the case in California and Louisiana.

Each spouse is still entitled to hold as separate property all property he or she owned before marriage, as well as any property either received as a gift or by will during the marriage. All other property received during the marriage becomes community property.

As for ownership of the house, the test is whether or not community property funds paid for the house, and not whose name is on the deed. Both signatures are always necessary to transfer good title to a house.

When you move from a community property state to a common law state, all community property remains community property. Subsequently acquired property in the new state will be governed by common law principles.

If you move from a common law state to a community property state your separate property remains separate property. Only property subsequently acquired in the state will be governed by the community property law of your new state.

Distribution of community property after death varies among the different community property states. Generally either spouse may dispose of one-half of the community property by will. If there is no will, on the death of either spouse the surviving spouse takes one-half and one-half goes to the estate of the decesased spouse.

With personal property the law of the state where the spouses live governs. However, with real estate, whether or not community property law governs depends on the law of the state where the property is located.

7. Trusts

In addition to absolute transfers of property the law provides for transfers whereby a settlor may invest the legal title in a *trustee* for the use and benefit of another who is the beneficiary of the property. This type of transfer is called a *trust*.

If the trust is to take effect during the life of the settlor it is called a *living trust*. A trust in a settlor's will, to take effect only after the settlor's death when his will takes effect, is called a *testamentary trust*.

Anyone who has the legal capacity to transfer property can transfer it in trust. Anybody who has the legal capacity to own property may be a trustee. Anyone, even without capacity, may be a beneficiary of a trust, since the very purpose of a trust is often to provide for incapacitated persons.

A trust must be for lawful purpose, and can be set aside if its purpose is to defraud creditors.

If the settlor fails to make the trust revocable then it will be irrevocable and have all the effect of any other transfer of title.

Beneficiaries other than *spendthrift* beneficiaries may successfully request the court to terminate the trust.

If a living trust relates to real estate the trust must be in writing to satisfy the statute of frauds. This writing is called a trust agreement or trust deed. The title to real estate in a trust must be validly transferred to the trustee.

A testamentary trust (one in a will) must meet all the requirements of the particular state's statute of wills.

The use of the living trust is another method, along with joint estates already discussed, for avoiding probate. The trust deed to the trustee may provide that upon the settlor's death the property is to pass to named beneficiaries. Even if the trust is revocable, if the settlor dies the property is not included in any inventory to the probate court. Of course, the settlor may place all of his property, both real and personal, in trust and thus avoid probate altogether upon his death.

8. Straws

Another form of joint ownership of property involves a *straw* holding of bare legal and record title while the real party in interest holds the equitable title. This way the real party's name never appears in the open, in cases where this is advisable.

Since it is the straw who obtains the mortgage and signs the mortgage deed and note, the real party in interest escapes personal liability to the mortgagee bank. Later, the straw conveys to the real party in interest. This deed is not recorded until the disability or death of the straw.

The use of a straw offers another opportunity to avoid probate. For example, if the owner in fee simple wishes his son to have his property upon his death without the delay and expense of probate proceedings, and yet the owner still desires complete control while he is alive, he could use a straw to accomplish this in the following way. First the owner conveys his fee simple estate to the straw. Then the straw conveys back to the owner a life estate with remainder in fee to the owner's son.

Obviously, a straw must be chosen with care as to his reliability, and his credit rating or freedom of debt from possible attaching creditors. The straw ideally has little enough assets to render him practically judgment proof.

H. DEEDS. IS YOUR TITLE MARKETABLE?
REGISTERED TITLES; TITLE INSURANCE

A deed is the evidence of title to real estate, as a bill of sale is for personal property. Title does not legally pass without the delivery of the deed from the grantor (seller) to the grantee (buyer). The *recording* of the deed is for the protection of the buyer's interest against all other claimants to the property. The seller has the responsibility and expense of the preparation of the deed and usually must pay for the state excise stamps which must be affixed before recording. The buyer must pay a recording fee. Printed forms are normally used and the banks placing the mortgages usually insist upon the exact metes and bounds (measurements and boundaries) being copied from deed to deed. Normally, only the names of the parties and the ever newer title reference at the registry are changed on each successive deed. Only lawyers may draw a deed. All the terms and provisions of the conveyance are spelled out in the prior contract of sale.

A deed is only one way in which title to real estate may pass. The other principal methods are: by will or descent, by adverse possession and by eminent domain.

A title may be marketable and yet completely void on the record, as would be the case in a title by adverse possession. In the absence of agreement, there is no legal obligation on the seller's part to give a clear *record title*. Only a good *marketable title* is implied. A marketable title is one which a prudent person well advised as to the facts and the law (for instance, a bank) would take. It must be a title free from reasonable doubt.

Since the average buyer wants to receive a title which is clear on the record, some printed forms for purchase and sale agreements recite that the seller must furnish to the buyer on closing day a good and clear *record and marketable title*. Unlike the contract to give a deed, the deed itself requires no consideration and may be given as a gift.

Warranty Deed vs. Quitclaim Deed

Some states require the seller to give the buyer a *warranty deed*. This is a deed in which the seller guarantees that he is the legal owner, has

166

the right to convey, and that he will defend the buyer against the claims of all persons. Many states allow the seller to give a special type of statutory *quitclaim deed* to the buyer. This is a deed in which the seller merely agrees to quit whatever claim he may have and to guarantee to defend the buyer against any claims under him, but against none other. A straight quitclaim deed by which the grantor merely relinquishes whatever claim he may have but makes no guarantee whatever is used in the warranty deed states to correct or reform titles.

Is Your Title Marketable?

The court will not force a purchaser of real estate to buy a lawsuit. Private restrictions in the chain of title could make the title unmarketable, but zoning ordinances or building codes would not amount to a defect in the title which would justify rejection by a buyer. In states where dower and courtesy rights still apply, the absence of a signature by a spouse signing off this right would make the title unmarketable. A defect in a foreclosure sale would render title unmarketable. Title derived through an estate which was not probated would be defective. A substantial easement across the property would constitute a defect in the title. Outstanding attachments, mortgages, assessments and leases would also render a title unmarketable, as would the seller's inability to give substantially the amount of land agreed upon. In general, then, if a seller cannot furnish a clear record title, or easily show title by adverse possession, the title is not marketable. Many defects on title may be readily cured by enabling curative statutes available to your attorney.

Registered Land-Certified Titles

This is a system designed to eliminate much of the uncertainty involved in title searching and abstracting. Registered land provides a land court certified title which is indisputable and free of all claims. First adopted in Australia in the mid-nineteenth century, this *Torrens System* of land registration is available today in California, Colorado, Georgia, Illinois, Massachusetts, Minnesota, Nebraska, New York, North Carolina, Ohio, South Dakota, Tennessee, Utah, Virginia and Washington.

Title Insurance

The foregoing discussion of deeds and titles shows that many legal technicalities could threaten or destroy your ownership. *Title insurance* protects you from these hazards. The title insurance company defends your ownership when it is threatened. The company examines and approves your title, then indemnifies you against any loss due to a defect in the title. Only your own policy fully protects you. You may not depend on a policy which protects your mortgagee bank, even though you had to pay for it as part of your closing costs. In any event the bank's policy decreases as the mortgage decreases, so you could be really stuck years later when you might need the protection.

Chapter 37

PERSONAL RIGHTS AND LIABILITIES

A. ATTACHMENTS

In most states an unsecured creditor cannot attach your real estate until after judgment. However, in some states, the creditor may start suit by having his lawyer issue a writ and attaching or "tieing up" the debtor's property before trial. This harsh creditor action often comes unexpectedly fast and tends to strike panic in the alleged debtor—especially on the occasions when the privilege is abused by money hungry, overreaching, pirate-type businessmen who are deliberately trying to bluff or frighten an innocent victim into a settlement. All too often the mere threat of attachment with its attendant notorious publicity is enough to frighten, for example, an aged, penniless widow into paying an unjustifiable real estate broker's commission. It has happened like this to a client of mine:

—Telephoning broker: Mrs. Smith, your house is sold.

—Mrs. Smith: It is? Wonderful! What price did you get?

—Broker: $26,000. I already have a $50 deposit.

—Mrs. Smith: What—$26,000! I listed with you at $27,300 net to myself, I can't afford to sell for $26,000. One thing is certain, I never would be able to pay your commission at that price.

—Broker: Oh, that's all right, Mrs. Smith. Don't worry. I'll wiggle a little for you on the commission. We can always adjust the amount between ourselves.

—Mrs. Smith: But I have another broker coming back later today with a lawyer buyer and his wife to place a $1,000 cash deposit at my price, $28,900. I had planned, until you called, on accepting their offer. They are lovely people and they are putting $15,000 down, so I know the deal will go through. Best of all, I would get the amount of money I need to rejoin my family in the South.

—Broker (rather testily; he is now "taking the gloves off"): Now, Mrs. Smith, you know better than to try to pull anything like that. Your house is already sold to my buyer. You'd better not deal with that other broker or I'll *attach* your house and sue you for my full commission, 6 percent of $26,000. That will be $1,560 you will have to pay me, and you won't be able to sell your house to anybody until you do because I'll have it all tied up.

—Mrs. Smith (gasping for breath): Well, please don't do anything rash until I call you back.

The rest of the afternoon went like this: The unethical broker drove widow Smith to distraction with repeated threatening telephone calls at the office where she worked. Then the broker's lawyer told her she had better sign his client's agreement if she did not wish to find herself a big loser in a long-drawn-out court action, with her house all tied up in the meantime. The widow Smith was also reminded that if she did not sign up immediately she would, in any event, lose out on her new home in the South near her family to which she had hoped to retreat to better bear the recent great loss of her husband. A warning call was even made to the office of the broker who had the right buyer at the right price to lay off the deal because the house was already "sold."

Of course, everything worked out all right, for the following obvious reasons:

1. The broker with the low offer had, after all, only an offer. Only Mrs. Smith, the seller, had a right to *accept* the offer and thus form a legally binding contract, because the offer failed to meet the terms of her "open" listing agreement with that broker. Actually the broker knew this well all along. Nevertheless, he was trying to lie to, cheat and bluff the seller, his own lawyer and the worthy broker as well.

2. Mrs. Smith actually signed and accepted the proper offer at her terms, which she had every right to do.

3. The sorehead broker who never had a leg to stand on in the first place carried out his threat to sue the widow for a commission and he did abuse the privilege of attaching Mrs. Smith's house immediately, upon issuance of the writ by his lawyer.

4. Mrs. Smith simply placed a bond with the court covering the amount of the disputed commission, and went through with her sale.

5. The bad broker lost his case, of course. But, like too many others, he is still free to harass other innocent victims.

6. The only thing that saved Mrs. Smith was that she called her lawyer *before* signing anything for the unethical broker.

The story does point out that any innocent person at any time may be subject to attachment, especially in the many states that permit attachments before judgment. Some of these states have helped to protect the innocent by requiring the attaching plaintiff to post a bond to indemnify the loss to a victim of a wrongful attachment. The debtor, in turn, may remove the attachment by posting his own bond. The purpose of the attachment, of course, is to prevent a debtor from disposing of his property pending a lawsuit against him.

In most states attachment or garnishment may be used when an employee owes money and his creditor compels the employer to pay him the amount of the wages due the employee. It may be employed against any third person who owes money to, or is holding tangible property for, the creditor's debtor, to pay to the creditor the amount necessary to satisfy the creditor's claim against the debtor. The money is usually paid into court for the benefit of the creditor.

Attachment or garnishment is generally done *after* the entry of a judgment against the debtor. The states which permit this procedure *prior* to a judgment usually restrict the cases to those involving fraud, a nonresident or a debtor who is concealing himself.

When the procedure is allowed, there are usually exemptions which the debtor may claim. Every state has minimum exemptions which all judgment debtors may claim. These usually include part of his wages, his auto if he needs it to work, and the tools of his trade.

B. LIENS

Ordinary creditors are limited to attaching a debtor's general assets or earning capacity. However, creditors who classify as lienholders have special advantages against their debtors. Lienholders are called "lienors." They hold a preferred claim against particular property called a lien, and thus enjoy special protection ahead of unsecured general creditors. The lien could be against your house. It could be foreclosed like a mortgage. Like a mortgage, a lien must be paid off before you could give clear title to a buyer, or refinance your house. You must never let liens go unattended. You should make every effort to avoid them or get rid of them. The most common liens on your real estate are held by judgment creditors, tax collectors, mechanics and public welfare agencies. There are also liens against personal property held by warehousemen, tradesmen, hotel keepers, hospitals and so on.

Some recent cases offer a few helpful tips:

1. An original owner is not liable to a buyer who pays his real estate tax, when the tax lien is filed against the original recorded owner and not against the owner at the time the lien is filed.

2. The recording of a chattel mortgage amounts to constructive notice to a creditor of the homeowner.

3. The bona fide purchaser for value without notice is protected from a mechanic's lien not filed *before* the buyer's deed was recorded.

4. The wife's interest in a tenancy by the entireties is unattachable by her personal creditors while the husband lives. However, when the husband's creditor gets an execution he receives absolute control of the property while the husband lives because the husband has this control. But the husband's creditor cannot sell anything more than the husband had. So, if the husband's interest is sold at auction, and the wife survives her husband, she still gets all the property.

C. MORTGAGE FORECLOSURES

A mortgage is given as security for a loan or a debt. The debt itself is evidenced by a note. In the New England states and North Carolina a mortgage is a "conditional deed." That is, the mortgagee who gives the money actually gets legal title to the real estate of the mortgagor who borrows the funds. In all the other states the mortgage is merely a lien on the borrower's property. When the mortgagor gives legal title to the bank, he retains the equitable ownership—that is, the value of the property over and above the mortgage indebtedness. The mortgagor also retains the right to redeem his legal title upon the satisfaction of the mortgage conditions. These mortgage conditions, the strings by which the borrower may pull back his legal right to his property, or remove the mortgage lien in the lien theory states, usually consist of four basic, statutory requirements, plus any other special conditions the bank may insert in their tailor-made mortgage form, which the borrower must sign to get his money.

The Statutory Conditions

1. Mortgagor must repay the full amount of the loan plus interest.
2. He must keep up payment of taxes on the property.
3. He must keep the premises insured against fire in an amount at

least as much as the mortgage debt, in a company approved by the mortgagee.

4. He must refrain from committing "waste." Since the mortgagee actually has a conditional legal ownership, or a lien on the whole premises, the mortgagor may not remove or sell off any part of the property, including additions, subsequent to the date of the mortgage.

Typical Additional Bank Conditions

1. Mortgagor is required to pay taxes monthly in advance as part of his bank payment. In some States the bank gets free use of this money without paying interest until the tax payment date.

2. Mortgagor is required to pay for fire insurance one year in advance and continue to make monthly payments in advance to the bank toward the next annual prepayment of premium when it becomes due. The bank also gets free use of this money without paying any interest for it.

Mortgagee's Right to Foreclosure

The mortgagor never sees the mortgage form when he applies for the mortgage, or when his application is accepted by the bank. At the "closing" the bank conveyancer does flash the mortgage form in front of the mortgagor for his signature as well as his wife's. (They both must sign the "note" as well.) However, at this point the new home buyer is simultaneously beset with so many different papers to sign and figures to digest that his head is swimming and he has all he can do to maintain composure and the pretext that he understands everything that is going on.

One thing for sure is that he is not given time to read all the formidable and legalistic fine print in the mortgage. The conveyancer has another party waiting in the anteroom, and the buyer must get back to work, the buyer's wife must rush home to the kids. Nevertheless, for breach of any statutory condition, or any other bank condition contained in the fine print of the mortgage form, the lending bank has the "statutory power of sale." This usually means that after publication of a notice of public auction once a week for three weeks in the local paper the mortgage foreclosure sale may take place.

If the unfortunate mortgagor can manage to pay up all arrearage payments plus the bank attorney's fees prior to public notice of the auction sale, he can still save his house.

At the sale the mortgagor is entitled to bid back his property. Junior mortgagees may protect their interests by bidding in and buying at the sale. The bank conducts the auction "with right of reserve." In other words, if no one bids high enough to protect the bank's interest, the property may be withdrawn from sale. If the sale yields more than the costs of the sale, plus unpaid taxes, plus the first mortgage debt due, then the junior mortgagees share in their turn, beginning with the second mortgagee. If any proceeds from the sale are left after all debts against the property are paid, this excess money goes to the mortgagor. On the other hand, the mortgagor is liable for a judgment in the amount of any deficiency resulting from the sale.

The buyer at the mortgage foreclosure sale gets absolute clear title in fee simple by statute. Also the mortgagor waived any right of redemption when he originally signed the mortgage form.

Homeowners facing mortgage foreclosure proceedings must beware of the vulture type of private financiers who prey upon them in their unfortunate circumstances. These rogues will mislead the owners into believing that their homes will be saved through their superior credit capacity for refinancing upon the payment of a substantial fee. The dodge of this type of "Uncle Harry will help you" type of second mortgage racketeer is that he will pick up all the $300 or $500 fees he can while waiting for a live one to come along. The "live one" gives him his big score, because the present mortgage being foreclosed is so small that "Uncle Harry" can immediately refinance for a few thousand more through some mortgage banker friend.

He thereupon arranges a payoff to the foreclosing bank's attorney to stop the foreclosure sale, gets the beleaguered homeowner to deed the property to him, siphons off the profit from the new higher mortgage he places, then rents the house back to the original owner with a tempting option to buy—when the debtor "gets back on his feet." Meanwhile, the lease gives him the right to evict his new tenant upon the first late rental payment, which usually happens fairly soon. Now the scoundrel sells off the house for another big score of profit. Best bets for these racketeers are those persons whose own personal credit is ruined, alcoholics, and victims of marital breakups.

The right of redemption by a foreclosed mortgagor, even after the sale, is preserved in several of the states for varying periods between one-half and three years.

D. TAX SALES

Many state statutes provide for tax liens upon the filing of a written notice by the tax collector involved. These liens cover unpaid taxes on real estate, corporations, inheritances, estates and income.

A tax lien may be foreclosed which would result, after due public notice, in a tax sale. However, for most homeowners who have an outstanding mortgage, their bank would normally pay taxes due to protect their own security. This is an advantage more homeowners should think about before complaining about the bank's using their tax escrow money without payment of interest. It is the homeowner who pays his own taxes, who, as a practical matter, runs the risk of a tax sale to satisfy a lien for unpaid taxes.

The following tips should be helpful:

1. Failure to receive a tax bill is no defense against a tax sale resulting from the imposition of a lien for unpaid taxes.

2. Unintentional tax delinquency is no bar to a tax sale.

3. Mistake or absence of the delinquent taxpayer from the state does not operate as bar to a tax sale.

4. Most states do not require any court procedure to enable a tax sale.

5. A notice of sale, however, is required to be given to the delinquent owner, and to publicly advise prospective purchasers of the sale. Failure of notice would invalidate the sale.

6. The payment or tender of payment of delinquent taxes at any time before the actual tax sale would invalidate the sale.

7. The sale must be held at the exact time and place specified, otherwise it would be void.

8. The sale must be held at *public* auction. A private sale would be void.

9. Any conspiracy or fraud in the bidding would invalidate the sale.

10. The owner may oppose a court confirmation of the sale, if one is necessary, on the grounds that the taxing authority failed to comply with any one of the many technical requirements of the sale.

11. The buyer at the tax sale does not get a deed. All he gets is an assignment of the tax lien which entitles him to a deed only when the owner's time for redemption has expired.

12. The purchaser at a tax sale takes the property subject to existing mortgages. The purchase by a junior mortgagee at a tax sale is subject to a prior mortgage.

13. Many states have statutes requiring the sale to be made to the highest qualified bidder.

14. Any member of the owner's family other than a husband or wife may buy at the tax sale, in the absence of a fiduciary relationship or fraud.

15. The title of a present owner who is paying his taxes on time could

be defective and unmarketable because of a prior tax sale to a stranger who may be holding an outstanding tax deed.

16. Most bank conveyancers as a matter of policy will not approve a property for a mortgage with their bank if there was a prior tax sale in the claim of title.

E. LICENSEES

Chapter 31 showed how the landlord-tenant relationship with all of its rights and responsibilities could be created verbally, without a lease, on the very informal temporary basis of a tenancy-at-will. However, if an occupant does not even have *exclusive* use of the premises to the exclusion of the owner and the right to control of the premises, with his own individual means of entrance and exit, then the law declares that occupant to be a "bare licensee."

Examples of licensees run all the way from the roomer in Mrs. Kitooley's boarding house who pays a weekly rent to the high-annual-rent commercial concessionaire in a department store, airport or shopping center.

The big concessionaire may think he is a tenant on a long lease and even have a lengthy and complicated lease to try to prove it. However, the court held, in one famous case, that the test of the difference between a tenant and a licensee was whether or not the occupant held exclusive possession of the premises. The big music company concessionaire failed this test of tenancy, was in the category of only a licensee, and was subject to removal from the department store *forthwith*, without any notice at all.

Many owners have been known to vacate a licensee operator quickly and take over for themselves the profitable business he built on their premises.

It goes without saying that Mrs. Kitooley has the power to evict her licensee roomer forthwith, without notice.

As part of the new wave of consumer law, some states have granted the status of a tenant at will to a licensee who has remained on the premises for at least six months.

F. BUSINESS INVITEES

Your mailman, garbage collector, tradesmen and salesmen who come upon your premises are presumed by the law to be there with your permission for the special purposes of their visits. While they are on your property the law says that you owe them the legal duty to exercise *ordinary* care toward them, and conversely imposes liability upon you for accidents and injuries caused to them by your *ordinary* negligence.

Translated into common terms, this means that it would be your plain duty to warn the mailman or garbage collector concerning a dangerous instrumentality which you may know will beset him upon his regular path across your premises.

The measurement of ordinary care by the courts is that degree of care which one has a right to expect from an ordinary, prudent person under all the particular circumstances involved. The measurement of *ordinary* negligence is simply your failure to exercise ordinary care.

Tort (a legal wrong) damages in the law include all incidental and consequential damages. Recent court awards for *intentional* torts or *accidental* torts (negligence cases) have run into huge amounts of money damages—especially in automobile negligence cases, where the defendant is apt to be heavily insured.

Privately, many judges confess that our tort rule for damages which requires an ordinary person to exercise ordinary prudent care twenty-four hours a day, every day of the year, is an unnatural and unrealistically harsh requirement. After all, normally prudent ordinary persons do goof once in awhile. The fact is that no better or more equitable standard has ever been devised. Consequently all of us bear the onerous burden in tort law to be careful all the time if we wish to be free from substantial lawsuits.

G. GUESTS

In some jurisdictions under tort law principles your social guests are entitled to no more than *slight* care from you. To be legally liable in damages to them for accident or injury you must be guilty of *gross* negligence.

Apparently, the courts in establishing this standard of care or liability for the host-free guest relationship have taken judicial notice of the frailties of human nature as well as exercised understandable compassion for the position of the host who is providing valuable services or entertainment free to his guests. The courts are ready to impose some assumption of risk upon the free-loading guest. They seem to feel that, human nature being what it is, if guests could sue for the ordinary negligence of their hosts every insurance company in the country would soon be bankrupt.

176

Accordingly, while you are in the role of free social guest you must be particularly careful to look out for your own safety at all times.

An interesting restaurant case dramatizes the difference between the *ordinary* care owed to a business invitee and the *slight* care owed to a free guest. Two friends entered a cafeteria. One purchased food and sat at a table to eat it. His companion made no purchase, being content to avail himself in turn of the free services of the men's room, a glass of ice water, a toothpick and the telephone booth. While the two friends sat at the table they were both injured from the accidental tumbling of dishes off a passing waiter's tray. The court was satisfied that the waiter was guilty of ordinary negligence. The insurer of the restaurant company (the waiter's master) had to pay damages to the plaintiff who was eating at the table because he was there in the role of a *business invitee*. As such, he was entitled to *ordinary care* from the waiter (the servant of the restaurant company). However, the free-loading companion could not collect for his injuries since he was there in the role of *a free guest* and entitled only to *slight* care. Since the waiter was not found guilty of *gross* negligence the insurer of the restaurant company was not liable to the guest.

This actual case could serve as a useful guide to the extent of your liability in your home or apartment to a visiting business invitee versus a social guest. Just be careful to check with your State to see if it has legislated away this historic distinction between the social guest and business invitee. Massachusetts now requires ordinary care and finds liability for ordinary negligence in both cases.

H. TRESPASSERS

You are legally entitled to the quiet enjoyment of your property free from the intrusion of uninvited or unwanted persons. Such persons are liable to you in tort for trespassing if they come onto your private property voluntarily. However, the law protects those persons from liability whose invasion of your private property was brought about involuntarily on their part through the operation of some external instrumentality or circumstance.

Remember, you do not own the street or the sidewalk. These areas are owned by the town.

While you may have the legal right to sue a trespasser you cannot receive any more damages than you actually sustain.

Since trespass is a tort and children are liable for their own torts, and not their parents unless they are present and directing the child, don't waste your breath threatening parents whose children have wandered onto your property.

You may legally use only that force which is reasonably necessary under the circumstances to physically evict a trespasser from your property.

Your only legal duty to a trespasser is to refrain from willful, wanton and reckless misconduct.

Even gross negligence on your part would not constitute any legal liability.

I. BANKRUPTCY AND INSOLVENCY

Whenever your liabilities become greater than your assets, or you are unable to pay your debts and obligations as they become due, you are *insolvent*.

If you reach this unfortunate situation you must know something about bankruptcy proceedings and how they would jeopardize your house.

You may file a *voluntary petition in bankruptcy* or be *forced into bankruptcy* by your creditors. Either way, the court appoints a trustee in bankruptcy to receive your property and settle your affairs. Since 1898, the National Bankruptcy Act supersedes earlier state laws which are only important now to conveyancers making title searches.

The federal law assures fair treatment for all of your creditors and at the same time gives you an honest chance to start over again fresh, with most (not all) of your debts discharged.

The debts not discharged in bankruptcy which you would still have to pay are:

1. All federal, state and local taxes.

2. All dishonest debts arising out of embezzlement, fraud or false pretenses.

3. Obligations for injuries caused by your wanton, willful and malicious misconduct.

4. Alimony.

5. Child support.

6. Wages due your employees or salesmen within three months prior to your bankruptcy.

Normally, the bankruptcy court will order your other debts discharged, but not necessarily. Your trustee will approve you to the court if he does not find the following situations:

1. Within the past six years you have previously been discharged in bankruptcy.
2. You have transferred property with an intent to defraud creditors.
3. You have obtained credit or money by false statements.
4. There is an unexplained loss of your assets.
5. You have failed to obey a court order.
6. You have failed or refused to answer questions.
7. You have failed to produce adequate records.
8. You have committed any crime involving your filing for bankruptcy.

Usually the value of your house far exceeds the value of your *state homestead exemption*. Accordingly, the trustee normally sells your house free from your homestead exemption. After the sale the trustee sets aside for you out of the proceeds an amount equal to your exemption.

Property you may acquire after your petition in bankruptcy is filed, but before you are adjudicated a bankrupt, is exempt from your bankrupt estate. You, and not your trustee in bankruptcy, have title to this after-acquired property.

J. SEPARATION AND DIVORCE

A marriage may be terminated by:
1. An annulment
2. Voluntary separation
3. Court-awarded separation
4. Divorce

We can dispense quickly with annulment since this means that the court finds your marriage invalid from the beginning. Therefore the attempted marriage has no effect on your property or personal rights.

The husband and wife may separate any time they wish with or without a court decree, because the law cannot compel them to live together.

The property rights of the husband and wife are different for separation than they are for divorce.

Separation Agreements

If a husband and wife decide to separate, a voluntary separation agreement drawn by their attorneys is usually more beneficial than going to court for a separation. Any property rights are advantageously settled as part of the voluntary agreement, which also deals with custody of the children and support.

Grounds for a legal separation awarded by the court usually include anything that would constitute grounds for divorce. These grounds vary widely throughout the states but generally include: adultery, cruelty, desertion, drug addiction, idiocy, incompatibility, impotence, imprisonment, attempt on life, indignities, insanity, loathsome disease, refusal to cohabitate and willful neglect to support.

Unfortunately the cases vary so endlessly that there are no common denominators for amounts paid or property settlements.

If a house is owned jointly neither party will be able to sell it without the other party's signing off.

The marriage is still binding even though the separation is granted by the court. Therefore either spouse would have all the rights of a surviving spouse upon the death of either the husband or the wife.

Divorce

Only a court can grant divorce, which constitutes legal death to a marriage. The court decree normally provides for a property settlement, including the ownership and possession of your house.

A surviving divorcee is not a widow; hence she has none of the rights that would be enjoyed by a surviving widow. Obviously, a divorced husband can have no rights by surviving his ex-wife. The only exception to this occurs in some states which grant an innocent divorced wife her dower rights upon the death of her ex-husband.

K. UNLAWFUL SEARCH AND SEIZURE—DEFENSE OF YOUR HOME (YOUR CASTLE)

One of the bundle of rights of ownership you possess is the very important right to the *"quiet enjoyment of your premises."* This means that the law will protect your right to privacy. You are protected from illegal invasions of your privacy from government officials and intrusions by unwanted private individuals.

Earlier in this chapter we dealt with your liabilities to persons who lawfully entered upon your premises. Now we shall dwell upon your rights to expel unwanted persons and defend your right to peace and privacy.

No officer of the law, under any circumstances, has a right to search your house or seize your property without a search warrant signed by a judge. The law officer must present adequate evidence to persuade the issuing judge that there is probable cause for the granting of the search warrant. The party seeking the warrant must take an oath before the judge, or make a sworn statement in writing, either of which is subject to prosecution for perjury.

The police officer has no personal discretion to search any person, or any property, at any address not specifically spelled out in the warrant.

You are entitled to see the search warrant or make the officer describe its contents to you before permitting the search to take place. Otherwise the search would be unlawful.

You are protected from any unnecessary damage. You are entitled to have your premises restored to the condition they were in before the search. A search in the night time must be specifically authorized.

You may sue for damages in a civil action all persons involved in an illegal or unreasonable search and seizure, and you would be safe from prosecution by the evidence gained from the illegal search or seizure.

Earlier we discussed your right to use all reasonable force necessary against a trespasser on your property.

Whenever you are acting in fear of violence, in fear of a felony, or in self-defense, even homicide is legally justifiable in the defense of your home (your castle).

Chapter 38

NEW LAWS PROTECTING BUYERS AND TENANTS

RENT CONTROL

Across the country State after State has adopted rent control legislation chiefly for the benefit of tenants in larger cities. Many large metropolitan cities have adopted their own laws. Some States and cities have already revoked these laws in an effort to stimulate the economy and increase their property tax base. The purpose of rent control is to regulate both rents and evictions. The following type properties are usually exempt: Owner-occupied two and three family houses, luxury apartment houses, cooperative apartments, and new construction (usually from a date about one year prior to the enactment of the new rent control law).

The maximum rent a landlord is allowed to charge the tenant is usually pegged at that rent paid at a date six months prior to the start of the new law. The local rent control board is empowered to grant landlords increases in rent to compensate for increases in taxes, utility costs, and costs of improvements. Likewise, tenants may be granted reduced rents to compensate for reductions in quarters or services provided.

In order to evict a tenant a landlord must first win approval from the local rent board before he can start proceedings in a court. Evictions are usually allowed for failure to pay rent, damage caused by the tenant, landlord wanting possession for himself or family, illegal use by the tenant or a nuisance created by the tenant.

CONSUMER PROTECTION

New State and Federal Consumer Protection Laws apply to real estate sales and rentals of both residential and commercial properties. These laws make any unfair or deceptive practice on the part of a seller or landlord illegal. The new laws hit hard at landlords and usually provide stiff penalties for any of the following practices by building owners:

1. Charging increased rents for increased taxes in a manner which does not conform to the law.

2. Failure to comply with the State Sanitary code within a reasonable time from notice by a tenant or governmental agency.

3. Failure to provide agreed services to the tenant.

4. Failure to make agreed repairs.

5. Misrepresentation to tenant that the dwelling unit does not violate any law when, in fact, it does.

6. Misrepresenting a personal notice to the tenant as an official or judicial document.

7. Failure to provide tenant with a copy of the rental agreement.

8. Failure to return the tenant's security deposit.

9. Deducting damages from the security deposit without giving tenant an itemized list.

10. Refuses to allow tenant full use of the rental unit without first obtaining a court order.

11. Charges a late payment penalty before payment is 30 days overdue.

12. Failure to provide utility service.
13. Illegally enters tenant's apartment.

FAIR HOUSING

The Federal Civil Rights Act prohibits discrimination in all types of housing. This federal law supersedes State laws which have provided exemptions such as: owner-occupied two-family dwellings. It means that no landlords, whether single family, multiple unit, or commercial owners can refuse to sell, lease or rent. It also means that no brokers or salesmen can discriminate against persons for race, national origin, national ancestry, color, age, sex or member of the armed services, or veterans. Also, more of these characteristics may be recorded either written or verbal on applications for sale, lease or rental.

INTERSTATE LAND SALES

The Interstate Land Sales Full Disclosure Act regulates out of state sale or lease of developments of 50 or more unimproved lots.

This new law requires the developer to furnish prospective buyers with a report containing the following information: accredited financial statements, improvement commitments, water and sewerage facilities, utilities provided, and environmental reports. This same information must be registered with the U.S. Department of Housing and Urban Development. The new law forbids and penalizes fraud, deceptive practices, and misrepresentation.

The States have adopted their own special new laws covering interstate land sales and generally have them enforced by their State Boards of Registration for Real Estate. They are especially interested in how deposit monies are handled until the closing, and the terms and conditions of sale.

PART III

Practical Ways to Make Money in Real Estate

Chapter 39

WHY REAL ESTATE? IS IT YOUR BEST BET?

Ever since the early American settlers bought land for two cents an acre, real estate has provided the largest single means to the accumulation of individual fortunes in this country. Nobody has ever given sounder or more profitable advice than John Jacob Astor when he said: "Buy on the fringe and wait!" In fact, the largest handlers of private funds in the country, the banks and insurance companies, have always invested more heavily in real estate than anything else. Accordingly, it would appear to be more than ordinary prudence for the individual investor to consider most seriously the many proven ways to build a fortune in real property.

Furthermore, it takes money to make money, and the more money you invest in anything profitable the more you can make. Therefore, it makes a lot of sense to invest your small down payment along with the large amounts of mortgage money provided by senior and junior mortgage lenders. This enables you to quadruple your investment right at the start. You are now in a position to reap profits four times as great than if you were limited to your own small funds.

Also, it is very comforting to know that a large, experienced financial institution is willing to look over your shoulder, advise you, approve your investment and say, "Don't be afraid. We are willing to invest three or four dollars for every one of yours." In what other way will the banks let you use so much of their money to become rich? In fact, income property investors, today, typically put up only about 10 or 15 percent of the total investment. You should never be afraid to borrow money for a worthwhile purpose. Every business and government has always had to do this, both to start and to keep growing. What other enterprise could possibly offer you more safety than realty investment, where the foreclosure rate is currently less than one in a thousand?

Only through real estate investment can you enjoy all of the following benefits:

1. Greatest net cash return on your actual investment. Investment buyers normally demand 10 to 15 percent per year minimum clear net profit on their actual cash investment. Obviously this is far greater than the cash interest or dividends on bank accounts or securities investments.

2. Amortization—the total principal savings each year on all the mortgage payments you make, using your tenants' money.

3. Depreciation—usually 3 to 5 percent each year on the total investment. This tax deduction allowed on all income property acts as a very profitable offset to your income tax liability.

4. Appreciation—the ever-increasing value of most income property through general inflation. Real estate has always been the best hedge against inflation.

5. The availability of the maximum 25 percent capital gain tax so long as you hold the property at least six months.

6. The extra increase in value obtainable by buying in a growing area.

7. The ability to control your own investment. You can't tell your bank or the corporation you invest in how to run their business, much as you might like to.

8. The opportunity to use your wits creatively. Ingenuity pays off big in real estate investment when used to upgrade existing facilities or create new facilities.

In the next chapter we shall see how easy it is to accumulate a starting purse and be off to the races.

Chapter 40

HOW TO ACCUMULATE A STARTING PURSE

Actually, all anyone need do is stop paying money out in rent, and buy any kind of real estate—even a single house, if the location is good. No one could have started more humbly than the hero of our next chapter, who bought a very old $7,800 single house with nothing down on a G.I. 100 percent mortgage.

If you fix up the house at all you can sell it later for a profit, so long as the location is good. If you wait a few years to build some equity—that is, the difference between your ever-decreasing mortgage balance and the ever-increasing fair market value of your house—you can make a second profit. A third profit normally reaped by the homeowner is called appreciation; that is, the ever-increasing value of your house due to inflation. You will make this profit, too, if you take care to avoid declining neighborhoods. And remember, you are saving money, through income tax deductions on your taxes and mortgage interest payments, even while living in the house.

You are now in a position to either sell the house for a handsome profit, or remortgage the property for a higher amount. You pocket the difference tax-free when you remortgage. Either way you have a starting purse for some serious, really beneficial investing in income property.

However, there is a still faster way for the average person to build his first nest egg for investing purposes. All you need do is buy a small multiple-unit house of two, three or four apartments and live in one of the flats virtually rent free. You can finance up to four units, minimum down, through the V.A. or the F.H.A. If two or more veterans are buying together, one additional unit over the four is allowed for each veteran involved in the joint purchase. If you are a veteran but do not earn enough to satisfy the bank you are approaching for mortgage money, then you may include your parents or other financially responsible parties as co-owners to show enough earning power to swing the mortgage.

Let's take for an example the two-family house a client of mine should have bought at the end of World War II and unfortunately did not buy. How he wishes he had the chance all over again! This is why, with what he knows now, he would never have missed that golden opportunity!

The two-family house he almost bought sold in 1946 for $10,000. It was a large, well-built house in a rich town with a low tax rate. Today, it would sell quickly for over $50,000. With a twenty-year mortgage the house would be all paid for, so to begin with he could be $50,000 ahead. However, the single house he did live in cost him an average of $2,500 a year more in actual total housing expense, including miscellaneous items. So, over the thirty-year span he could have saved an additional $75,000 for a total savings of $125,000. Furthermore, many additional thousands could have been saved if he had cut his personal costs by living less pretentiously. When you add to all these savings the amounts of compounded interest he would have accumulated over those thirty years through the bank and securities savings he would have been able to make, you begin to appreciate how easy it really is for anyone to build a starting purse for real estate investment.

Remember, you don't have to wait twenty years. You can take a ten- or fifteen-year mortgage, or you can refinance after just a few years, for your starting cash.

Now let us see in the following chapter how I was able to help another client make some right moves that catapulted him from struggling obscurity to financial independence and success.

Chapter 41

STEP BY STEP FROM A $7,800 G.I. NO-MONEY-DOWN SINGLE HOUSE TO A FORTUNE IN REAL ESTATE WITH THE MAILMAN WHO DID IT IN TWO YEARS

The hero of this chapter, Alexander Paraskeva of Wakefield, Massachusetts, returned from World War II a young man of twenty-three, to find himself suddenly married, without a job and in need of a place to live. An apartment was nowhere to be found. He learned about the no-money-down opportunity to buy a house under Veterans Administration guarantee to the bank lending the full mortgage. His brother, who owned a grocery store at the time (he is now a big real estate tycoon), vouched for him as an employee. Soon he found himself the proud owner of a very old-fashioned single house, badly in need of repair, for only $7,800 with nothing down.

Young Alex lived in this house for many years and raised his family, always thinking about making it into a two-family because he needed the income. But he was stalled through lack of initiative, ignorance of what to do and how to go about it, and just plain fear. Finally, after sixteen years he decided to convert his single house into a two-family.

Inquiring at the city hall he found that his house was properly zoned for a two-family. The town building inspector, plumbing inspector and electrical inspector told him what would be required by law. Now he sought bids from three carpenters, three plumbers and three electricians. So far, his procedures were absolutely correct. You must always check the zoning ordinances and building codes, and get at least three bids from each type of contractor needed. Let's see what happened with the bids he received.

The high carpenter bid was $4,000. Alex chose a carpenter who did the job for $1,500. One plumber quoted $2,000; another, $1,000. A third plumber did the work for $850. One electrician bid $1,250. Another took the job for $600, and did more work than the first electrician was going to do.

Alex became very pleased with himself for overcoming his earlier fears and creating a needed extra income from the second apartment in his converted two-family. Today, he realizes where he made his first big mistake. If he had started with a run-down two-family instead of an old single house, he could have saved a fortune on carpentry, plumbing and electricial work. However, at that time, in the excitement of his new creative enterprise, his inexperience led him to his second big mistake. Reasoning that, if he was doing so well with one two-family house he would surely do better with two, he bought another run-down single house for $12,000 to create a second two-family and a total of three extra incomes for himself. He now realizes that he should have jumped to four or six units. He knows that he can fix up a six-family almost as cheaply as he can a two-family, since basic plumbing and wiring are much the same.

Let's sum up what Alex had learned about investing and upgrading:

1. Buy location. This is the prime requisite. You can change the house, but you can't change the location.

2. Never buy a single house and change it into a two-family. Buy a two-family to begin with.

3. A converted two-family is all right, but insist on separate heat and utilities.

4. Never buy a two-family if you can afford a larger building. Preferably you should start with four or six units.

Alex's thinking was now absolutely correct. At this point, he came to me for assistance in selling his first two-family. He told me that he was employed as a mailman, and living in his second house while converting it into a two-family. He wanted to use the proceeds from the sale to buy at least six units and start building a real estate empire. He had adopted his wife's Mormon religion. He _____ in living and hard working. His health and strength were the best from his regular job of walking his mail route in his own home town. His wonderful wife, and now grown children, stood closely by him and gave him great assistance. He knew he was properly prepared and ready for real estate investment, remodeling and upgrading. He knew the rewards would be well worth the effort. He had the necessary confidence to succeed. I immediately sold his two-family for him at $22,900. His original $7,800 full mortgage was almost all paid off. His profit was enormous. Fortunately, I had at that particular time a listing of a seven-unit, old converted house in a good location. This would be perfect for Alex. The seller wanted only $23,000 for what amounted to a lucrative opportunity with plenty of room for remodeling and upgrading of rental income.

Now, it is very difficult, indeed, to obtain new first mortgages on old worn-out multiple frame dwellings. Some banks will go only to four units. Few will go above four units, especially if the building is not brick, does not have separate furnaces in the basement, or is very old or in poor condition. Banks generally prefer large, modern, brick apartment buildings. Consequently, the bank holding the existing mortgage would not rewrite a larger mortgage for my buyer, nor would a host of other banks that I had inspect the property—and these were banks where I had friends. Meanwhile, the seller was getting very worried. His insurance company had already notified him that they would not renew their policy on his old building due to its poor condition. The seller's wife was working against him rather than for him. With all this pressure on him the seller kept going over my head to inform my buyer, Alex, that he would sell for less for a fast deal. The more eager he was to reduce his price for quick action, the more determinedly would Alex— who was dying to buy the building immediately—wait him out. Finally, the seller came down from $23,000 to $18,200. At this point, Alex snapped up the building. What a buy for him!

Alex's own bank, based on their confidence in him, gave him a new mortgage, plus construction money to remodel. He painted the outside, installed new front steps, and replaced the gutters. With all the work done by himself and family, the actual out-of-pocket outlay was very small to repair the exterior. His only costs were for paint and lumber.

Alex took the cheap, quick, easy way out in renovating the interior of this old "dump" of a building. He used inexpensive plywood to cover interior walls where the walls were really bad, and paint alone where inside the front door it helped a lot. Alex replaced some supporting timbers in the basement to keep the place from tumbling down. The rest of the job was largely a matter of installing colorful inexpensive modern appliances in the kitchens.

Alex did one flat at a time as it became vacant. He increased rental income dramatically and collected by the week to squeeze an extra week's income out of every three months. Also the tenants were willing to pay a higher rate by the week. When he had finished, after a few months, he had generated a $100 per week net profit for himself. Now he was really eager to get five more buildings just like this one. Six months later Alex turned down an offer I had for him of $33,500. However, the next property I chose for Alex was to become much more fruitful an investment for him than he ever dared to dream.

A bank in a nearby town was stuck with a foreclosure on two old nursing homes. For three years every broker, contractor, and remodeler in the area had successively turned the property down. The bank was into the property to the tune of $47,500—and there were no takers. The location was perfect—plenty of grounds in the richest residential section of the town. Adjacent houses sold from the thirties to $100,000. The only real problem militating against these two huge old houses was the limitation of two-family zoning. What in the world would you do with all the extra rooms? One building had twenty-six rooms, the other building had twenty-one rooms. This property represented a real challenge to me, so I began to prosecute the following inquiry.

Checking at the town hall, I found that if two detached garage buildings were either torn down or removed, there would be no impediment to creating two additional building lots. I knew that these lots would be worth between $8,500 and $10,000 each in that choice area.

In other words, if I could get those large old houses for Alex with 100 percent bank financing, which a bank is legally allowed to give only when it is stuck with a foreclosed property, he would then be in a position to raise $17,000 cash on the sale of the two extra lots, after investing no cash down at all. Of course I became more and more fascinated and intrigued with the potential profit in this property that all the "pros" had rejected.

I succeeded in getting the bank to accept an offer of $41,800, even though they were stuck for $47,500. I had the two extra lots approved by the town. I found out that Alex could not only make two full apartments out of each building under the two-family zoning, but that, in addition, he could rent out the extra rooms by the week. Since these were old nursing homes there were almost enough baths to match the additional rooms. In that fine location he could command up to $25 per week just for a room and bath. With this kind of income for a room and bath, who needs apartments?

Subtracting the $17,000 for the two extra lots, Alex won those two buildings for a total of $24,800, with no money down. In less than six months, doing most of the work in spare time with his own family, he remodeled the two buildings, filled them with tenants to the tune of over $13,000 per year. In addition, he has already raised his first mortgage by $20,000 of tax-free cash, and the total property now has a fair market value of approximately $120,000. Less than one year ago he paid only $41,800 with nothing down.

Contrary to the fears of all the experts, the roofs did not fall in, nor did they need to be replaced. The boilers in the basements did not blow up. The plumbing remained sound. So did the wiring. In fact, the houses were better built than you could afford to build them today. Once again Alex scored with paint outside and inside, and some interior plywood. The rest was largely a matter of modern kitchen appliances.

Following this same pattern Alex has accumulated $400,000 worth of real estate holdings in the two years since I sold his first converted two-family for him for $22,900. And he originally bought that house, if you will remember, for $7,800, G.I., with no money down. Lately, Alex has been scoring a big hit as guest speaker at my real estate course for buyers, sellers, and investors at Massachusetts Institute of Technology in Cambridge, Massachusetts. A humble mailman with little spare time or money, but enormous energy, confidence and determination, he has turned his own modest dwelling into a fortune in real estate holdings—in only two years. This young ex-G.I. from World War II who slept at the switch for sixteen years finally got started, so that now, at the age of forty-four, he is sure to become a millionaire while he is still young enough to enjoy it. If he had only started sooner, he would be a millionaire already. Well, at least he is well on his way, and he loves the $18,000 a year income he now gets from his property as a handy supplement to his $7,800 a year mailman's salary.

My good friend and client Alex Paraskeva would like to pass on these tips to you:

1. Stick to multiple dwellings.

2. Never, never, as a novice, buy stores in older established areas. Walk down the main street of any town and note the vacancies. Don't buck the trend to shopping centers.

3. Avoid resort or seasonal—two or three months of the year—deals. Hotels and motels are businesses, not real estate investments.

4. Stick to modest rentals. The lower the rental the better because demand is so much greater and maintenance is so much less. You will be able to avoid expensive mechanical gadgets, like garbage disposals, dish-washers, air-conditioners, etc., while simultaneously avoiding higher utility charges.

5. Avoid, like the plague, high interest rate commercial second mortgages. Low rate seller's second mortgages are more advantageous. Frequently these can be even lower than bank first mortgage rates.

6. As a beginner avoid multiple mortgages on the same property.

7. Don't be afraid to borrow money. If you start with small cash and the foreclosure rate is less than one in a thousand, you will never get a safer risk. You can't be an armchair enthusiast. You can't run the gauntlet with scared money.

8. Think positively! Think Big!

9. Be ethical. You will be surprised how much it helps.

10. Two heads are better than one. Make your wife your partner.

11. Do not become satisfied. Remember your goal.

In the next chapter we shall see that you do not have to be the young vigorous, energetic masculine type like Alex Paraskeva to get rich in real estate.

Chapter 42

HOW THREE GRANDMOTHERS STRUCK IT RICH BY BUYING LOW AND UPGRADING

About three years ago a house burned out in a good location near my brokerage office in Melrose, Massachusetts. All the seasoned alleged expert brokers in the area recommended that the building be demolished as a lost cause as far as rebuilding was concerned.

A grandmother client of mine who had dabbled somewhat in real estate in the past, on her own, decided to buy the property with another grandmother friend. She thought it would be an interesting challenge to buy it very low, remodel it, then sell it for a profit. I must say that I admire her courage and her wisdom for flying in the face of all the lazy, scared professionals who said that it couldn't be done.

And so the two grandmothers, one of whom was embarking upon her very first venture in real estate speculation, pooled $3,000 each to buy the burned-out house for $6,000. The property had already been condemned by the Board of Health. All the floors and ceilings had burned out, so that the kitchen stove was half in the kitchen and half in the basement, while the beds were half upstairs and half downstairs. Nevertheless, the two grandmothers, who lived in the city themselves, knew that in that location there was not even an empty lot available for $6,000, the price they were paying. They also knew that if they could rebuild this seven-room, four-bedroom house it would have to bring at least $20,000. This gave them $14,000 to play with, and they knew that many brand-new houses are built on top of the land for that kind of money. Actually, the two grandmothers bought the house from the outside only, due to its good location. They never even bothered to go inside the house.

Immediately upon closing the deal, arrangements were made to have all debris cleared away. Next, the ladies removed the partition between the hall and old-fashioned small living room to make a large modern living room. Bids were obtained for a complete remodeling job from three carpenters, three plasterers, three plumbers, three electricians, and even three masons to put a new cement floor in the basement. The roof turned out to be in satisfactory condition. The interior walls were replastered with a skim coat, then papered in keeping with the colonial style of the house. A new kitchen and new bath were installed. Where a huge pantry had been downstairs the space was put to good use with a new half-bath plus a laundry room. Forced hot water by oil baseboard heat was installed along with a completely new 220-volt electrical system.

My office sold the house the first day for $21,000 and it was fully approved by the F.H.A. The local bank advised the ladies that they ought not to sell because they should get more. What an interesting turnabout for all these experts who said it could not be done! The good grandmothers, with understandable discretion, do not care to name the exact figure of their profits. Let's just say that they were more than pleased with their rather handsome profit from their four-month pastime.

Feeling like world champions over their truly marvelous accomplishment the two ladies took in a third grandmother friend. They placed profit from the sale of the remodeled house, along with an equal contribution from the third friend, into a corporation formed for further speculation. They immediately purchased six houses in a package deal from an estate.

The girls were getting smarter all the time, and on this purchase they used "nominee clauses" in their purchase and sale agreements. This meant that if they could resell the six houses individually, at a profit, before their ninety-day closing date, the new buyers could close for them with the estate, thus saving closing costs for the three grandmothers. They actually succeeded in saving closing costs on five of the six houses. They did have to close, themselves, on one house. In the end they lost $100 on the one house, but they made a quick, neat profit on all of the other five houses which they resold before they would have had to close themselves.

These three amazing grandmothers have gone on to make many more successful transactions of this type. They are not only piling up substantial profits but are also enjoying their lives immensely compared with their previous boredom. They would like to pass along the following advice:

1. You can make over the house, but not the location.

2. Screen buyers carefully as to the sincerity of their intentions and their probable ability to obtain financing and actually perform on closing day. (The ladies learned the hard way!)

3. Always visualize the type of buyer to whom you will be appealing. Then make sure that the house, lot and location will suit this type of buyer's need. In other words, put yourself in the shoes of the buyer.

4. Expect that you might have to take a $1,000 fast profit on a single low-priced house. Make it up on volume. After all, builders of new houses are often happy to average $2,000 profit on a house.

5. If you take on many transactions, you learn more on each sale, and one bad break will never kill you.

In the next chapter we shall see how you can do it, too.

Chapter 43

HOW YOU CAN DO IT, TOO!

BUY MINIMUM DOWN

One of the important advantages of investing in real estate is that you need not risk all your money. The bank providing the mortgage is quite willing to go most of the way. So why not take advantage of this unusual opportunity to make money with other people's money to the fullest possible extent? This will conserve your own cash for additional investment, or as a reserve or emergency fund.

In the Boston area today banks give a maximum of 80 percent of the sale price, or their evaluation, whichever is lower. This is for well-located newer type brick apartment buildings. Older buildings, or buildings in less desirable neighborhoods, get less mortgage money, and stores get less than apartment houses. Consequently, most investment properties today are actually sold on the basis of existing financing, including one or more junior mortgages, the last of which is usually taken back by the seller himself. In most cases this allows the buyer to come in with approximately 10 percent cash down. Obviously, you can buy three buildings instead of one if you pay 10 percent down instead of 30 percent or more. In fact, sometimes our office makes sales where the buyer puts cash down of only 5 percent. This kind of leverage is a great advantage to the buyer.

One way the buyer can get this great leverage break even with brand-new financing is through the Veterans Administration or the Federal Housing Administration. These agencies guarantee or insure the bank against loss on properties up to four dwelling units with minimum or even nothing down. The Veterans Administration even allows one extra unit above four units for each veteran when two or more veterans buy jointly. Of course the buyers are expected to live in these multiple-unit properties themselves. As we have already seen in an earlier chapter, this opportunity makes it easy for even the little fellow to get started in real estate investment. Many, many post-war real estate fortunes were started in just this way.

START WITH AS MANY INCOME UNITS IN THE BUILDING AS YOU CAN

A two-family house, providing an extra income to take the sting out of the monthly bank payment, is a better income proposition than a single family house, where everything is outgo and there is no income at all. By the same token a three-family is better than a two-family and a four-family is better than a three-family.

In fact, the more units in the building the better off you are. The reasons are obvious. The overhead and many of the fixed expenses are relatively cut down and minimized when spread over more income units. These fixed items include: One lot, one tax bill, one charge to get utilities into the building, one boiler, one oil tank, one basic plumbing system, and one basic wiring system. True, these costs become larger for larger buildings, but the fact remains that the costs per income unit decrease in direct proportion to the number of units. Consequently, if you buy for minimum cash down the greatest number of units you can get for your money, you are always ahead of the game—as long as the building meets all the tests that I shall now outline for you.

PICK WINNERS BY USING THESE 20 TESTS

1. Always start with the actual, effective gross income. You must reduce the raw gross, or projected or alleged gross income by the common sense vacancy and management expense for the particular building. Does the property have a history of 3 percent vacancy, or 30 percent or more? How many vacancies are there right now? How long have they

been vacant? Can you really manage the building yourself? Management expense, if you need it, runs 5 or 6 percent of actual rents collected. Remember, appraisers of income property always deduct vacancy and management expense from the projected gross income to arrive at the true gross income.

2. Never pay more times gross income than similar properties are actually selling for. While appraisers belittle this rule of thumb measurement of the fair market value of income properties, most buyers and brokers swear by it. Of course, it is the net income, rather than the gross, that is processed, or capitalized, into fair market value by appraisers. Yet, it is a fact of life that if new brick apartment buildings in the area, at the time, are actually selling for seven times their annual gross income, it would certainly be foolhardy to pay more than this for a similar building. In this way the "times gross" rule of thumb does establish a practical upper limit of value beyond which only a fool would venture.

3. Be sure you are including all expense items, and at fair, realistic amounts, in order to reduce your effective adjusted gross income down to the true net cash income. In all my experience of examining thousands of sellers' and brokers' statements on buildings offered for sale, I have never seen one which listed all the expense items an appraiser would use. In addition to the usual items listed for taxes, heat, insurance, water, hall lights and janitor, you must also consider the following items which are usually not listed:

    a. Operating expenses such as advertising costs and uncollected rents.

    b. Maintenance expenses for the building, the furnishings, the appliances, yard and ground care, snow removal, and swimming pool service.

    c. Reserves for replacements of building components, furnishings, equipment, furniture, and appliances.

4. Use fair economic rent for the area, if this is lower than the actual unit rents listed.

5. Consider future assessment and tax rate increases.

6. Use normal insurance cost if this is greater than the insurance expense listed.

7. Use normal heat cost, if greater than heat expense listed. Be sure the seller is not being supplied by two oil dealers and showing only one dealer's bill.

8. If the building and grounds look ill cared for, increase the janitor expense enough to allow for proper care.

9. Are you providing enough expense for supplies and miscellaneous?

10. Do you have an emergency "kitty"?

11. Check the safety of the financing. Avoid balloon balances on the mortgages. Will you really be able to retire the various mortgages as they become due? Are there "lifting clauses" on the junior mortgages permitting you to refinance the first mortgage? Does your first mortgage have an "alienation clause" forbidding you from selling "subject to the mortgage"?

12. Are you getting enough cash return on your investment? Never buy for amortization only. Certainly you are entitled to at least 10 percent net cash return on your investment, when you consider your risks and the nonliquidity of your investment. Shrewd buyers look for 15 percent net cash return on their investment (after allowance for vacancy and repairs) even on well-located good buildings. Obviously you should require greater cash return for inferior location, construction or condition.

13. Will this location provide for "appreciation"? Avoid declining neighborhoods like the plague. Get into the path of "growth."

14. Will this building make "upgrading" feasible? That is, will you be able to charge more for existing units or create additional rental units?

15. Have you checked out the local zoning ordinances for number of units, height of the building, parking spaces, and so forth?

16. Does this building conform to the local building codes?

17. Does the present type occupancy constitute the "highest and best use" of the land?

18. What is the remaining economic life of the building? Residential units are generally considered to have a total useful economic life of fifty years. What is the actual "effective age" of this building? Subtract this from the total economic life to arrive at the "remaining economic life."

19. Have you had a "pro" check the quality of the construction and the condition of the building in relation to the price you are paying?

20. Does this type of property best suit your investment needs, your management ability, your ultimate goal?

Remember—seasoned, successful investors frequently look for a year or more, and reject many, many properties for each one that they buy. A real estate investment is much like a wife. If you choose wisely your life can be a heaven on earth, but if you pick a "lemon" your life can be a living hell.

WHERE YOU CAN FIND THE RIGHT BUYS

1. Public auctions as advertised in the local papers. These are not bank foreclosures, but settlements following divorces, and so on.

2. Estate sales; check the probate courts and your local papers.

3. Bank foreclosures.

4. Federal Housing Administration foreclosures.

5. Veterans Administration foreclosures.

6. Through lawyers.

7. Through personal friends.

8. Owner ads.

9. Your own "real estate wanted" ads.

10. Brokers

11. When you see a building that appeals to you, find out from the janitor, superintendent or a tenant who the owner is and approach him directly. After all this is precisely the way the brokers get most of their listings.

HOW TO CUT THE ASKING PRICE DOWN TO THE RIGHT PRICE

Asking prices of investment properties offered for sale are notoriously higher than the ultimate sale prices. The following tips should help you:

1. Most investment brokers are willing to take notes for their commission if they cannot get the required cash down. This makes it possible for you to offer less cash down. These brokerage commissions are quite considerable, and therefore offer the key to sizable price reductions. Brokerage fees are usually 5 percent of the first quarter-million, 3 percent of the sales price between one-quarter million and three-quarters of a million, and 2 percent on the sales price above three-quarters of a million. Of course, this is for units of more than six families. Brokerage commissions for units up to six families are usually computed on the residential rate of 6 percent.

2. Check the Registry of Deeds or the city hall, as the case may be, for the amount of the State Excise Tax Stamps on the recorded deed. This reveals the true price the present owner paid. State Deed Stamps vary in price. If the property was previously sold "subject to a mortgage," the stamps are for the equity above the mortgage only. Once the seller knows that you know how little he paid for the building his whole hand is tipped.

3. The seller is, of course, entitled to try to get the very best price he can for his property. Just never forget that, by the same token, you are entitled to try to buy for as little as you can. Since he is starting higher than he is willing to accept, as a general rule, you must make your first offer lower than you are willing to pay. Subsequent negotiation should enable you to arrive at a fair market price.

4. Determine what you are looking for, then try to find it yourself. Just be sure that, in order to save a $15,000 brokerage commission, you are not overpaying $30,000 or more for the building. If you are inexperienced, get an independent appraisal, and use a "pro" to negotiate for you.

5. Confront the seller or broker with the true, adjusted gross income, considering actual vacancies and all the deferred maintenance. Explain all the expenses he has not included. Then emphasize the much lower, real net cash income (if any). This should help you get that dream price down.

6. Complain about where the money is going to come from to retire the balloon balances on all the junior mortgages when they become due. Show how if you pay off any principal on these mortgages there will be no cash return at all.

7. Show how the rents are rather high for the area. Suggest that this is probably the cause of those vacancies.

8. Explain how your tax bill can go only one way—up. Point out why you will need more insurance for your new higher mortgages.

9. Complain about the lack of parking facilities, storage space, public conveniences or anything else that the building lacks.

10. If it is an older building, stress the fifty-year limit to the total "economical life" of the building, and the short remaining economic life.

11. Stress the fact that· you are willing to put some cash into the deal—at the right price.

12. Make sure that the seller and broker know that you have your eye on "another building."

13. You should now be able to figure a few more arguments for yourself. Good luck!

Chapter 44

BEWARE OF THESE SELLER AND BROKER TRICKS

1. The seller's statement is always based on full occupancy. One fast visit to the premises shows the number of vacancies. Closer inspection

and inquiry reveal the extended length of time these vacancies, and others in the past, have lasted. In other words, the seller's alleged gross income is often a dream figure; yet his entire statement, including the high price you are asked to pay, and the misleading cash return you are supposed to get for your investment, are too often based on this absolute fiction.

2. You will never believe the money he has spent on advertising, and the valuable time he has wasted in vain efforts to fill those vacancies. You don't really expect him to emphasize this, do you? So, you had better make it your business to find out.

3. Every seller and every broker glosses right over "vacancy and repairs" with the excuse that no one can accurately predict these expenses, and that they, therefore, prefer to leave that up to the buyer. They then proceed with their raw, unadjusted, unreal gross income to paint a beautiful picture of low expenses and high returns. In fine print, at the bottom of every statement or advertisement is the legend: "These figures are before allowance for vacancy and repairs." Remember to check carefully into the actual expenses for these two items. This could be the area where the whole difference lies.

4. Make sure the rent schedule represents "fair economic rent" for the area. If it is higher than this it will have to come down or create a vacancy problem.

5. You can check tenants yourself, and demand verified accountant statements of income for these tenants. The seller knows this. So, the rents you have to watch closely are the ones he claims you will get for the vacancies. Just get out of your car and talk with the next door tenants. You may be surprised to find that an existing tenant is paying far less, for better quarters, than what you are being told you will get for the vacancy.

6. Beware of low tax assessments. In brand-new buildings, the low assessment may be for only part of a year, or part of a building. In older buildings the temporary abatement the seller had may vanish as soon as you take over. Many cities and towns reassess as soon as a new higher sales price takes place.

7. Expect increased assessment and taxes if there has been recent substantial remodeling or additions. Always check the assessment at the city hall.

8. Is there a second fuel oil supplier whose bill is being withheld by the seller?

9. Does the insurance bill include public liability, etc.?

10. Does the building violate the local zoning ordinances?

11. Are there any complaints on the building at the building inspector's office?

12. Is the roof all right? How long will it last?

13. Will the boiler hold up? I know of one right now that needs immediate replacement. I wonder if the buyer of that building will know about it—in time?

14. Don't forget to check for water in the basement and sewage disposal problems.

15. The amazing truth is that unlike houses, which are carefully and personally listed by the broker, large buildings are listed via telephone by the broker, or by the seller's written statement on the building. Again, the buyer, though he is given full opportunity for thorough inspection of a house, is shown only a small part of the apartment complex or shopping center, whereupon he is expected to make his offer and give a deposit check. Often the broker accompanying the buyer is seeing the property for the first time himself. Under these circumstances you must check everything carefully.

16. Sure there is a cash return, but would there be if you were paying any principal off in those balloon balance mortgages which are going to come due some day—all too soon?

17. Many older buildings, especially in certain parts of the country, and especially if they are of frame construction, cannot be remortgaged, and the seller usually knows this. The broker *should* know it. Just make sure, in this type of situation, that you are not planning on refinancing later.

18. An otherwise neat little store block can be hit awfully hard by new, much larger and more glamorous shopping centers nearby—even though the store block is modern, brick and in a new growing area.

19. Be on the alert for the infiltration of inharmonious influences in the neighborhood.

20. What is the zoning on the empty land next to you?

I honestly do not believe that most sellers and brokers would deliberately go out of their way to hurt you as a buyer. But the fact remains that the seller is usually under no obligation to volunteer help to you in an arm's length transaction. You must bear in mind, too, that the broker is the legal agent of the seller, plus the fact that you can hardly blame him for being somewhat anxious that the sale should go through. You can sue in tort for damages if they deliberately deceive and defraud you. In some states, Massachusetts for one, you may rescind the contract and get your money back—even for innocent misrepresentation of a material fact, and even though the contract has been fully executed and you have moved in. Nevertheless there is still on the Massachusetts books the interesting old case of the buyer who found termite damage in his building but could not prevail in a suit against the seller because the seller never told him that the building was free of termites. So, *caveat emptor* is still very much with us.

Be sure to ask questions, get the facts, get the seller and the broker to make positive statements of fact which they will have to back up. Learn to brush off the seller's and broker's "personal opinions" and "seller's puff," which they don't have to back up.

Chapter 45

WHY YOU SHOULD SEE YOUR LAWYER BEFORE SIGNING

It is a general practice for residential brokers to wrap up a deal quickly and with the least amount of commotion—while the buyer is hot and "under the ether." It is always feared that, if he is allowed to get outdoors and whiff a little fresh air, the whole deal may cool off. Accordingly, broker associations as well as individual brokers have adopted a simple one-page purchase and sale agreement, so that the broker himself, without any "interference" from the seller's or buyer's attorney, can quite intentionally wrap up the whole deal in a few painless minutes. Under this system, all the pain comes later.

One mark of a good investment property brokerage firm is that the broker insists that the purchase and sale agreement be drawn up at a conference between the seller's and buyer's attorneys. This means that you cannot become fully committed as a buyer until your attorney has had the opportunity to verify income and expenses and all the many crucially important factors involved. Also, as a seller you just do not become involved with a buyer who cannot really perform on your terms.

Consequently, when you get interested in an investment property to the point of desiring to know just how low you can buy it (and you have not yet carefully checked out everything important) you should submit an offer and deposit check to the broker only with the following precautions:

1. Your deposit check should be made out to the broker, not the seller.

2. The broker should hold the check in escrow until he gets an acceptance from the seller, and your attorney has had the chance to draw up a purchase and sale agreement satisfactory to you.

3. On the back of your check you should write the following, or a similar legend:

"To be used only as a deposit on an offer to purchase property located at—" (insert the street address, city and state).

"Price—" (insert price you are willing to pay).

"Cash down—" (insert here the difference between your offered price and the total of all mortgages involved).

"Subject to verification of figures and signing of purchase and sale agreement wholly acceptable to me."

4. Try to keep the check down to $500, at this point. No matter how big the building is keep the check as low as possible and insist on an "out" such as outlined above.

5. If your offer is accepted have your attorney get together with the seller's attorney promptly.

6. Never let a broker "wrap you up" all by himself when you are merely at a stage where you and your attorney should start checking out everything thoroughly, with as much information and time as the situation may require.

If you do not have an experienced real estate attorney be sure to get one. I have seen attorneys inexperienced in the practical problems of real estate commit some unbelievable "boo-boos" at closings. A very humorous book could be written on this subject if the consequences were not so serious and tragic.

Remember that a contract is formed the moment acceptance is communicated back to the offerer. Until this moment, you are free to revoke your offer. Don't ever let a seller or broker bluff you about this.

The acceptance must be unequivocal and in conformance with the terms of your offer in order to be binding upon you. Any other type of acceptance constitutes only a counter-offer and gives you the privilege of accepting or rejecting.

Once your offer is rejected by the seller, or his agent, the broker, the offer is dead, and they cannot revive it and accept it later. Never let the seller or broker bluff about this.

However, once your offer is legally accepted your only "out" is the one you carefully provided for in the terms of your offer.

If you become bound on a full purchase and sale agreement you may not only lose your deposit but be forced to complete purchase through the doctrine of "specific performance" in equity court. This rare remedy is available to you against the seller as well.

Obviously, you need an experienced real estate attorney. Only a fool would make an offer and give a check before seeing his attorney.

Chapter 46

HOW TO BE A SUCCESSFUL LANDLORD

The great majority of tenants behave in an admirable way and pay their rent on time. I know many apartment house owners who have yet to lose one month's rent on a bad tenant.

However, the vast amount of litigation in our courts involving the landlord-tenant relationship attests to the necessity of a landlord adhering strictly to the adage that an ounce of prevention is worth a pound of cure.

The following checklist should be helpful:

1. If the building is relatively small and the tenants come into personal contact with one another, it is usually wise to let the apartments on a tenant-at-will basis rather than a lease when you start a new tenant. The reason for the widespread use of this method, whereby the landlord forgoes the protection of a lease, is the fear of every landlord that one bad tenant could soon empty his building. After you get to know the tenant, it is then safer to enter into a long-term binding lease.

2. When you do let your premises on a tenant-at-will basis it is always wise, since there is no written lease, to have the tenant sign a written set of house rules. Tenants are usually willing to sign anything when they first move in.

3. Another important advantage of the tenant-at-will arrangement for a landlord is his ability to raise the rent at will. Under this type of letting the tenant still enjoys the same exclusive use of the premises that a tenant under a lease does. Both parties are entitled to a length of notice (in writing) to vacate equal to the established interval of the rent payment. There is usually a two-week notice statute covering non-payment

of rent. The tenancy-at-will is so very widely used by small landlords because they feel it gives them much greater flexibility than a lease does. Many tenants-at-will stay on for a great number of years. The point is, if you want to raise the rent, you can. Also if you must get rid of a tenant to save your entire building, you can.

4. Larger scale landlords, with many tenants who are not in personal contact with one another, prefer the written lease for one or more years. The lease, of course, spells out all the terms, rules, and regulations, as well as the total rights and responsibilities of both the landlord and tenant. In many states, like Massachusetts, a lease must be in writing to be enforceable. If there is no writing then a tenancy-at-will is created.

5. Good landlordship calls for the exacting of a security deposit at the signing of the lease. This security most often amounts to an extra month's rent held by the landlord. Frequently two months' rent or more is required. Everything naturally depends on whether there is a waiting list of tenants, or a vacancy problem. Obviously it is better to have a fully occupied building with fewer security deposits than a high vacancy rate with more security money. On commercial leases, the security deposits often amount to six months' rent or more. Sometimes with a big lessee you hold one of his bankbooks for $10,000 or more as security against his business failure or any other form of lease-breaking.

6. You must insist on prompt payment. You should get very stern about only a short delay in payment. This way the tenant is trained to let someone else wait for payment, but not you.

7. The lease should be drawn to run not for exactly one year from the date of signing but rather for the number of additional months which will make the anniversary date fall at a convenient time of the year for you to relet the premises.

8. The lease should allow you to show the premises "at reasonable times" during the period of notice of termination required by the tenant—and before he actually moves. This can eliminate vacancy time.

9. Since there is no duty for the landlord to repair, you should be very careful about what you undertake voluntarily. There is a growing tendency to "allow the tenant to redecorate his own premises."

10. Remember, the tenant is responsible for liabilities arising out of that part of the premises "under his control"—whether interior or exterior.

11. If you take a $250 deductible insurance policy you can drastically reduce your insurance cost.

12. Whenever possible make the tenant responsible for grounds care, rubbish removal, and snow removal for that part of the exterior premises provided for his use.

13. Spell out strict rules regarding noise, pets and children, if you want a fully occupied building.

14. Try to raise your rents moderately. Raise the rent more often rather than a big amount all at once. The tenant has to feel that it would be more expensive to move than pay the increase.

15. If you are an absentee landlord, get in the habit of inspecting your buildings once a week. This way you catch up on broken windows or tenants' "complaints" early enough to prevent more serious and more costly problems from arising.

16. Usually it is better for you not to live in the building yourself. After all, you are depriving yourself of the normal rental income for the apartment. All you will succeed in doing is to stimulate complaints and nuisance calls.

Chapter 47

UPGRADE AND REFINANCE FOR TAX-FREE PROFIT

Everyone agrees how difficult it is, under today's tax laws, to generate any kind of tax-free money. One very obvious method is to apply the same principle that a homeowner uses when he raises the mortgage on his house by rewriting it for a higher amount. With an income property you simply have more opportunity to do this because you are dealing with a larger mortgage which is being paid off and reduced by more substantial amounts, paid for by your tenants. You pocket the difference, tax-free.

Also, with an income property there is greater opportunity to get still more cash on a mortgage rewrite due to appreciation of the fair market value of the building. This new higher value can be deliberately and intentionally created by you, without depending upon general inflation or even local expansion of all real estate prices. What I am referring to here is "upgrading." As mentioned in the beginning, one of the big advantages of investing in real estate is your ability to control your investment and use your ingenuity to enhance the value of your property.

Upgrading is normally accomplished by an owner in two main ways. First, you can manage your building better or improve your rental units to the point where you can demand higher rents. Second, you can actually increase the number of rental units through more efficient use of overall space. Either way, your gross annual income is increased, and mortgage lending institutions base their loan maximums directly upon the total gross income of the building. For example, depending upon the policy of the bank and the characteristics of the particular building, the maximum amount of loan would be between four and five times the gross income generated by the building. Meanwhile, all the money you have spent to upgrade your building is tax deductible either immediately or over a period of years.

In this way, you do not need to sell a winner and face a capital gain tax in order to raise money. You simply hold on to your good investment while rewriting the mortgage for a higher amount which yields you principal tax free.

Chapter 48

HOW TO SELL FOR MORE PROFIT

1. Beware of overpricing; the faster you sell the better. A long drawn-out period of showing your building will irritate your tenants, empty your building, and make it a "dog" on the market. Experience proves that in the end you will take less than you could have had in the beginning. In addition, you will have lost time and money along the way.

2. Use a qualified appraiser to establish the fair market value of your building. Your buyers will tend to believe a professional appraiser more than they will believe you, themselves, or their friends and advisers.

3. If you are not showing a high cash return on the buyer's cash investment, you will have to repackage your offering. This can be accomplished by:

    a. Lowering the cash down requirement.

    b. Lengthening the mortgate payment period.

    c. Reducing the mortgage interest rate.

d. Charging "interest only" on the mortgage you take back.

e. Increasing your rents.

f. Decreasing expenses.

4. If you think it's unnecessary for me to remind you to prepare your property for showing to prospective buyers, you should follow me around for just one day. Recently, I had a buyer who reduced his offer on an apartment building from $550,000 to $475,000 due to lack of attention by the janitor and minor deferred maintenance in the rear hallways. What a price to pay for negligence!

5. Always check out all the tax angles with your lawyer or tax accountant. There are many ways to create a tax avoidance or postponement.

6. Take back a bigger mortgage yourself rather than lower your price too much. If you need cash you can discount the mortgage.

7. Sell through several large first-rate investment brokerage firms who are active and know what they are doing. This way you retain the privilege of selling yourself. You will be amazed at the help and the education you will receive from these competent brokers. Do not hesitate to seek their advice. Just be sure to check it out for accuracy and sincerity.

Chapter 49

WHY YOU SHOULD START NOW

For more than a quarter of a century real estate prices have been steadily increasing. All experts are in agreement today that, due to ever higher costs for materials and labor, steadily increasing land costs and general inflation, real estate prices will continue to increase for as long a time ahead as anyone can forecast. Therefore, any delay in realty investment will be costly to you.

Furthermore, it is now possible to buy real estate on 5 or 10 or 15 percent margin. In addition there are numerous tax advantages in real estate investment.

No one can say that these favorable conditions of low cash down, preferential tax benefits and almost certain appreciation will last forever. So the sooner you get started, the longer time you will have to profit by this existing, and foreseeable, favorable climate.

If you wish to buy and sell for quick profit there is no better period than now to depend on certain appreciation. About the only way you could lose, today, would be to carelessly pick a poor location in a declining area. On the other hand, if you wish to buy and hold, the climate may never be better for this.

In the next part of the book you will learn how to have your cake and eat it, too, through early refinancing for taxfree cash, then coasting home for the full score at the end of a new ten- or fifteen-year mortgage paid for by your tenants.

Chapter 50

TYPES OF PROPERTY: ADVANTAGES AND DISADVANTAGES

BUILDING NEW VS. BUYING USED

In order to build new on a paying basis, your land cost, land development and utility cost cannot exceed 20 percent of your total overall cost per unit. In other words, your total land cost must fall in range according to what you are going to build. If all things are equal and you keep within this range then you will save at least 15 percent by building new. The trouble is all things are seldom equal due to the following chronic problems of the builder:

1. Water.
2. Rock ledge.
3. Soft land, such as peat or marsh.
4. Green lumber.
5. Plaster cracks.
6. Sub-contractors who fail to show up on time.
7. Materials that do not arrive on time.
8. Bank construction money payments that are now delayed.
9. Redoing work to please town or bank building inspectors.
10. Most F.H.A. builders wish they had never started as they are

harassed with ever more demands for additional paperwork, and they are continually delayed in reaching completion O.K. This means that they stay under initial 10 percent or more bank financing longer than they planned on, before they can qualify, as under 21-D3, for 3 percent F.H.A.-backed money.

Remember the above problems start *after* you have finally found the land and obtained the necessary zoning, which in itself is normally a very time-consuming and drawn-out undertaking. In fact, today with the added problems of inflationary prices, scarcity of buildable land in demand locations, high interest rates, and new stricter zoning laws, such as snob-zoning and environmental protection laws it has become almost prohibitive to build new.

If you do build new, be sure to get three bids from subcontractors who are experienced in the particular type of building. It is my belief that only one person in a thousand has the required amount of patience, time and business astuteness to build new successfully. Therefore, I suggest that for the average investor it is much easier and more practical to buy already-built properties.

APARTMENT HOUSES

The novice should always go into apartment units. He will understand the problems of providing shelter better than other concepts less familiar to him.

Properly priced, well constructed apartment buildings in or near big cities are in great demand today, as they always are in good times. In a depression, of course, they lose tenants; if a depression were to occur, the current low national average vacancy rate would be greatly increased, and for a long period of time.

Apartment units are usually assessed lower than store units but higher than guest houses. The tenants require more sevices and generate more complaints, problems and expenses than do store or professional tenants. However, a vacancy is usually easier to fill and will not hurt you as much as an empty store.

The number of apartment renters is presently growing faster in proportion to total population than ever before. There is an unusually good opportunity in this investment area to buy low, remodel, then upgrade the income to permit a profitable sale or tax-free cash grab through refinancing at a higher amount.

Investors expect 10 to 15 percent cash return on their cash investment, after allowance for vacancy and repairs for well located good buildings. The trouble is, today, sellers and brokers generally have the problem of selling buildings that show from minus cash return to less than 5 percent cash return on this good type of property. Twenty to 25 percent or more net cash return is expected on cash invested when dealing in inferior buildings or locations. Remodeling or upgrading speculative type properties should provide even higher returns. Banks lend up to 80 percent mortgages on modern brick apartment buildings, and less for older or frame buildings.

STORE BLOCKS AND SHOPPING CENTERS

Net cash returns are relatively higher on store blocks because the tenants usually provide their own heat through separate heating systems. Also, store tenants normally provide their own utilities, interior repairs, redecoration and maintenance, snow removal, and grounds care.

However, this type of building is usually assessed higher than apartment houses, and this high assessment, of course, increases the owner's expenses.

Busy executive type investors are interested in the time savings aspects of owning this type of property in preference to apartments. Also, they like the opportunities for longer leases, greater security deposits and possible "overage" clauses in the leases. Through the use of the "overage" clause the owner exacts higher rent on a predetermined scale as the tenant's gross sales exceed a certain amount.

However, one vacancy at a relatively high rent can hurt you badly. Store vacancies usually linger longer than apartment vacancies. These are some of the reasons why banks usually lend a maximum 60 percent mortgage on older store blocks.

The big difference between an apartment tenant and a store tenant is that the apartment lessee needs merely to continue to live there and pay his rent to you, but the store lessee must in addition operate a successful business. The business mortality rate is, of course, much higher than the foreclosure rate in real estate investment.

You must always beware of store blocks in declining neighborhoods, including once-flourishing downtown areas. Even new shopping centers can suffer in the face of still newer and better shopping centers.

This type of property sells normally at slightly higher prices in relation to gross income than do apartment units. Making the right investment in this area is complex and tricky compared with investing in apartment houses.

PROFESSIONAL BUILDINGS AND OFFICE BUILDINGS

In recent years, with many suburban areas reaching the saturation point on new apartment buildings due to unavailability of apartment zoned land, builders have turned to professional buildings to get zoning as well as higher income on the building.

The professional tenant—doctor, dentist or lawyer—stays on longer than an apartment lessee. He can afford to pay more per square foot of space. He gives a bigger security deposit, and accepts tax escalation clauses in his lease. He improves the building with substantial improvements to his part of the premises. And he maintains his suite in excellent condition.

However, when a vacancy does occur, you are hit with very substantial renovating costs to suit a new tenant, and the vacancy remains longer than an apartment vacancy. Professional tenants can drive up heat and utilities costs, as well as facilities and maintenance costs. Parking requirements are greater than for apartment tenants.

If you are able to fill your building, you reap more gross income and therefore have a more valuable property. You must be very careful not to grant exclusion clauses too freely to the first tenants in the building. They will demand them, but if you limit your opportunities to take on needed additional tenants, you may wind up owning a white elephant. Well-located, well-constructed, and well-rented professional buildings will sell for more money, and their higher gross income tends to be more stabilized than apartments or stores.

GUEST HOUSES

The guest house offers a relatively high cash return on investment. Assessments are usually lower than for apartment houses. So are sales prices in proportion to gross income. Management is simpler than most investors realize. Some rooming houses are actually run by one person in return for a free room. Vacancy is the only real problem. If you have the right location and building for high occupancy, this can be one of the simplest, yet most overlooked opportunities for making a handsome return on your real estate investment.

REST HOMES AND NURSING HOMES

There is a bona fide new demand for this type of real estate investment. And it is true that the cash return can be lucrative. However, it is most important for the would-be investor to research thoroughly the entire field of Medicare and Medicaid. Similarly, all local, state and federal regulations must be known and complied with, as well as local zoning laws. Failure to comply with any one of these regulations or laws could represent a catastrophic loss in this very specialized area of investment.

INDUSTRIAL PROPERTY

This is an area reserved for the truly sophisticated investor. Novices should stay clear. Successful industrial property investment requires very specialized knowledge of the problems of manufacturing. For the sophisticate a lucrative area of investment lies in the conversion of large old mill sites, bought at $1 per square foot, into remodeled office buildings.

LAND

There is common agreement that suburban land has increased in value in recent years faster than any other kind of real estate investment.

The advice to "buy on the fringe and wait" has paid off handsomely. However, some adversely located land has failed to enjoy this great overall increase in value.

Landholding offers tax shelter, and the opportunity to develop "capital gains" for the rich. However, the land must be carefully chosen so that substantial appreciation in value will take place within ten years, in order for the investor to break even. Land investments throughout the U.S. have doubled in the last ten years. Many especially promising and rapidly developing areas like Cape Cod, Massachusetts have experienced a 300 percent increase in value over the last ten years.

However, the great Southwest has been the fastest growing area of all since World War II. Individual lots commonly multiplied in value twenty times in skyrocketing cities like Albuquerque and Tucson, while in Palmdale, California (North Los Angeles County) land prices jumped from $15 an acre to $8,000 and more, just since 1950.

The whole trick in land investment is to buy where the value is increasing rapidly.

SEASONAL PROPERTY

The big lure to investors here is the quick ten- or twelve-week cash return which equals the return on year-round property that you have to

213

wait fifty-two weeks to get. Meanwhile, you are relieved of tenant problems and complaints for nine or ten months of the year. Another advantage is the ample time you have to make repairs, since the property is vacant most of the year.

Usually these resort locations have more liberal or practically no building restrictions or requirements. Also, in a vacation area, tenants are less fussy, more easily satisfied.

On the other hand, close attention to the property is required each week during the season. This could be burdensome for some investors who prefer long-distance, remote-control operations. The property has a higher non-liquidity rate; that is, it is not so readily marketable as year-round property. The selling season is restricted practically to April, May and June. Further, there is a higher risk factor involved due to dependence upon unpredictable weather conditions. Thus, the usual vacancy risk is aggravated by cancellations due to cold or rainy weather. Normally, the mortgage span of ten to fifteen years is shorter than for year-round property. Hence, cash flow is less, but amortization, or forced principal savings, is greater than with year-round property.

Chapter 51

SPECIALIZE FOR MORE PROFIT: YOU SHOULD HAVE A GOAL

Actually each of the specialized areas of real estate investment discussed in the previous chapter is a field unto itself. The conditions and requirements for successful buying, managing and selling are different enough and sufficiently complex to justify specialization within a particular area for maximum efficiency and success. Many of the lessons that the investor must learn are best taught by actual experience. Obviously this rich, actual experience is more readily transferable from one building to another similar type building than to another of dissimilar type.

Your maintenance crew will have specialized experience, which can bring you economies. So can homogeneous, volume purchasing of materials and supplies. Also, the more experience you have with a particular class of tenant, the easier it is for you to maintain high occupancy with satisfied tenants who will stay.

Specialization helps you to reach your overall objective or goal. You should know what that goal is, and never become satisfied until you reach it.

Two main goals of real estate investors are:

1. Developing income to augment a present inadequate income.

2. Conserving or increasing capital: creating capital growth to develop a capital gain tax situation which will be lower than your high individual tax bracket, or creating a tax shelter by paying taxes on land you are holding for future use. If you can afford it, instead of taking tax deductions each year, you can add the taxes to your cost, thus increasing your basis as you go along and ultimately paying a low capital gain tax on a smaller amount of profit at the time of future sale.

Chapter 52

HOW TO APPRAISE INCOME PROPERTY

The most valid approach to income property appraisal is obviously the "income approach," even though a "comparable sales" and "cost" approach are also used as guide lines.

Buyers, sellers and brokers frequently use a rule of thumb method called the "time gross" system. Under this technique it is contended, for example, that a modern brick heated apartment building has a fair market value of seven times its gross income, because similar type buildings have actually sold recently in that area for seven times income.

Now, your kid brother would know that this method is neither accurate nor valid enough to be treated as a final measurement of value. For it is what is on the bottom of the "sheet" as "*net* income" that really counts, rather than the figure on the top representing raw, unadjusted, ineffective gross income. And two similar buildings with the same gross income may have vastly different expenses and, therefore, widely different "net cash" incomes.

The professional appraiser's income approach, of course, deals with the processing of the actual cash *net* income into a final capitalized fair market value.

The basic formula for straight capitalization using straightline depreciation is:

$$\frac{capitalization\ rate}{net\ income} = fair\ market\ value$$

To apply this formula properly you must use the following steps:

1. Adjust the alleged annual gross income by reducing it to an actual, effective gross income through a 5 or 6 percent management expense, plus an appropriate vacancy allowance. Do not use a rule of thumb percentage for management or vacancy. Use a realistic deduction which reflects the actual vacancy history of the particular building. The percentage could be from 2 to 10 percent for management and 3 percent or as high as 30 percent or more of gross income.

2. Now, subtract *all* the real expenses of the building from the adjusted effective gross income to find the true *total* net income. These expenses should include: fixed items, operating expenses, maintenance bills, reserves for replacement of component parts of the building, plus reserves for furnishings and equipment. Don't forget the resident superintendent's free apartment and salary, if there is one. Remember, many of these expense items are never listed on the usual statement of the building. Also, it is par for the course that you will have to allow more for taxes, heat and insurance than the figures indicate on a sales statement.

3. Now, break down the *total* net income into the net income which is imputable to the investment in the land, and the remaining net income which is attributable to the building improvements. This is called the "building residual method" by appraisers, and is generally used because you normally know the value of the land investment, or can readily find out through comparable land sales. For example, if recent comparable land sales indicate that the subject land is worth $100,000 then multiply this amount by 8 percent or whatever percentage investors are currently demanding in your area as interest return on their total real estate investment. Appraisers consider the full value of the property for this purpose—not just the amount of cash actually put up by the owner. The resultant $8,000 would be labeled *net income imputable to the land investment*.

4. Now subtract the net income imputable to the land from the total net income. If the total net income happened to be $30,000, for example, then the remaining or residual net income of $22,000 would be considered the true *net income imputable to the building*. It is this amount that is used for net income in the basic formula above. In other

words, when you divide this $22,000 amount by an appropriate capitalization rate, you would get what is actually the *fair market value of the building only*. Afterwards, you add the known value of the land to arrive at *the total fair market value of the property*.

5. You are now at a point where you must know how to build a capitalization rate. The "cap rate" consists of two parts: the interest rate investors are currently demanding on their total realty investment, plus an amortization rate which will guarantee a return *of* their total investment at the end of its "remaining economic life." For example, if 8 percent happened to be the proper interest rate to use as a "return *on* the investment," and the remaining economic life of the building were twenty-five years, then an amortization rate of 4 percent per year would be required to insure a full 100 percent return *of* the total investment at the end of the twenty-five years. The total of the 8 percent return *on* the investment plus the 4 percent return *of* the investment would indicate an appropriate "capitalization rate" of 12 percent.

6. Thus, in the example in 4 above, the "net income imputable to the building" of $22,000 would be divided by 12 percent to arrive at a fair market value *for the building* of $183,333.

7. Now, add the $100,000 known value of the land and you get a *total property fair market value* of $283,333.

Chapter 53

LOOK FOR DANGER SIGNALS BEFORE BUYING

1. Why is the seller selling? He probably knows that he should never sell a winner (see Chapter 55). It is, therefore, most important for you to find out why the seller is letting this alleged money-maker go. There may be a valid reason.

2. Is the store block in an old declining central retail district which *used* to have 90 percent of the business? Is most retail business now being done in the new shopping center on the outskirts?

3. Is a new shopping center about to be put up nearby?

4. If your potential purchase is a shopping center, how does the

overall business cycle look? A downturn in the economy can turn a profitable shopping center into a losing proposition.

5. If you are depending heavily on a major national company tenant, be sure you know what the future planning and policy of that company is going to be regarding locations.

6. If your choice is an apartment building, are the rents in line with those for comparable quarters in the neighborhood? If they are too high in comparison with the rents for other buildings—already in existence or about to be built—can the building stand a decrease in the rent schedule and still show a return?

7. If it is a new building will the seller guarantee 100 percent or 90 percent, or even 80 percent occupancy? If he will not, are you safe in depending upon full occupancy? If he will give you an occupancy guarantee, how good is his guarantee?

8. Be sure you are allowing sufficient time to fill a new building.

9. Are you providing sufficient expense money for advertising, leasing commissions, and so forth to fill a new building?

10. Do certain tenants have burdensome "exclusion" clauses which would render it most difficult for you to fill the remainder of a new building, or to replace tenants if vacancies should occur?

11. Will you face a new tax assessment immediately upon buying, or at the first of the next year? If so, what will it probably be, and will the return be able to stand it?

12. What is the future of the city's tax base? What is the philosophy and policy of the tax planners?

13. What is the physical condition of the building? Can you afford to rectify deferred maintenance at the price you are paying?

14. Does the statement provide for necessary reserves for replacement of component parts of the building furnishings and equipment?

15. Are you leaving yourself without reserve capital in case of an emergency? Many buildings have been lost in precisely this way.

16. Is the building so old in terms of frame construction, poor condition, and so on that no bank will touch it? If so, be sure you are not depending on refinancing it later.

17. If the building is selling for more "times gross income" than similar buildings are actually selling for in the area, forget it. The price must be "in line" for safe resale, no matter how much you personally like it, or are willing to pay for it.

18. Do the tenants plan to stay on? Exercise options at the end of their leases? Be sure you discuss this with them and not just with the seller or broker.

19. Now that you have been brainwashed as to all the good points of

the building, what can neighbors, or brokers who do not have the listing, tell you about the bad points?

20. What can they tell you at the city assessor's office or the building inspector's office, or the planning board or the appeal board? Are there any violations or complaints? This could be highly interesting or important information.

21. Check parking carefully. Is it adequate for both present and future needs? Above all, do not plan on adding rental units if lack of additional parking space will bar building permits.

22. Is your assessment lower than the standard ratio for your city? Remember, tax abatements or preferential arrangements have a way of vanishing more quickly than you may be planning on.

23. Is the building "stacked" with tenants who are relatives or friends of the present owner?

24. Have you talked with the janitor, and the janitor who left, and the fuel oil supplier, and the tenants, and some previous tenants?

25. Do the maps at Urban Renewal headquarters, the Department of Public Works, and so on, indicate that the building is in the path of a future taking? Remember that when government negotiators start notifying tenants that a building is scheduled for a "taking," you may expect the building to suffer a sudden high vacancy rate.

26. Are you sure you can safely meet the big balloon balances on those junior mortgages when they become due? Beware of "interest only" junior mortgages. They show a false high cash return on the statement.

27. Will the existing mortgage instruments permit you to lift the junior mortgages for refinancing of the first mortgage at a later date if it becomes necessary or desirable?

28. Those small "first mortgage" payments, spread over twenty years, are very convenient, but if it is really a ten-year mortgage (with twenty-year payments), what will you do if the bank decides to exercise its prerogative and terminate the mortgage after ten years?

29. Remember, the first year's principal reduction on a twenty-year mortgage is only about 2¼ percent, and on a fifteen-year mortgage only about 4 percent. Do not depend on higher amortization than you are actually going to get in the early years of the mortgage.

30. What will the cash flow be after you allow for vacancy, management, correction of deferred maintenance, repairs, supplies, all necessary reserve accounts, adequate janitor service, advertising, leasing commissions, miscellaneous expenses, emergency fund, and so forth, in addition to the few basic expenses shown on that seller's or broker's statement?

Surprisingly, despite all of the danger signals and pitfalls listed above, there are always many fine real estate investment opportunities available. You must be prepared to reject many offerings before finding a winner. You must learn to read "between the lines" on the statement of the building. Just take off a compensating amount from the price asked, or the cash-down asked, to make up for the "difference," so that you will actually receive a fair cash return on your investment.

Chapter 54

SHOULD YOU OWN AS AN INDIVIDUAL, PARTNERSHIP OR CORPORATION?

INDIVIDUAL OWNERSHIP

No other method of ownership can match 100 percent ownership and control if what you want is maximum control for yourself. However, seasoned, experienced investment property owners (who themselves have made a mistake now and then and have been burned) believe sincerely that two heads are better than one. They also know that there are times when the individual owner simply cannot break away to personally tend to an emergency situation, whereas the man in partnership with another is free to do so.

Tax-wise, as an individual owner you should be a small investor, in a low tax bracket, and without plans to expand; or a wealthy investor desiring "depreciation" to offset your other high tax bracket income. By using "depreciation"—and you could use up to 5 percent in some situations—you are postponing payment of taxes on your property. When you do pay the tax you are paying at capital gain rate maximum of 25 percent.

PARTNERSHIP

Under this system of income property ownership, you are deliberately making an equal division of the income in order to reduce the tax via lower tax brackets. You are cutting your opportunity for personal profit and control. But you will find that two heads *are* better than one, particularly on those occasions when you are too pressed for time to effectively act alone. Many investors have found that half of a good profit is better than all of nothing.

CORPORATION

Tax-wise, this system becomes necessary when you own a lot of real estate and you are in a high tax bracket or facing a future high tax bracket. For example, you may have only $10,000 of your own cash down on a $1,000,000 property, but when the mortgages are all paid off in twenty years and you have $1,000,000, you will have a major tax problem.

When you are in a high tax bracket as an individual, you simply keep the profit in the corporation which pays a lower tax rate. Meanwhile, over the years, all your property can be passed on to your children without a penny in tax payment. If you are married, both you and your wife can give $3,000 each, in stock, to each child every year as a tax-exempt gift. In addition, both you and your wife may give a lifetime gift of $30,000 each. And the value is the value at the time of the gift.

MASSACHUSETTS REALTY TRUST

This entity is used primarily in Massachusetts where there is no state income tax on rental income from a realty trust. However, the realty trust is considered a corporation for federal income tax purposes. The trust has transferable shares. Ownership can be passed on to the family to decrease equity. Deeds do not have to be recorded. If, for example, you have ten certificates and you wish to give away 20 percent of the property, you simply endorse two certificates. There is no publicity.

"Irrevocable" trusts can be dangerous if, for example, the trust unexpectedly grows big. "Revocable" trusts are more flexible and better. So "short term" trusts are used for a minimum of ten years and a day, or longer. Now, the trust is irrevocable for ten years. Income goes to the beneficiaries, so the rental income from the property is taxable to the beneficiaries of the trust, who are in a lower tax bracket. The owner could be the grantor, his children the beneficiaries. After ten years and a day, the property would revert back to the grantor.

Obviously a tax attorney should be consulted in all of these situations.

Regrettably, many income property owners are paying more taxes than they should, or were ever intended to pay.

Chapter 55

FOR THE SOPHISTICATED INVESTOR

NEVER SELL A WINNER

Remember how long and hard you searched to find that winner. If you ever counted up the value of the time alone you put into it, it would be a very significant amount. Now, you may as well realize that replacing this winner with another winner is going to be just as difficult and costly. And you may never succeed. Can you afford the time and risk? Ask yourself, is this sale necessary? If you must sell off something, why not sell a loser? It may take more effort. You may have to take less than you would prefer. However, the chances are you will still be better off than selling a winner.

Never forget that any real estate investment is valuable. When you sell, you dissipate your "net worth" and destroy your borrowing power. Also, you face a capital gain tax. Remember, if you must sell, you can take the sting out of the tax bite by selling on the installment plan. If you do not take over 30 percent at the time of the sale, you may pay the tax each year on the lower installment amounts.

REFINANCE AND PYRAMID

As an alternative to early selling for a capital gain, an owner may elect to refinance for tax-free cash profit. Now, you can actually have your cake and eat it, too. You are free to use your cash profit gained from the new, higher financing any way you like, and still keep the building. At this point many sophisticated investors take a shorter term first mortgage— from ten to fifteen years—and ride it out all the way until they finally own the property free and clear. Often, by the time they refinance, good management plus inflation has increased their gross income faster than their expenses. At least, the total gross income is a larger amount than the total expenses, so, in any event, their net profit is larger than when they first bought the building. This enables them to handle the new larger mortgage on a shorter term.

Instead of spending the cash gained from the refinancing, if they do not need the money they should use it—or part of it—as a down payment on an additional building. There is no better way for you to pyramid your holdings, earnings, and tax savings. As your net worth grows, your borrowing power grows. Your bank's confidence in you is increased. They are eager for your new and larger deposits in your accounts with them. You may now "write your own ticket" when it comes to raising additional financing.

KEEP INCREASING YOUR LEVERAGE

Whether you buy additional buildings with the profit made from refinancing or from outright sale, be sure to constantly strive to obtain the maximum number of units for the amount of cash you are investing. For example, if you can buy a half-million dollar, forty-six unit apartment building for only $20,000 cash down, your opportunities for gain and savings are greatly enhanced over what a $100,000 ten-unit building could offer you for the same $20,000 cash down. You would be buying the half-million dollar property for only 4 percent cash, while the $100,000 building would cost you 20 percent cash. The smaller the percentage of cash down you pay, the greater "leverage" you have to reap larger net worth borrowing power, the more dollars of net cash return you receive, and the larger the forced principal savings you make through higher amounts of amortization.

HOW TO CUT YOUR INSURANCE COSTS

As you accumulate additional buildings you can get a lower insurance rate per building by having several buildings insured under one "package" policy and one premium payment.

Another way to cut premium payments is to use a "$250 deductible" policy. By paying for your own broken windows, and other low cost miscellaneous claims, you can cut your premium bill almost in half. If there are several high-priced buildings involved, you start off each year many thousands of dollars ahead in insurance costs. This takes care of a lot of broken windows and other items, and still leaves you a handsome saving. If you think this makes sense, why not try it on your own buildings?

GOOD MANAGEMENT MAY COST A LITTLE MORE, BUT NEGLECT CAN KILL YOU

Back in Chapter 48 you saw how an owner lost $75,000 at the time of the sale of one building due to minor deferred maintenance caused by neglect. For a small fraction of that $75,000 loss the required maintenance could have taken place on time. In addition to this one-time saving, the owner could have enjoyed a lower vacancy rate, higher gross income, more net cash return, happier tenants, and a better reputation for the building and for himself as an owner and manager of income property. Word gets around fast. Once the word reaches the mortgage bankers in your town, your reputation and borrowing power is at stake. Don't be pennywise and pound foolish. Property management requires time, effort, thought and care, plus the willingness to spend a little money to gain the full benefits of 100 percent occupancy by satisfied tenants who will stay and make you rich.

Chapter 56

ARE YOU ENJOYING THESE TAX SAVINGS?

CAPITAL GAIN

In Chapter 54, and elsewhere in this book, several examples of the "capital gain" tax rate at a maximum of 25 percent were given as extremely beneficial inducements to realty investments, whenever the investor's ordinary tax rate would be considerably higher. This great tax saving, alone, to the high tax bracket owner makes property investment abundantly advantageous.

DEPRECIATION

Using depreciation as a direct offset to ordinary income tax liability, you are saving at the ordinary rate each year. When you sell, you are paying a maximum 25 percent capital gain tax. You can take up to 5 percent depreciation a year. If you still own at the time of death, and you have depreciated your property down to zero, the Internal Revenue Department will appraise the property for estate tax purposes. Your heirs can now start depreciating the property all over again on the new "basis" as determined by the estate tax.

Example:
   You have an equity of $78,000 in a $500,000 property which in twenty years may be worth $1,000,000. You and your wife each own $39,000 in a corporation. You have three children.
   $18,000 can be passed on to the three children each year via tax-exempt gifts, at the rate of $3,000 to each child from each parent. In addition, each parent can give one lifetime gift, tax-exempt, of $30,000. Now, there is no tax on a half-million dollar property. The children can draw salaries from the corporation to further reduce the net profit. The savings on your estate tax are tremendous.

BEWARE OF EVASION

Tax avoidance is legal, and expected by the laws and regulations of our sophisticated Congress, Courts and Internal Revenue Department. Tax evasion, however, is illegal and severely punishable. The seasoned, wise property investors are saying that you cannot get away with anything on Uncle Sam, today. Accordingly, it would appear to be wise practice not to succumb to the temptation of the unethical practices of some owners who charge personal expense items of supplies, maintenance and repairs such as fuel oil, wall to wall carpeting, plumbing, electrical work, appliances and fixtures, and the like, to their income property expenses. These practices are not only unethical, but strictly illegal.
   In order to exploit the tremendous tax benefits in real estate investment to the fullest extent it is necessary to use a qualified tax consultant.

Chapter 57

HOW A DOCTOR WHO STARTED WITH $5,000 IS BECOMING A MILLIONAIRE

The following story is not a one-shot-in-a-million fairy tale. It has now been similarly lived by so many modern Americans, in all walks of life, that certain common denominators and standard guidelines have evolved.

Dr. Condon, a middle-aged client of mine, was already a successful young doctor when he first became fascinated by real estate. He saw the opportunity for an all-year-round hobby that, at the same time, would make him rich.

It was in 1951 that he took his first plunge in a real estate investment. It was a modest $5,000 speculation. Together with a partner he purchased an old hotel which had been converted into 19 two-room apartments.

For $10,000 cash down the two young enterprising partners bought the old building for a price of $15,000. They had a $5,000 mortgage.

The small apartments consisted of a bedroom and kitchen. However, there were only four baths servicing all nineteen units. As rents came in, the apartments were gradually remodeled, inside and out. The rents were raised as soon as each apartment became remodeled. Within one year their first building was on a profitable basis. Then they purchased their second acquisition, an estate sale of two houses, with a lot in between.

The estate cost $22,000, but they were able to procure a $21,000 mortgage, so they needed to take only $1,000 cash out of their new business. One of the houses in the estate was a single-family, which they quickly sold for $13,000. They used the proceeds of this sale to reduce the $21,000 mortgage to $8,000.

The other house was a large three-family. They turned this into nine efficiency apartments which are now worth $29,000. They did not have to sell this building. They also kept the lot in between, which is now worth $6,000. The lot was hot-topped to bring in parking revenue, both from their new tenants and outsiders.

At about this time they purchased, on a no-money-down mortgage takeover, an old six-unit apartment building for $12,900. As the rent money kept coming in, they upgraded this six-unit building from $40.00 a month rents to $95.00 a month. The annual income rose from $2,600 to $6,800. To accomplish this miracle they simply installed a new heating, plumbing, and electrical system, and redecorated, all with cash coming in from the business.

In only five years after the $22,000 estate was purchased, the remaining $8,000 mortgage on it was paid off. The remodeled nine-unit house in the estate was remortgaged for $10,000. At this point, six years after they started, the two partners had back, tax-free, their original and only out-of-pocket investment of $5,000 each. None of the doctors' cash was in the business, now. Sixteen years after they bought that first converted hotel, the two partners owned free and clear $100,000 worth of real estate from this, their first enterprise.

Meanwhile, in 1956, five years after he made his first investment in real estate, the doctor formed a second corporation. He raised $100,000 in cash together with three other associates, and bought 120 apartment units for a price of $500,000.

Ten years later, in 1966, the doctor's second corporation purchased its second building, worth $400,000, for $360,000 from a bankrupt owner. The 66 percent vacant, all-electric, luxury apartment house required only $30,000 cash down, which came out of profits from the business.

In a very short time the doctor and his group filled the luxury building with tenants and put it on a profitable basis. No tricks or gimmicks were needed, just good management which the former bankrupt owner had failed to provide.

At this point, the doctor's overall operations were profitable enough to enable him to buy out one of his three associates in his second corporation. The retiring associate did rather well for himself, too. His original $25,000 investment brought him $175,000 in ten years, besides the salary he had received out of the business all along the way.

Thus, sixteen years after the doctor started with a $5,000 investment in that old converted hotel, he and his remaining two associates had an equity of $500,000 in real estate worth $1,200,000.

In a few years all buildings, constituting 150 apartment units, will be completely paid off.

The doctor is currently seeking new investments so that he can reach his personal ambition to become a millionaire. He contends that almost anyone can do the same thing.

You have read about "Practical Ways to Make Money in Real Estate." Why not get started yourself, now?

PART IV

10 Ways to Make a Killing in Real Estate

Chapter 58

HOW TO BEGIN

In today's high-priced market you should have at least $5,000, either in hand or within borrowing reach, as a good starting purse. Of course, you can get a bigger, faster start for $10,000 or $20,000, as demonstrated throughout this book; and, conversely, you could even get a pretty good start with $2,500.

Does that sound high? It shouldn't. *Don't put this book down if the most you can raise right now is a few hundred dollars.* Surely, if you can raise *anything*, so can some of your friends or business associates. One of the best ways of pulling together the kind of money you need for a small but sufficiently substantial investment is to form a group of, let us say, ten people, each of whom contributes $500.

For we might as well be realistic and settle on a total initial investment of $5,000. Even though $2,500 is reasonable starting money, it doesn't give you the cushion you should have. A starting purse of $5,000 allows for reserve funds that are almost certain to be required for emergency use. For instance, your first building venture may suddenly need a new roof or a new boiler; plumbing or electrical repair may be required; bills may have to be met sooner than anticipated; painting and gutter work tend to crop up fast; and a sudden vacancy, plus an uncollected rent payment, may occur at any time. If it were not for these contingencies—which must be provided for in our safe and foolproof methods for making your killing—you could get started for even less, as many of my clients have done (see Chapter 64, "How to Buy for Minimum Cash Down"). But, with a $5,000 starter, you can make a lot of money.

WHERE YOU CAN GET IT

At the outset, you must understand that the biggest investors in real estate—those who invest to the tune of billions of dollars, as, for example, the banks and insurance companies, as well as heavy individual investors who make cash down payments of $50,000 and up—never, never invest their own personal funds. All of them use other people's money. The insurance companies use their policy holders' money. Individual large-scale investors nearly always borrow their cash down money from the bank for about nine percent interest. All of these investors make huge profits on the difference between the small cost of the money they use and the large returns they make out of their real estate holdings. You, too, may make a three-year personal loan at your bank.

If there is some reason why your commercial bank does not want to go along with you, you may try a home modernization or improvement loan at the bank that holds the mortgage on your house. If this does not provide you with the needed cash, you may do what all big real estate investors do when they need cash—increase your mortgage. (See Chapter 67.) If you do not have a mortgage, or it is already too high to provide for any further increase, borrow from the cash and loan value in your own life insurance. This is generally considered to be the most efficient way of personal borrowing available today. The interest rate is certainly low enough and your basic protection is not lost.

Another system which works well when you simply cannot get enough cash to get started on your own is to take on one or more partners. The three grandmothers, whose first joint venture was recounted in Part III, "Practical Ways to Make Money in Real Estate," just reported to me that they closed six deals in the last five weeks that were all very profitable. Moreover, many investors believe that two heads are better than one, and that it is always helpful to have a partner who can tend to a problem when you simply cannot get away yourself to handle it.

In other words, if you are among the great majority who just cannot save regularly and accumulate your own starting purse, you are not precluded from making your fortune in real estate.

In fact, if you find yourself hemmed in by limited income and ever higher costs of living the very best way out for you is to benefit from the greatest hedge against inflation there ever was—real estate investment. The sooner you get started the quicker you, too, will become rich.

Now that you have your starting capital, let us see in the next chapters exactly how you can turn it into a larger fortune than you ever dreamed possible.

The following recommended ways have been tried and proved by thousands before you, over the years. They are the safest and most foolproof methods. Always remember that the foreclosure rate in real estate is about one in three hundred. No other business investment gives you so much advantage and protection. Even if you were to fail, you would not be wiped out, because you have only made a minimal investment.

Most investors who have successfully applied the systems outlined in this book have retrieved their original small cash investment within a year, or a couple of years, and then gone on to build their fortunes on other people's money.

Chapter 59

ADVANTAGES OF GETTING A LICENSE

Everybody knows how lucrative the brokerage business can be at six percent selling commissions. The average house today nets a broker over $1,500 in commission, and the fees for the sale of investment properties run into several thousand dollars. Yet it is amazingly simple and inexpensive for anyone to obtain a broker's or a salesman's license in most of our fifty states. Almost anyone over twenty-one years of age can qualify as a broker, while virtually any eighteen-year-old can be a real estate salesman. The requirements for both broker and salesman differ very slightly and are, as I outlined in my previous book, extremely easy to meet. Only in a few of the stricter states does the licensing examination require as much as the equivalent of a high school education, followed by a rapid training course or a careful reading of a training manual.

What most people do not know is that every broker periodically runs into special opportunities to buy low and quickly resell for a big profit or hold for long-term investment.

There are always some sellers who are ill-informed in this fantastic ever-rising market, in a big hurry, or just plain desperate. Just being a broker in a given area permits you to be the first one to recognize and know a bargain when one is offered to you to sell. As long as you are open and aboveboard, reveal yourself as the buyer, and refrain from trying to act in the dual capacity of broker and principal, you are legally free to take full advantage of these situations.

All you would have to do is subtract your selling commission from the owner's asking price, then deduct a further significant amount for the convenience to the seller of an immediate cash deal. Most sellers are happy to avoid the waiting and anxiety between a sale and a closing. They know that, too frequently, expected sales fail to take place due to lack of financing or buyer's change of circumstances.

The case histories outlined below illustrate typical money-making opportunities available to every broker.

1. An elderly gentleman came into my Melrose, Massachusetts brokerage office and said, "I want to sell my two-family house. It is not very fancy. I lived in it for many years, and a lot of improvements could be made. All I want is out. I can't wait to get up into New Hampshire, in the country, so I can retire in peace. I should like to get $15,000 for myself, but I would take $14,000 for an immediate sale, if you would like to buy it yourself for speculation." When I told one of my salesmen to call a speculator client, a sale resulted within a half-hour at $15,500. The fortunate buyer simply placed it right back on the market for $20,900 without spending any money on it at all.

In case you think opportunity like this only knocks once, consider this next case:

2. The owner of a seven-unit income property was being prevented by his wife from undertaking some needed repair expense; meanwhile his fire insurance company was threatening to discontinue his policy due to his failure to repair. The poor, frustrated old man, broken-hearted from the lack of consideration he was receiving from his newly acquired younger wife, reluctantly listed the property with me for sale at the ridiculously low price of $23,000. One of my speculator buyers immediately offered to snap it up at the price. While my buyer and I were busily engaged in attempting to raise a mortgage on the property despite its run-down condition, the seller began to press the panic button. Unsolicited, he desperately volunteered to lower his price to facilitate financing. Every couple of days he would offer to take off another thousand dollars or so. My buyer soon caught on and started to drag his heels about raising his financing. Sooner than any of us dreamed it would happen, the seller was voluntarily down to $18,500. At this point my buyer did not dare risk losing the deal, and came up with a construction money mortgage from his own bank, based solely upon his own credit.

The fortunate buyer spent nearly $5,000 on improvements, but six months after his purchase at $18,500 he refused a $33,500 offer from a new buyer I produced for a quick resale.

The big point to remember is that these chances for killings are not exactly isolated cases. They have come up in the regular course of events several times every year in my own brokerage office. These phenomenal shortcuts to fortunes from shoestrings are commonplace daily opportunities all over our country.

I have been content with the brokerage or legal fees involved, allowing my clients to make the big score from buying and reselling, or holding for profitable investment. With an easily obtainable broker's license you could elect to take the full measure of profit available. You could still make many brokerage commissions selling less desirable profit opportunities to others.

Chapter 60

THE MOST PROFITABLE TYPES OF BUILDING TO BUY

In Chapter 67 of this book I emphasize that the maximum achievable number of units for the amount of cash you have to invest is normally the most profitable investment for you. Right now, I want to concentrate on the specific kinds of buildings that normally make the most profitable buys.

WHY OLDER BUILDINGS ARE BETTER BUYS

Let me say at the outset that if you expect to make any money out of buying buildings today you must buy used, or older, buildings which were built when bricks and boards were cheap. New buildings, today, involve such high prices for land, labor, materials, taxes, developer profits and mortgage money that you just cannot touch them. In fact, it is my experience that when a rich doctor comes to me for a nice, new, well-located, trouble-free building that only has to carry itself without showing any cash return at all, it is impossible to find one anyplace in my area. Every time I think I have finally found such a building for one of many eagerly waiting buyers, thorough appraisal invariably indicates it would actually cost the buyer a net cash loss annually. The last one was a 23-unit building for $335,000 that the doctor buyer, who liked it and wanted to buy it very much, had to reject because his banker, attorney, and accountant convinced him that it would create an annual out-of-pocket loss of $4,500 per year. Even though the doctor would have still benefited greatly from tax shelters which he desperately needed, he complained that such an investment just did not make fiscal sense to him.

There is so much high tax bracket money and "hidden money" in our affluent society bidding for the few new, well-located buildings available for sale that the prices tend to preclude any cash return at all. This kind of money must benefit from large, preferential tax deductions for depreciation, and other real estate tax shelters, in order for its owners to avoid unacceptably high tax burdens. For all of these reasons, and more, the best profit opportunities lie in older buildings.

Most novice, unsophisticated, and lazy buyers are afraid to tackle an older building. This reduces the demand, thus driving prices down. Meanwhile, tax assessors are more lenient; and rentals, established many years ago, frequently fall below fair economic rents for the area today. Other advantages awaiting the astute buyer lie in the frequent opportunities for upgrading rentals through modernization and improvement of the present units; or even actually increasing the number of rental units through more efficient use of available building or land space.

The plain facts are that these older buildings were built when land, labor, and materials were much cheaper than they are today. Owners who have already milked huge profits out of the buildings, allowed deferred maintenance to pile up, or proved to be inefficient building managers, are frequently willing to let go at fair market value, and sometimes even less.

Of course, new buildings are being sold every day to buyers who are neither doctors nor tax dodgers. However, my experience is that these other types of buyers are all too frequently being sold a "bill of goods" by tricky sellers and brokers, as outlined in Chapter 66.

WHY APARTMENT BUILDINGS ARE BETTER BUYS

Let's face it—today, the little fellow is frozen out of the housing market. He either lacks the current high cash down payments required by most banks, or the financial ability to pay the sky-high monthly bank payments brought on by high prices, big mortgages with the highest interest rates in the history of the country, and confiscatory local real estate taxes. The bankers say, "Let 'em rent."

Many who could afford to buy houses prefer luxury apartments for "closer in" easier living at overall housing costs 15 per cent less than home ownership, according to recent U.S. Department of Labor surveys covering metropolitan areas of the country. Add to this the lack of available land in desirable locations, and prohibitive building costs, and you begin to see why builders are putting up twice as many apartment units compared to single family dwellings as they did in 1960.

Yet so great is the demand for apartments in today's housing market that vacancy rates are at an all-time low. Many more apartments are needed than are being built: completion time of new apartment buildings is doubling because of insufficient numbers of skilled workers in the building trades. Add to this the apartment builder's problems with stingy local zoning officials, and greedy bankers who stick them with exorbitant interest rates—up to ten percent—plus a "piece of the action" (a share of their profits over a fixed amount, usually at ten percent); and you begin to see why new apartment buildings are at a premium. Of course, all of these factors keep the value of older apartment buildings surprisingly high.

Another important consideration is that most investors understand and feel familiar with the problems of shelter. On the other hand, most of them know very little about the specialized and complex problems of commercial and industrial buildings.

For all of these reasons, plus many more, it is hard to get "stuck" today if you stay with apartment buildings. When you consider the present five percent inflation rate which is ravaging the country the only way you could possibly lose on an apartment building, bought at a fair price, would be due to structural failures in the building itself, or a declining neighborhood.

WHY FOUR-UNIT DWELLINGS ARE SO GOOD

The public law governing Veterans Administration and Federal Housing Administration financing of residential construction specifically singles out owner-occupied one to four-unit dwellings for preferential treatment and assistance to mortgage applicants (with the V.A. one additional unit may be purchased for each additional veteran buying jointly).

This means that exceptionally high mortgages, requiring correspondingly low cash down payments, are available from participating banks which are protected against loss by these governmental agencies.

The interest rate on these mortgages is kept uniformly low throughout the country by public law. For this reason many banks do not cooperate with V.A. or F.H.A. mortgage financing. Other banks which will lend these mortgages require several "points" as a bonus charge. Each "point" is one percent of the face amount of the mortgage. However, buyers under V.A. or F.H.A. financing should be aware that the public law tolerates a maximum charge to the buyer of only one "point." The additional "points," when required, are legally payable only by the seller or the broker. Further details of the advantages of this type of governmental financing for residences up to four units are explained in Chapter 64, "How to Buy for Minimum Cash Down."

The four-unit residential building is ideal for the beginner who is limited in cash down money and building management experience.

WHY COMMERCIAL BUILDINGS WITH NET NET LEASES ARE SOMETIMES GOOD

The prime consideration with many well-heeled, sophisticated investors who have no time or inclination for building management is that the building must be maintained by the tenants, who are under long-term leases with unquestioned ability to pay. The commercial net net lease building fits this requirement.

Under a net net lease the tenant, a long-term business, normally spends large sums of money improving his part of the building. Of course, these improvements add to the value of the building for the owner, and act to lengthen the tenant's stay. This type of tenant pays for his own heat, parking area maintenance, grounds care, snow removal, maintenance of both the interior and exterior structure, and the water bill. He frequently pays for his share of the real estate tax, and insurance on the building as well. Under these conditions his lease is sometimes referred to as a net net net lease. This leaves the happy owner with nothing to do but make his mortgage payment to the bank. He then pockets all the remaining rent payment. Sounds good, doesn't it? However, remember that the loss of such a tenant at the expiration of his lease, or before then, due to an unanticipated contingency, could be extremely hurtful to an owner unable to fill the vacancy promptly. A general business recession or individual tenant bankruptcy could be disastrous. At best, the owner is locked in to a stabilized investment, usually at a conservative cash return annually. All the excitement of personal building management is gone, along with the opportunity to creatively and imaginatively upgrade the gross rental income.

A WORD TO THE UNWARY

Industrial buildings, usually highly specialized in structure, frequently become white elephants at the expiration of a lease if the original tenant fails to exercise his option to renew the lease. This highly specialized and complex field of investment should be avoided by all except the extremely well financed and knowledgeable investor. Besides the commercial building hazards of business recession and individual bankruptcy, any sudden or violent change in the labor market, local governmental regulation, transportation pattern, taxation policy and a host of other hazards could bring on total disaster.

Rooming houses and seasonal property have made a fortunate few highly specialized and astute investors wealthy, but on the whole they are fraught with the ever-present peril of high vacancy rates caused by plant layoffs, student vacations, and the vagaries of the weather.

Chapter 61

HOW TO MAKE SURE PROFITS IN LAND

WHY INVEST IN LAND?

Available land supply is constantly diminishing. At the same time the demand for land for housing, commercial, and industrial use is growing by leaps and bounds. The inescapable result is that any precious land that is not altogether impossible by way of bad location or poor condition must continue to increase in value. Well-located good land increases in value even faster, while land in the path of growth is pure gold. Even abandoned quarries, gullies, gulches and swamps are currently in demand for sorely needed dumping grounds. Suburban land ringing our sprawling metropolitan areas has been increasing in value faster than any other type of real estate.

Land investment opportunities are everywhere—in the great growth areas of our Southwest, the booming Southern California desert, former New England hinterland, the islands in New York Harbor, overcrowded Washington D.C., and booming Florida.

By the year 2000 A.D., only 23 years away, there will be 500 miles of Times Square between Boston and the District of Columbia. The population in this area will nearly double to 71,000,000 persons. A megalopolis of 25,000,000 people will stretch across the barren coastline between Santa Barbara, California and the Mexican border. California, already the most populous state in the Union, will triple to a population of 60,000,000.

Everywhere the story is the same—more and more people, and more and more commercial and industrial activity having to settle for less and less available land. In a situation like this it does not require a great deal of brain power to appreciate the opportunity in investment in land. The only question remaining is, "Where are the best places to invest?"

THE SOUTHWEST

The fastest growing area of all since World War II has been the fabulous sun land of California, Arizona, and New Mexico. Since 1940, while the population of Boston, for example, actually decreased, Tucson increased from 35,000 to one-quarter million people. Albuquerque's metropolitan population skyrocketed over ten times from 30,000 to over 300,000. At the same time, individual building lots in these fast-growing areas commonly multiplied 20 times in value.

THE FIRE ISLAND, NEW YORK STORY

In Saltaire, Fire Island, tiny lots 20 x 85 ft. are currently selling for over $5,000. Only ten years ago these same lots sold for $250 to $400 depending upon location. In the neighboring community of Kismet similar small lots are also selling for the same price of over $5,000 each. However, ten years ago the same lots in Kismet sold for only $80 each. This is an unbelievable example of land multiplying 50 times in value in one decade—the last decade—and right under our very noses.

Within the last few years lots on this magic island have increased in value thousands of dollars each. Predictions are that in spite of these recent dramatic increases land will become so scarce in Kismet and Saltaire a few years from now that prices are almost surely bound to double again.

Another view Saltaire, Fire Island, N.Y.

BUY ON THE FRINGE AND WAIT

John Jacob Astor is responsible for the time honored advice to "buy on the fringe and wait!" Subsequent real estate events have certainly made this slogan eligible for the title of "the understatement of all time."

Actually you should not buy on the edge of town. Prices are already too high there. Also land developmental costs will still be under the control of the big city or town—and normally too high to permit sufficient profit to a developer.

The trick is to buy land not inside the path of growth where it will be prohibitively expensive, but outside and beyond the path of growth *in the direction of projected growth*—where you can still buy low enough to make a profit. In many recent examples around the country investors needed to wait only five years for the growing city to reach them.

Remember, if your land does not double in value in ten years, you have not made a good investment because annual real estate taxes keep increasing and add up fast. And your money should be making money. So the first important step is to research carefully enough to make sure you are dealing with the fringe of a city that is growing fast.

RESORT AREAS

Land on Massachusetts' famous Cape Cod summer resort has increased in value 300 percent in the last ten years. The lake resort areas of New Hampshire have likewise been experiencing spiraling increases in land values. The story is the same for every summer resort area throughout the country. Wherever you have ocean, lake, or riverfront property reachable by the city dweller you also have continuing rapid price rises. The same is true of winter resort areas throughout the country. This trend is bound to strengthen due to our population explosion compared to the limited supply of vacation land. The rapid increase in apartment dwellers, our affluent society, and our ever-increasing health fanaticism are further factors guaranteeing future big increases in value of any vacation land.

GOVERNMENT OWNED LAND

Much of the best remaining available land is owned by the Federal, State or Local governments. This does not preclude this land from private use.

What most people do not realize is that the government is often interested in building revenue. All of our states have extremely active departments of commerce where high priced talent is working tirelessly to attract industry, trade and travel to build up needed tax revenue. As a result, it is possible to purchase or lease from the government very desirable valuable land with fantastic profit potential, especially recreational type land. As privately owned available land continues to dwindle in supply, the smart money boys will work more aggressively on our politicians to part with more and more government owned land.

OUT-OF-STATE INSTALLMENT LAND SALES

It is true that many people have made profits on this type of investment in spite of the big gamble they have taken, especially when they have bought unseen land. It is likewise true that many others have lost their money for the following principal reasons:

1. The development company was big, well-known and had the backing of governmental agencies, but was nevertheless prosecuted in the courts for selling land under water, switching lot numbers, and a variety of other illegal practices.

2. The company went in for large scale promotion and advertising. It also went into bankruptcy before the installment buyers finished paying for their lots. So a lot of people never did get title, and lost all of their money.

3. The company is still going strong, but many of the installment buyers found themselves unable to keep up their payments, and so lost everything.

The big lesson here is never, never buy land you have not seen. Never sign any land contract or turn over any money without advice from your attorney. And never buy land that is covered with snow. Wait until spring so that you will at least know if the land is buildable.

The only time you should even get involved to the point of seeing the land, or checking out the development in out-of-state installment land purchases, is when you know for a fact that you are buying in one of the fastest growing localitites in the country. Even then it would be better to buy outright so you could own and resell for a profit while the boom is on.

Of course, it is usually much better to go to the area yourself and buy locally. Now, you are not paying for some company's fantastic overhead to pay for salesmen, free dinners, free bunny girls, free trips, and heavy advertising and promotion bills.

Chapter 62

WHERE TO FIND THE RIGHT BUYS

Good small buildings that can be bought for small cash investments and are sure to yield quick and certain high percentage returns on cash invested are just what the doctor ordered for the shoestring investor.

Even smaller *new* buildings are very high priced today and usually require substantial cash down payments. One good way to beat the game is to come up with good small *older* buildings—well located, and at low prices, with small cash down requirements.

The two best finders of this especially juicy type of real estate investment in my town happen to be clients of mine. They both own and operate a "junk and disposal service" business. I can assure you they make much more profit out of the real estate investments they come by through the operation of these businesses than they ever make out of their disposal services.

It works like this. Someone contemplating a move—or perhaps a new widow or widower who finally stops grieving for the deceased spouse—calls the disposal service to clean out the basement or attic, or the old furniture and so forth. Over the telephone, the caller says, "We are moving," or "Our aunt just died." In the course of these arrangements the disposal service operator is often the first to know of the owner's intention to place the property on the market for sale. I guess you get the picture from there. Since these particular disposal service operators are extremely astute and successful real estate speculators in that particular area, they can spot a chance for a quick resale or upgrading profit a mile away—blindfolded. The big secret of their unusual success is that this type of investment opportunity is difficult for the average speculator to come by—in time. Today, there are literally hundreds of investment buyers for every profitable parcel of real estate coming on the market. In this situation ingenuity and imagination on the part of the income buyer or speculator is absolutely mandatory.

Other successful methods my clients use are:

1. Watching death notices in the newspaper. Frequently, the attorney handling the estate is mentioned in the notice. If not, these buyers inquire of friends, relatives or neighbors of the deceased, or the surviving spouse, to ascertain the name of the attorney. Then, these determined buyers make their pitch to the attorney who may have to dispose

How To Buy FHA-Acquired Properties Available for Sale or Rent.

FHA FORM NO. 1220-1
Rev. 12/68

DEPARTMENT OF HOUSING AND URBAN DEVELOPMENT
FEDERAL HOUSING ADMINISTRATION

FHA-ACQUIRED PROPERTIES AVAILABLE FOR SALE OR RENT

Notice to Interested Parties. The attached list of FHA-acquired properties
is published and made available solely for public information. The listed
properties are under the jurisdiction of the local FHA Insuring Office identified on Page 1 and are available for purchase subject to prior sale, renta
change in price, or removal from availability for some other reason. This i
not a binding offer to sell or rent, nor is it to be construed as any type c
agreement. This list will be revised from time to time to add newly acquire
properties or to delete properties sold or rented.

WHO MAY PURCHASE OR RENT AN FHA-ACQUIRED PROPERTY. ANY INDIVIDUAL OR ANY
COMPANY OR CORPORATION, REGARDLESS OF RACE, COLOR, CREED, OR NATIONAL ORIGIN
MEETING THE DOWNPAYMENT, CREDIT OR OTHER REQUIREMENTS OF THE FHA MAY OFFER
TO BUY OR RENT AN FHA-ACQUIRED PROPERTY. OFFERS TO PURCHASE MAY BE SUBMITTE
DIRECT TO FHA WHEN THE PURCHASER CANNOT SECURE THE SERVICES OF A QUALIFIED
BROKER. THE SALES PRICE AND TERMS WILL BE THE SAME IN EITHER INSTANCE.
HOWEVER, ONLY THOSE PROPERTIES SO INDICATED ON THE ATTACHED ARE AVAILABLE
FOR RENT.

Physical Condition of Properties. The general policy of the FHA is to sell
properties in a livable condition. The purchaser of an FHA-acquired proper
can expect to occupy the property without the need to make extensive repair

Sales Procedures. FHA policy is to market all acquired properties on an
"Open" basis with offers to purchase being submitted through qualified or
licensed local real estate brokers, except as noted above. Information
about any of the properties listed may be obtained from the FHA Insuring
Office identified on the attached Page 1. When making inquiry to the FHA
office, the specific property should be identified by giving the FHA case
number and the property address. Local brokers will probably have information which the FHA office may not have and which will be of interest,
such as schools, churches, transportation and shopping.

Financing the Purchase. There are three methods under which FHA-acquired
properties may be purchased:

(1) The purchaser pays all cash; or

(2) The purchaser obtains a mortgage loan from a private lender
and uses the mortgage proceeds to buy the home from FHA; or

(3) If private financing under 2 above cannot be obtained within
thirty days after acceptance by FHA of an offer to purchase,
the FHA may accept a mortgage given by the purchaser.

How To Buy Properties Direct From The Veterans Administration.

VETERANS ADMINISTRATION
REGIONAL OFFICE
JOHN FITZGERALD KENNEDY FEDERAL BUILDING
GOVERNMENT CENTER
BOSTON, MASSACHUSETTS 02203
October 15, 1968

YOUR FILE REFERENCE:

IN REPLY REFER TO: 301-263

·TO: ALL SALES, PARTICIPATING & PROPERTY   Loan Guaranty Division
MANAGEMENT BROKERS   Letter #21, 1968

SUBJ: EARNEST MONEY DEPOSITS ON SALES OF VA PROPERTIES

1. Earnest money deposits must not be submitted with VA Form 26-6705, "Credit Statement of Prospective Purchaser and Contract of Sale". Instead, you are authorized to retain this deposit in a Special Trust Fund.

2. Earnest money deposit will be handled as follows:

    a. Acceptance of Offer: - Upon submission of three copies of Form 26-6705, broker will be notified by postcard (FL-22) that offer has been accepted subject to satisfactory credit and employment. Earnest money deposit will be retained by broker until final approval has been granted, at which time a letter will be forwarded confirming acceptance.

    b. Rejection of Offer: - When you receive a letter of rejection, return the earnest money deposit to your client.

3. Please take the following action on all VA Forms 26-6705 submitted on or after this date:

    Items 26-27: Include your name, address and telephone number.

4. This procedure will expedite the receipt and processing of any offers (VA Form 26-6705) submitted by you, enabling us to give you and your client faster and more efficient service.

Joseph A. Miller

JOSEPH A. MILLER
Loan Guaranty Officer

of the real estate in the deceased person's estate. In this way, they become the first to buy, and even avoid a real estate broker's commission. They report that it is rare for the lawyer to insist on any type of commission.

2. They work closely with local attorneys on a personal basis. These attorneys frequently offer properties for sale on behalf of out-of-state and other type sellers who prefer not to handle the sale transaction themselves, or to hire a real estate broker.

3. They work closely and personally with the brokers in the area. They find it helpful to keep reminding the brokers that they are repeat customers. They also bait the brokers with promises of tips on where buildings are for sale which they are not buying themselves. With these techniques they frequently exact the brokers' better offerings, and even get some brokers to cut their regular commission rates. They also offer immediate cash bonuses to the brokers' salesmen to look out for them.

4. They watch the papers for public auctions, for bank foreclosures and divorce settlements. Actually, they build up friendly contacts directly with bankers and lawyers in town to get the jump on other buyers who find out about opportunities for the first time in the papers.

5. They check in the Probate Courts for filings of deaths and divorces.

6. They follow Federal Housing Administration and Veteran Administration foreclosure sales. Today, these agencies which take back the properties that cooperating banks get stuck with, actually renovate, remodel and practically make like new many of their foreclosure properties before they are offered for sale. Since these properties, like regular bank foreclosures, are offered at or near 100 per cent financing, they can be very juicy investments indeed. If you bid on a V.A. foreclosure, you may wish to bid a few hundred dollars over the asking price for a good parcel that is sure to draw still competitive bidding. The Veterans Administration is bound to accept the best offer. With the F.H.A. foreclosures you do not get this chance to clinch your purchase. They insist on drawing the lucky offer out of a hat in front of the assembled bidders. They will sell only at the advertised price.

7. They use mailmen and other "spotters" to advise them of vacant buildings. Then they trace the owners through the local assessors and tax collector offices. If this does not work they contact neighbors and friends of the owner who has moved away.

8. When they see an income building that particularly appeals to them, they find out who owns it from a tenant, or janitor, or at the tax assessor's office.

Since good buys are so few and far between, and are likely to be found in the most unusual places and circumstances, the only safe thing an investor or speculator can do is to keep hustling. In the end, no amount of knowledge or professionalism will ever prevail against the determined, aggressive pusher who is in there trying all the time, and playing every angle.

Real estate investment or speculating today is so complex, difficult, and fraught with hidden perils that a shy, squeamish, or scared buyer might just as well stay home and forget about trying to make a killing in real estate on a small investment. Yet it can be done, as many of my clients have proven. But it will never be accomplished successfully with scared money, or by an investor who is afraid to borrow and use other people's money.

Look for a four to eight-unit residential building for a starter. Stay away from new property. Buy something that was built 50 years ago at low cost. Plumbing facilities should be there, even if old. It is a lot cheaper to remodel plumbing than to install it. Remember, it is easy, today, for anyone to paint, paper or panel. Kitchens and baths are most important. Modernize as much as possible. Beautify as much as possible.

Buy your property within a radius of ten miles. The best place to buy is in your own home town. Make your real estate broker work and earn his commission.

Remember you can always fix a poor building, but you cannot fix a bad location. Avoid declining neighborhoods and slums like the plague. If banks and insurance companies do not want this kind of property, how can you afford to gamble with it? Check the property around the building you are considering. Professional appraisers give tremendous weight to the value of the properties on either side and across the street. It works like this: the bank appraiser recognizes a house to be worth $30,000, but he values the house on either side at only the high teens, and the property across the street in the low twenties. His final estimate of value for the subject property now becomes $25,000, just half way between what the house is worth by itself, and the value of the surrounding houses.

Remember, you can make as much profit out of a two or three room apartment as you can out of a five or six room apartment and have a lot less headaches to boot. Large apartments are rented by large families who drive up your heat and maintenance bills.

In small buildings, in particular, the lease is better for the tenant than the landlord. Leases can be broken easily by the tenant. Yet, if you are chained to one bad tenant by a lease, he could empty your building for you.

Always take two months rent in advance. Keep one month for security to insure 30 days notice to vacate by the tenant, and against possible damage. Screen your tenants. A credit report costs only a few dollars and it may save you hundreds of dollars and many headaches.

Do not overextend yourself. Guard your credit. It is your most important single asset as a real estate speculator.

Above all, when you find a good buy, do not get cold feet. Remember, the Prudential Insurance Company has over ten billion dollars invested in real estate mortgages. Don't you be afraid to invest a mere shoestring. If you start with apartment units, and avoid declining neighborhoods, you will have a great deal of trouble getting hurt. There is no such thing as an apartment vacancy today. As I have been writing this very page— on a Sunday afternoon between Christmas and the New Year—my real estate office in Melrose, Massachusetts has included two apartment rentals in its newspaper ads for the day. By noontime twenty telephone inquiries had come in. Both apartments were rented at once. By the way, the office does not usually bother with rentals, except to accommodate owners who have bought through our real estate office, or who happen to be my legal clients. The reason we do not handle apartment rentals, normally, is that they are too difficult to get. The owners do not need us. If they ever do get a vacancy, one short ad in the local bugle for about $1.50 will bomb them with desperately eager renters.

The result is that with older small residential buildings with moderate rentals in good areas you actually have no costs for either management or vacancy allowance.

Chapter 63

HOW TO BUY AT ROCK BOTTOM PRICES

At today's inflated price level very few income property buildings "appraise out." By this I mean that their asking prices are so ridiculously high that when you estimate their true fair market value by accepted appraisal techniques the invariable result is that if you bought the building you would actually be out of pocket a significant amount of cash each year. Now, this may still be all right for a big investor in a very high tax bracket who has special tax axes to grind. But, it certainly is not the right cup of tea for the little guy, starting out, who is trying to make his fortune on a minimal investment.

Consequently, I shall emphasize in this chapter that you cannot afford to buy at all, unless you are buying at the right price.

HOW TO APPRAISE INCOME PROPERTY AND DETERMINE YOUR OFFER

The very first thing that the novice must understand is that virtually all advertisements in newspapers and so called "statements" or sales proposals on buildings being offered on the market, either directly by the owners, or by income property brokers, are completely misleading. They all abuse the legally allowed privilege of "seller's puff." They all withhold essential information and say only enough to present a picture of huge net cash annual returns, and unbelievably fantastic total annual returns, including mortgage amortization, tax depreciation allowances—plus other tax shelters—and annual appreciation in value due to inflation.

When the average person first reads these ads or proposal statements, his first impulse is to dash off a deposit check forthwith and send it posthaste to the seller or seller's broker, with a hurried scribbled entreaty to "please hold this one for me before it gets away." How different the buyer's reaction would be if he were to actually see the building; talk with the tenants; know the actual, fair economic rentals for those accommodations in that area; know about the concessions and expenses the owner underwent to obtain the tenants he does have; know about the true vacancy rate, and the true length of vacancies; know the true amount of management and uncollected rent expense; know *all* the expenses, not just the few that are usually outlined; know the true amounts of even the few expenses admitted to; know the tremendous amount of deferred maintenance expense; know the shocking total cost of allowing for replacement of component parts of the building, plus furnishings and equipment which are never indicated by a seller or broker; and know the true maintenance, miscellaneous and janitor expenses just to keep the building and grounds from total ruination This is just to mention some of the hidden problems involved in buying income real estate at the right price.

One good way to determine the amount of your offer is to visualize the transaction a little ahead. In other words, just assume you have bought and you are now applying for the necessary bank financing. You must do this even though the seller or broker is deliberately throwing you off this track by offering to let you take over the existing financing. They actually keep a straight face and act as if this is doing you a big favor.

So, now, the bank appraiser is looking at the property to decide how much mortgage money his bank should allow you. I am assuming that your personal credit is as good as gold. I'll tell you what he does.

First of all he is very liberal about accepting at face value the alleged total gross income. He then subtracts a very modest "standard" amount for vacancy allowance, such as five or ten percent of gross income. This is not always sufficient to account for the actual, true vacancy expense. From this relatively high adjusted gross income figure the average bank appraiser subtracts somewhat more total expense than the seller or broker has indicated, but rarely as much as an independent professional appraiser would use in thoroughly protecting a buyer client. The bank appraiser would in this way ascertain a relatively high *net* annual income of the property.

Into this net annual income figure the bank appraiser would divide a "standard" capitalization rate to arrive at the "capitalized value" of the building, in other words, its present worth based on future probable net income.

A few years ago, many so-called appraisers completely unscientifically used a standard rule of thumb capitalization rate of ten percent for most older buildings. In this way they would declare an income building yielding a $10,000 annual net income (before financing expense) to have a fair market value of $100,000. Today, these same routine bank appraisers are widely using a 12 percent capitalization rate on run-of-the-mill older buildings.

Now let's apply their formula to an actual case:

Total Gross Income	$20,000
(which the bank appraiser elects to accept without questioning)	
Less vacancy allowance @ 5%	
(this appraiser is liberal)	− 1,000
Adjusted Effective Gross Income	19,000
(Note: This appraiser is not deducting the usual 6% management expense allowance)	
Less total operating expenses	7,500

(The appraiser has increased the alleged tax bill to the prevailing rate for the area, and added a flat 5% of gross for repairs. However, many necessary expenses

as outlined in this chapter have not been provided
for)

Net Annual Income   11,500
  Before Financing

At this point the bank appraiser usually omits some important refine-
ments that an independent fee appraiser would normally make. For
example, he probably would not bother to apportion the total net annual
income of $11,500 into the proper separate amounts attributable to the
land and to the building. This is important in scientific appraisal work
since the land does not depreciate but the building does.

So, the bank appraiser would simply apply the basic straight capitalization formula including straight line depreciation as follows:

$$\frac{\text{N.I. (net income)}}{\text{r (capitalization rate)}} = \text{F.M.V. (fair market value)}$$

Using 12 percent for the capitalization rate—which, as we said above,
bank appraisers are typically adopting as a rule of thumb "cap" rate on
smaller, older buildings—our figures in this example would be:

$$\frac{\$11,500. \text{ (N.I.)}}{.12 \text{ (r)}} = \text{F.M.V.}$$

or $95,833 equals the Fair Market Value of the Property.

Actually, this is a low estimate of value for a building generating
$20,000 annual gross income. $96,000 (you always round off figures in
final estimates of value) is less than five times the gross income.

In the Boston area, for example, this would apply, in reality, to a
relatively poor building, or an inferior location, or both. Well-located,
good buildings will actually sell at prices of at least six times gross
income. Newer buildings often sell at prices of seven times their gross
income, or even more for plush apartments in prime areas.

However, it is important to remember that the low estimate of fair
market value that the bank appraiser came up with in our example is in
reality par for the course for bank appraisers. They do, notoriously,
come in on the low side in their opinions of value. Then they become
stingy about the maximum percentage of this low total value that they
will actually lend in a first mortgage (usually 60 to 70 percent.) That is for
income property.

Since financing the building is the key issue in the entire purchase
transaction, you may as well sit up and take notice of the rather dismal
view of value that the bank is going to take. Remember, the lower the

allowable mortgage amount, the higher the cash down payment for you, and the less juice by way of annual cash return on the cash invested.

As I said before, do not let the seller or broker sidetrack you from making this appraisal the way the bank man would—for a run-of-the-mill older building with the relatively high capitalization rate of 12 percent. Some brokers typically would tell you, as they have told clients of mine who did not see me early enough, that eight percent, for example, would be the proper and usual capitalization rate to use in our formula above. You will note that the lower the "cap" rate you use, the higher your fair market value would be.

Now, right here and now I am going to explain just how silly it would be to use an eight percent capitalization rate; and at the same time, explain why banks so often use a 12 percent "cap" rate on older buildings—which high rate does in effect decrease their estimate of value for these buildings.

In the first place, you must understand how the capitalization rate is actually arrived at in the formula:

$$\frac{\text{Net Income}}{\text{Capitalization rate}} = \text{Fair Market Value}$$

The "cap" rate is actually composed of two rates. First, there is the estimated *fair interest return on the total capital investment* in the real estate. Secondly, the investor is also entitled to *a return of his total investment in the property.*

In our example of the $96,000 older building above, the appraiser would have to use seven to eight percent as the fair annual interest yield (since the buyer could get 5¼ percent in a bank or 6 percent for just clipping bond coupons.)

Let's be conservative and take only seven percent for the fair annual interest yield on the $96,000 price we are paying for our building, above. (Actually the national average demanded by investors has been running seven and one-half percent.) Now to this seven percent we must add our second factor, the additional annual percentage figure, to properly amortize the building so that when it no longer will yield $20,000 annual income, we can get our $96,000 total investment back.

In our example the bank appraiser would probably be unwilling to assign any longer than a 20-year remaining economic life to the building. This would indicate a five percent amortization rate. In this way our 12 percent total capitalization would have actually been constructed by the appraiser as follows:

7% — interest return on investment

250

BANK APPRAISER'S INCOME AND EXPENSE FORM

LOCATION _____

RENT SCHEDULE

(1) _____   (6) _____   (11) _____   (16) _____
(2) _____   (7) _____   (12) _____   (17) _____
(3) _____   (8) _____   (13) _____   (18) _____
(4) _____   (9) _____   (14) _____   (19) _____
(5) _____   (10) _____   (15) _____   (20) _____

GROSS ANNUAL INCOME $ _____

Less ___ % for vacancies $ _____

EFFECTIVE INCOME $ _____

EXPENSES

Taxes (% of gross)	$ _____
Heat (No. Oil)	_____
Insurance	_____
Water	_____
Electricity	_____
Janitor	_____
Repairs (%)	_____
Mtg. (%)	_____
Miscellaneous (%) _____	_____
Total Expenses	$ _____

NET INCOME $ _____
Valuation ____ % $ _____

Loan Recommended _____ for _____ yrs. @ ___ %

ANNUAL DEBT SERVICE $ _____

RETURN ON EQUITY   _____ %

BROKER _____   **APPLICANT** _____

5% — amortization rate to provide ultimate return of investment

___

Total   12% — capitalization rate

Now, do you begin to see why you must use such a high total capitalization rate—as the bank appraiser does. These high cap rates keep the value of the building down. If the bank sees the value low, *you* had better learn to see it low—or you will wind up overpaying.

Accordingly, your offer must be on the low side. Always use the bank appraisal, as explained above, as your excuse. Even if you are willing to pay more, you must start at a lower figure in order to negotiate successfully with the seller, as for example, offering to "split the difference" between his high asking price and your low offering price.

In practice you will find that you must inch up slowly and reluctantly from your first low offer. Otherwise, the seller will detect your anxiety and willingness to pay even more.

HOW TO HANDLE THE BROKER

Don't start off by kicking the broker around. Remember, he owes you nothing, except the same fair legal duty he owes to any other citizen. That is, the duty to refrain from actively defrauding or cheating you in any way. The broker's plain legal obligation is his fiduciary (best interests) duty to his principal, the seller. The law contends that the broker is in an arm's length transaction with the buyer. No broker ever owes any duty to a buyer to see to it that the buyer makes a good deal, or a profitable deal, or keeps from suffering loss as a result of a purchase through the broker. Briefly, as long as the broker refrains from any positive misstatements of material facts he remains clear of legal attack from the buyer.

Always beware that the broker, like the television, or billboard advertiser is entitled to his own personal opinion regarding the value of his wares.

Accordingly, it is wise to lure and entice the usually all too willing broker away from his plain legal duty to act in the best interests of the seller, if you wish him to beat the seller down in price for you.

Remember, you have no legal right to demand this type of dastardly performance by the broker.

Unfortunately for all sellers, as soon as the buyer even looks like he might give a cool reception to the seller's asking price, most brokers start begging for a low offer—*any* offer. So, actually, it is not too

252

difficult, with just a minimum display of restraint and lack of enthusiasm for the building, or its price, to get that broker plugging to obtain for you a significant price concession from his principal, the seller, in order to insure the sale and his commission.

Now, at this point it is well for the buyer to realize that standard income property commission rates for the broker as recommended by the trade are as follows:

6 percent commission on dwellings between one and four units.

5 percent commission on the first quarter-million of sale price.

3 percent commission on the sale price between one quarter million and three quarters of a million in sale price.

2 percent commission on all sale price over three quarters of a million dollars.

The recommended commission rate for land sales is 10 percent.

Now, as anyone can plainly see, these rates generate exceedingly high amounts of commission, for example: a commission of $12,500 on a quarter million sale, or $20,000 commission for selling a half-million dollar property. So for heaven's sake make the broker fight for you, protect you, and earn his commission.

Of course, you must understand that the biggest income property firm in your area, if it is anything like mine, frequently takes a $5,000 commission when they are due $20,000. And they often take their commission in the form of an extended promissory note instead of immediate cash. All of this becomes necessary in practice, as distinguished from the theory that these big-shot brokers preach, because of the unrealistically high prices of property, sellers and brokers becoming trapped at the closing by their own lies and deceit, and the reluctance of most brokers to lose the sale altogether. C'est la vie.

Additional pointers on how to reach rock bottom price:

1. Make your offer so low that you will provoke the seller or the broker into screaming out the absolute lowest price he would consider under any circumstance.

2. Demand an independent fee appraisal.

3. Obtain the book and page reference at the Registry of Deeds from the local tax assessor's office. An inspection of the deed to the present seller on the public records will usually reveal the amount of excise stamps on the deed. Some crafty lawyers put the stamps on a copy of the deed which they hold in their safe, where the state law allows this. Current Massachusetts legislation makes this practice illegal. Until December 31, 1967, all deeds recorded had to account for .55¢ in federal tax stamps for each $500 of sale price, or fraction thereof. Sales subject to mortgages require the stamps only for the cash equity involved. For

deeds recorded after January 1, 1968 (when federal stamps were discontinued) use your State excise tax stamp (usually $2.00 or $3.00 per thousand) in the same manner to ascertain the true price paid by the seller when he bought the property. Once you know this you are looking down the seller's throat instead of him looking down your throat.

4. If you are bashful, shy, or timid, it will pay you to hire an experienced "pro" to negotiate for you.

5. Embarrass the seller or broker with the obvious deceit in his "statement of his building." With most building statements I have seen—and I have seen thousands of them—your kid sister would have no trouble at all pointing out overstated income and understated expenses. In my classes at M.I.T. in Cambridge, Massachusetts for investors or appraisers I usually pick at random statements on buildings offered for sale by many leading income property firms. First, I put on the blackboard the statement, as is, with it's usual claim of fantastically high cash and total annual returns to the investor. Then, on the same wide blackboard, I adjust the alleged figures on the statement to reflect realistic amounts—always much lower for adjusted, effective gross income and much higher for common sense expenses. Then I add more actual expense items and necessary replacement reserves for parts of the building and its furnishing and equipment. Without fail, every time I do this for my class the huge phony profits turn into sizable net annual losses. Then we all stand in amazement wondering how these income property touts get away with all the chicanery. Why don't you do the same thing for yourself, using this chapter as your guide, the next time you are contemplating the purchase of an income property.

6. Emphasize the unsafe financing structure, particularly of the secondary financing, at the asking price. Ask the seller where the money is going to come from to pay off the balloon balances on the junior mortgages when they become due. He will always tell you how easy it will be for you at that future time to refinance the first mortgage for a higher enough amount to accomplish this. However, the truth is—particularly on older properties—that the banks are getting less and less liberal on the amounts of their mortgage loans, while at the same time interest rates are skyrocketing. So be sure you are allowing for all these facts of life while the seller and broker are leading you down the primrose path. Face the rascals with the true financial facts of life and demand a justified price concession to make the financing safe.

7. It is always wise to find fault with particular problems of the building. Try to win some price reduction for each individual fault, one at a time. This way, no matter how small the concession you obtained for each complaint, the total saving could be quite significant.

254

8. Please remember that you do not have to buy any particular property, and you are certainly in no hurry to buy. The whole trick in this business is to find a seller who *has* to sell, and in a hurry. If you do not remember anything but this you will automatically always be buying at rock bottom price.

Chapter 64
HOW TO BUY FOR MINIMUM CASH DOWN

Returning to the thesis of this book—how to make that killing on the smallest possible investment—it becomes obvious that a smaller, lower priced multiple structure will always permit a relatively low cash down payment.

However, professional appraisers are in general agreement that a two-family house just does not "appraise out" for an absentee owner. This means that the gross income from only two units is so limited, while the expenses are so relatively high (the opposite of "leverage," which I recommend in Chapter 67,) that the absentee owner would normally profit more from an alternative investment.

THE 4-UNIT DWELLING IS AN IDEAL SHOESTRING INVESTMENT

The point I wish to emphasize here is that good, older, lower priced four-family buildings without too many strikes against them locationwise actually perform well in earnings for even absentee owners. In my area, clients of mine have purchased many of these ideal low-cost investments for as little as two to five thousand dollars cash down, and have seen these investments yield annual cash returns of $1,000 and more; plus all the other savings through mortgage amortization and appreciation in value due to inflation; plus depreciation allowance, and other tax benefits.

The reason for the low down payment requirements is that the total

SECTION 203

Section 203 of the National Housing Act provides three separate programs of mortgage insurance. *Section 203(b)* is the basic and most commonly used FHA program. Proposed construction must meet the FHA Minimum Property Standards, but there are no special qualifications for borrowers. Any family which can demonstrate the ability to make the required cash investment and the payments on the mortgage can be approved. *Section 203(h)* provides a program designed to provide replacement housing for victims of disasters, with no down payment. *Section 203(i)* permits construction meeting less rigid standards than 203(b) and is designed primarily for use in rural areas.

MORTGAGE LIMITS

	Section 203(b)	Section 203(h)	Section 203(i)
Single-family homes	$33,000.	$14,400.	$16,200.
Two-family homes	$35,750.	Not applicable	Not applicable
Three-family homes	$35,750.	Not applicable	Not applicable
Four-family homes	$41,250.	Not applicable	Not applicable

LOAN-TO-VALUE RATIOS

Within the above limits, the following ratios are applied to the sum of either FHA or VA's estimate of the value of the property and FHA's estimate of the closing costs. This permits the buyer to include a portion of his closing costs in his mortgage.

OCCUPANT MORTGAGORS

Plans approved by FHA or VA prior to construction *or* dwelling completed more than one year on date of application.

Plans not approved by FHA or VA prior to construction *and* construction completed less than one year on date of application.

Veteran	Non-Veteran		Veteran	Non-Veteran
100% (-$200)	97%	first $15,000	90%	90%
90%	90%	next $10,000	90%	90%
85%	80%	over $25,000	85%	80%

(The special terms for veterans are available only for the purchase of single-family homes by those who have been certified by VA as eligible. Qualifications are less stringent than those for eligibility under the VA home loan programs, and there is no limit on the number of times an eligible veteran can use his eligibility in FHA programs.)

MORTGAGE TERM

30 years

OPERATIVE BUILDERS

FHA does not normally issue firm commitments to insure mortgages in the name of the builder. In most areas, construction financing is available on the basis of FHA conditional commitments. In unusual situations, when no construction financing is available otherwise, FHA may issue firm commitments in the name of the builder. If the mortgage is ultimately insured in the builder's name, however, the mortgage amount is limited to the non-occupant amounts above, and the mortgage term is limited to 20 years.

APPLICATION FEES

Though fees are under review for possible changes, the current fees are $45 proposed construction, $35 existing construction, $15 when property is approved by VA, and a CRV is presented to FHA.

SECTION 221(d)(2) HOME MORTGAGE INSURANCE

Section 221(d)(2) of the National Housing Act provides mortgage insurance for the purchase of homes by families displaced by government action and by low- and moderate-income families in general. Properties must meet the FHA Minimum Property Standards for Low-Cost Housing. This fact, and the lower mortgage limits available under this program, generally limit the use of the program to families with lower incomes, but there are no specific income requirements for eligibility. The program can also be used to finance rehabilitation of substandard properties.

MORTGAGE LIMITS

	Standard Limits	High-Cost Areas
Single-family homes	$18,000.	$21,000.
(Families of 5 or more	$21,000.	$24,000.)
Two-family homes	$24,000.	$30,000.
Three-family homes	$32,400.	$38,400.
Four-family homes	$39,600.	$45,600.

Cash Down Requirements and Maximum Mortgages Under The Federal Housing Administration.

The limits for high-cost areas shown above are available only in those areas in which construction costs are such that suitable housing cannot be constructed within the standard limits. This determination is made by FHA, and limits are established separately for each area. The limit may be less than the above high-cost area limits, but they will never be lower than the standard limits.

LOAN - TO - VALUE RATIOS (Subject to the limits above)

Plans approved by FHA or VA prior to construction *or* dwelling completed more than one year on date of application.

Displaced Families: Appraised value plus closing costs, or appraised value plus closing costs plus prepaid expenses minus $200 per unit, whichever is less.
Others: Appraised value plus closing costs, or 97% of appraised value plus closing costs plus prepaid expenses, whichever is less.
Operative Builder: 85% of appraised value plus closing costs. Under this program, an operative builder can qualify for a mortgage in the full amount available to an owner-occupant if the property is to be sold to an owner-occupant under an approved lease-option agreement which provides for equity accumulation. Plans not approved by FHA or VA prior to construction *and* completed less than one year on date of application.

REHABILITATION

Displaced Families: Appraised value before rehabilitation plus closing costs plus estimated cost of rehabilitation; or appraised value after rehabilitation plus closing costs plus prepaid expenses minus $200, whichever is less.
Others: Appraised value before rehabilitation plus closing costs plus estimated cost of rehabilitation; or appraised value after rehabilitation plus closing costs; or 97% of appraised value after rehabilitation plus closing costs plus prepaid expenses, whichever is less.

Operative Builders: Least of: 85% of appraised value after rehabilitation, plus closing costs; five times estimated cost of rehabilitation; or 85% of sum of purchase price or appraised value before rehabilitation, whichever is less, plus estimated cost of rehabilitation, plus closing costs. See also the note above concerning sales under lease-option plans.

MORTGAGE TERM

30 years

APPLICATION FEES

$45 proposed, $35 existing.

INFORMATION SOURCE

HUD Area Office or HUD-FHA Insuring Office.

ADMINISTERING OFFICE

Assistant Secretary for Housing Production and Mortgage Credit—FHA Commissioner.

January 1971

☆ U.S. GOVERNMENT PRINTING OFFICE: 1971–704-085/144

HUD-97-F(3)

prices of most of these four-unit older, valuable buildings are only in the thirty or early forty thousand dollar price range to begin with. Many banks will give up to 80 percent mortgages for one to four-unit dwellings. Best of all, the Veterans Administration and the Federal Housing Administration will protect the lending bank against loss on one to four-unit dwellings. Of course, to benefit from these government-backed loans providing maximum mortgages, and minimum down payments, you have to buy with the intention of occupancy. Otherwise, you cannot buy V.A. at all, and your F.H.A. mortgage would be only 85 percent of what it could be if you intended to occupy the building yourself.

Now, right here, is a wonderful opportunity for any G.I. buyer to get a 7 percent mortgage, or F.H.A. buyer to obtain a 7½ percent mortgage. The F.H.A. buyer pays one-half of one percent for the F.H.A. insurance which protects the bank against loss. Banks are protected by the V.A. out of public funds. What is wrong with a fellow who is trying to start on a shoestring living in his own little apartment building for awhile?

I'll promise you one thing. If more people would do this in today's skyrocketing market, it would not take very long for them to be moving on into their own palatial single.

Consider Alex Paraskeva, the Melrose, Massachusetts, mailman whose story is told in Chapter 41. He started by living in small multiples himself. Well, today, after only six years of activity, Alex has gone from his first little multiple to nearly one million dollars in real estate. He now lives in a $150,000 showplace single house in the Park section of Wakefield, Massachusetts. Yes, all this really took place in the last four years—and from *less* than a shoestring start.

G.I. CASH DOWN REQUIREMENTS

Many banks, even today, will still grant G.I. 7 percent mortgages with only ten percent cash down. I deal with one wonderful bank which has granted five percent cash down G.I. loans to veterans throughout this entire mortgage crunch period, which started in mid-1966. And what is more this bank does not charge one single bonus point for granting the loans. Of course, the V.A. itself would protect a bank on a 100 percent loan to a veteran, but the banks will not go along without some investment by the veteran.

FHA CASH DOWN REQUIREMENTS

The F.H.A. has a formula for maximum allowable mortgages and minimum required down payments which is illustrated in the table on page 256. Briefly it requires only $1,000 cash down on a $20,000 property, $1,500 down on a $25,000 price and $2,500 down at $30,000.

WHY MOST INCOME PROPERTIES ARE SOLD SUBJECT TO EXISTING FINANCING TODAY

Obviously, most investors and speculators are not veterans; do not wish to occupy the income property themselves; and try hard to get more than four units on the same lot to benefit from leverage (see Chapter 67.)

All of this means that the purchase prices they have to pay are relatively high in today's highly inflated market. Cash down payment requirements would be quite high, if new first mortgages had to be obtained. The reason for this is that banks usually lend only between 60 and 70 percent mortgages on non-owner occupied income property. How, then, can my thesis of *minimal* investment by the buyer possibly be genuine and valid?

Quite simply, the answer is that small investors just do not obtain new first mortgages. In fact, most leading income property brokerage firms in my area will not even *list* an investment property, unless the present owner is willing to sell subject to his existing mortgages.

Actually, the seller himself normally takes back an extra new mortgage; sometimes it is the fourth or even the fifth mortgage. It is all of this secondary financing that keeps the down payment so low. Believe it or not, while most of us worry about coming up with one mortgage payment every month for our own little homestead, investment property speculators think nothing of three, four, or five mortgage payments on each of their buildings. Of course, they have one big advantage. They never have to pay their own mortgage payments themselves. Their tenants pay off their mortgages for them. This is precisely why these investors must eventually become very rich, after benefiting greatly each year, as they go along, from high cash returns plus several types of tax deductions.

Obviously, you can buy three buildings instead of one if you pay only 10 percent down instead of 30 percent or more.

Most important of all is the opportunity that this type of financi provides for the little fellow to get started on a relatively small investment.

Some additional pointers on how to buy for minimum down payments are as follows:

1. When you see a run-down building that is well-located, tell the owner you will agree to repair and upgrade the building if he will take a large first mortgage himself.

2. When you know an owner is preparing for retirement, emphasize the tax advantages to him of taking a large first mortgage himself.

3. If the owner is uninterested in taking the first mortgage in the above situations, perhaps he will take back a large enough second mortgage to keep your cash investment low.

4. Buy bank foreclosure properties. The foreclosing bank is legally allowed to, and frequently will, grant up to 100 percent first mortgage money.

5. Buy Veteran Administration foreclosure property. They grant up to 100 percent first mortgages at their low rate of interest as well.

6. Buy Federal Housing Administration foreclosure property. They grant maximum first mortgage loans.

7. If you still do not have enough cash down to swing the deal, take an "option" until you can raise enough cash down, or better financing.

Try to avoid the old seller and broker trick of falsely kiting the price in the sale contract in order to obtain a higher first mortgage than you could if the true price were used. Most banks will not be fooled anyway. At best you will destroy your reputation for integrity at the very place where you are going to need it the most—your own bank.

Chapter 65

WHAT TO PUT IN YOUR CONTRACT OF SALE

Before we get into any of the fine points, let's get a few fundamentals straightened out first.

AVOID BINDERS

To begin with, an income property buyer, unlike the typical house

Used extensively by brokers who are always in a hurry to get you married to the deal before you have had a chance to check everything out. You are intended to be naked as far as having any protection is concerned.

OFFER TO PURCHASE

I offer to _____ 19 ____

_____ for the property located at

_____ in the City of

_____ town

containing about _____ sq. ft. of land with the buildings thereon, $ _____ to be paid as

follows: $ _____ cash, $ _____ first mortgage _____ years at _____ %, with payments of

$ _____ quarterly
        monthly

I hand you $ _____ to bind this offer, to be returned to me, if it is not accepted before

_____ 19 ____ If it is accepted, I agree to sign your usual real estate agreement to

carry this out and take title within _____ days, and to make an additional deposit of

$ _____, the deposits to be applied to the purchase price. Signed in triplicate.

_____

Accepted on _____   _____   _____
            DATE   SELLER   BUYER

_____   _____
HUSBAND OR WIFE   HUSBAND OR WIFE

_____
REALTOR

261

buyer, should be smart enough to avoid the use of a binder entirely and go right into a full, formal, and final purchase and sale agreement. This is the only kind of agreement that gives him the certain right to compel the seller to perform in an equity proceeding called "Specific Performance." For example, the Massachusetts Supreme Judicial Court has denied specific performance where it was shown that the parties intended to further agree, as with a formal purchase and sale agreement to follow.

While some binders may be enforceable, they are frequently either doubtful or downright unenforceable. The big point to remember is that even when a binder actually is a complete and enforceable contract it still fails to cover most of the material matters that are covered in a professionally drawn purchase and sale agreement contract.

TYPICAL BINDER

Used extensively by brokers who are always in a hurry to get you married to the deal before you have had a chance to check everything out. You are intended to be naked as far as having any protection is concerned.

Certainly it would be foolhardy to commit your deposit, and your liability in damages, without being fully protected yourself, or at least certain that you will want to or be able to perform.

GO DIRECTLY INTO A CONTRACT OF SALE DRAWN BY YOUR ATTORNEY

The only safe practice for the buyer is to enter into a full contract as soon as possible. No buyer should ever attempt this, however, without the services of a competent real estate attorney.

Most printed contract forms are prepared primarily for distribution and sale to brokers for their use. It is the brokers who fill in most of the contract of sale forms which they then have signed by the buyer and seller. Relatively few buyers are intelligent enough to have their contract of sale drafted by an attorney at law.

Most others are reckless and ignorant buyers who appear to be completely unaware of the risks they are taking when they let the broker sign them up.

The printed forms used by the brokers are at best incomplete and inadequate protection to a buyer; and at worst no protection at all, sometimes amounting to vicious overreaching of the unwary buyer. Buyers seem to forget that the broker is the legal agent of the seller, and in practice usually looks out for himself first.

The following pages are an example of better type of agreement used by some higher type brokers. Compare author's list of "Minimal Protections Every Buyer Needs in His Contract of Sale" at end of this chapter. You will notice how even this seldom used very lengthy and complicated agreement form is heavily weighted in favor of the seller and broker, and why you need your lawyer.

This   day of   19

hereinafter called the SELLER, agrees to SELL and

hereinafter called the BUYER or PURCHASER, agrees to BUY, upon the terms hereinafter set forth, the following described premises:

1. **PARTIES**
   (fill in)

2. **DESCRIPTION**
   (fill in and include title reference)

3. **BUILDINGS, STRUCTURES, IMPROVEMENTS, FIXTURES**

   (fill in or delete)

   Included in the sale as a part of said premises are the buildings, structures, and improvements now thereon, and the fixtures belonging to the SELLER and used in connection therewith including, if any, all venetian blinds, window shades, screens, screen doors, storm windows and doors, awnings, shutters, furnaces, heaters, heating equipment, stoves, ranges, oil and gas burners and fixtures appurtenant thereto, hot water heaters, plumbing and bathroom fixtures, electric and other lighting fixtures, mantels, outside television antennas, fences, gates, trees, shrubs, plants, and, if built in, air conditioning equipment, ventilators, garbage disposers, dishwashers, washing machines and driers, and
   but excluding

263

4. TITLE DEED
(fill in)

Include here by specific reference any restrictions, easements, rights and obligations in party walls not included in (b), leases, municipal and other liens, other encumbrances, and make provision to protect SELLER against BUYER'S breach of SELLER'S covenants in leases, where necessary.

Said premises are to be conveyed by a good and sufficient deed running to the BUYER, or to the nominee designated by the BUYER by written notice to the SELLER at least seven days before the deed is to be delivered as herein provided, and said deed shall convey a good and clear record and marketable title thereto, free from encumbrances, except

(a) Provisions of existing building and zoning laws;

(b) Existing rights and obligations in party walls which are not the subject of written agreement;

(c) Such taxes for the then current year as are not due and payable on the date of the delivery of such deed;

(d) Any liens for municipal betterments assessed after the date of this agreement;

*(e)

5. PLANS

If said deed refers to a plan necessary to be recorded therewith the SELLER shall deliver such plan with the deed in form adequate for recording or registration.

6. REGISTERED TITLE

In addition to the foregoing, if the title to said premises is registered, said deed shall be in form sufficient to entitle the BUYER to a Certificate of Title of said premises, and the SELLER shall deliver with said deed all instruments, if any, necessary to enable the BUYER to obtain such Certificate of Title.

7. PURCHASE PRICE
(fill in); space is allowed to write out the amounts if desired

(provide for payment by certified or Bank's Check acceptable to the SELLER, if required)

The agreed purchase price for said premises is

dollars, of which

$ have been paid as a deposit this day and

$ are to be paid at the time of delivery of the deed in cash.

$

$ TOTAL
_____

8. TIME FOR PERFORMANCE: DELIVERY OF DEED (fill in)

Such deed is to be delivered at   o'clock   M. on the   day of
     19   at the   Registry of Deeds,
unless otherwise agreed upon in writing. It is agreed that time is of the essence of this agreement.

9. POSSESSION and CONDITION of PREMISES.
(attach list of exceptions, if any)

Full possession of said premises free of all tenants and occupants, except as herein provided, is to be delivered at the time of the delivery of the deed, said premises to be then (a) in the same condition as they now are, reasonable use and wear thereof excepted, and (b) not in violation of said building and zoning laws, and (c) in compliance with the provisions of any instrument referred to in clause 4 hereof.

264

10. **EXTENSION TO PERFECT TITLE OR MAKE PREMISES CONFORM**
(Change period of time if desired.)

If the SELLER shall be unable to give title or to make conveyance, or to deliver possession of the premises, all as herein stipulated, or if at the time of the delivery of the deed the premises do not conform with the provisions hereof, then any payments made under this agreement shall be refunded and all other obligations of the parties hereto shall cease and this agreement shall be void and without recourse to the parties hereto, unless the SELLER elects to use reasonable efforts to remove any defects in title, or to deliver possession as provided herein, or to make the said premises conform to the provisions hereof, as the case may be, in which event the SELLER shall give written notice thereof to the BUYER at or before the time for performance hereunder, and thereupon the time for performance hereof shall be extended for a period of thirty   days.

11. **FAILURE TO PERFECT TITLE OR MAKE PREMISES CONFORM, etc.**

If at the expiration of the extended time the SELLER shall have failed so to remove any defects in title, deliver possession, or make the premises conform, as the case may be, all as herein agreed, or if at any time during the period of this agreement or any extension thereof, the holder of a mortgage on said premises shall refuse to permit the insurance proceeds, if any, to be used for such purposes, then, at the BUYER'S option, any payments made under this agreement shall be forthwith refunded and all other obligations of all parties hereto shall cease and this agreement shall be void without recourse to the parties hereto.

12. **BUYER'S ELECTION TO ACCEPT TITLE**

The BUYER shall have the election, at either the original or any extended time for performance, to accept such title as the SELLER can deliver to the said premises in their then condition and to pay therefor the purchase price without deduction, in which case the SELLER shall convey such title, except that in the event of such conveyance in accord with the provisions of this clause, if the said premises shall have been damaged by fire or casualty insured against, then the SELLER shall, unless the SELLER has previously restored the premises to their former condition, either

(a) pay over or assign to the BUYER, on delivery of the deed, all amounts recovered or recoverable on account of such insurance, less any amounts reasonably expended by the SELLER for any partial restoration, or

(b) if a holder of a mortgage on said premises shall not permit the insurance proceeds or a part thereof to be used to restore the said premises to their former condition or to be so paid over or assigned, give to the BUYER a credit against the purchase price, on delivery of the deed, equal to said amounts so recovered or recoverable and retained by the holder of the said mortgage less any amounts reasonably expended by the SELLER for any partial restoration.

13. **ACCEPTANCE OF DEED**

The acceptance of a deed by the BUYER or his nominee as the case may be, shall be deemed to be a full performance and discharge of every agreement and obligation herein contained or expressed, except such as are, by the terms hereof, to be performed after the delivery of said deed.

14. **USE OF PURCHASE MONEY TO CLEAR TITLE**

To enable the SELLER to make conveyance as herein provided, the SELLER may, at the time of delivery of the deed, use the purchase money or any portion thereof to clear the title of any or all encumbrances or interests, provided that all instruments so procured are recorded simultaneously with the delivery of said deed.

265

Until the delivery of the deed, the SELLER shall maintain insurance on said premises as follows:

Type of Insurance   Amount of Coverage

(a) Fire   * $
(b) Extended coverage   * $
(c).

Unless otherwise notified in writing by the BUYER at least seven _____ days before the time for delivery of the deed, and unless prevented from doing so by the refusal of the insurance company(s) involved to issue the same, the SELLER shall assign such insurance and deliver binders therefor in proper form to the BUYER at the time for performance of this agreement. In the event of refusal by the insurance company(s) to issue the same, the SELLER shall give notice thereof to the BUYER at least two _____ business days before the time for performance of this agreement.

Collected rents, mortgage interest, prepaid premiums on insurance if assigned as herein provided, water and sewer use charges, operating expenses (if any) according to the schedule attached hereto or set forth below, and taxes for the then current year, shall be apportioned and fuel value shall be adjusted, as of the day of performance of this agreement _____ and the net amount thereof shall be added to or deducted from, as the case may be, the purchase price payable by the BUYER at the time of delivery of the deed. Uncollected rents for the current rental period shall be apportioned if and when collected by either party.

If the amount of said taxes is not known at the time of the delivery of the deed, they shall be apportioned on the basis of the taxes assessed for the preceding year, with a reapportionment as soon as the new tax rate and valuation can be ascertained; and, if the taxes which are to be apportioned shall thereafter be reduced by abatement, the amount of such abatement, less the reasonable cost of obtaining the same, shall be apportioned between the parties, provided that neither party shall be obligated to institute or prosecute proceedings for an abatement unless herein otherwise agreed.

A commission, according to the present schedule of commission rates recommended by the Greater Boston Real Estate Board, is to be paid by the SELLER to

the Broker(s) herein, but if the SELLER pursuant to the terms of clause 22 hereof retains the deposits made hereunder by the BUYER, said Broker(s) shall be entitled to receive from the SELLER an amount equal to one-half the amount so retained or an amount equal to the commission according to such schedule for this transaction, whichever is the lesser.

The Broker(s) named herein warrant(s) that he (they) is (are) duly licensed as such by the Commonwealth of Massachusetts.

15. INSURANCE
* Insert amount
(list additional types of
insurance and amounts
as agreed)

16. ASSIGNMENT OF INSURANCE
(delete entire clause
if insurance is not to
be assigned)

17. ADJUSTMENTS
(list operating ex-
penses, if any, or at-
tach schedule)

18. ADJUSTMENT OF UNASSESSED AND ABATED TAXES

19. BROKER'S COMMISSION
(fill in space)

20. BROKER(S) WARRANTY
(fill in name)

-2-

266

21. DEPOSIT
(fill in, or delete reference to broker(s) if SELLER holds, deposit)

All deposits made hereunder shall be held by the broker(s) as agent for the SELLER, subject to the terms of this agreement and shall be duly accounted for at the time for performance of this agreement.

22. BUYER'S DEFAULT; DAMAGES

If the BUYER shall fail to fulfill the BUYER'S agreements herein, all deposits made hereunder by the BUYER shall be retained by the SELLER as liquidated damages unless within thirty days after the time for performance of this agreement or any extension hereof, the SELLER otherwise notifies the BUYER in writing.

23. VETERANS FINANCING
(fill in blank spaces or delete entire clause)

The BUYER, being a Veteran, intends to use his so-called Veterans Administration loan benefits to finance the purchase of said premises; it is understood and agreed that if on or before _____ a Certificate of Reasonable Value for not less than the purchase price shall not be issued by the Veterans Administration Loan Guaranty Division and if an accredited lending institution shall not approve and accept a mortgage loan of $ _____, payable in _____ years at a rate of interest not to exceed _____ % per year, based upon the aforesaid Certificate of Reasonable Value, then all payments hereunder by the BUYER shall be forthwith refunded and all other obligations of all parties hereto shall cease and this agreement shall be void and without recourse to the parties hereto.

24. F.H.A. FINANCING
(fill in blank spaces or delete CLAUSES 24 & 25)

The BUYER agrees to apply promptly for a U.S. Government Federal Housing Administration insured loan for not less than $ _____, payable in _____ years at a rate of interest not to exceed _____ % per year, and if he shall not be able to obtain a firm commitment for such loan on or before _____ then at the BUYER'S option, all payments hereunder by the BUYER shall be forthwith refunded and all other obligations of all parties hereto shall cease and this agreement shall be void and without recourse to the parties hereto.

25. F.H.A. APPRAISAL STATEMENT
(fill in amount or delete Clauses 25 & 24)

(the wording of this clause is required verbatim by F.H.A. Rules & Regulations)

It is expressly agreed that, notwithstanding any other provisions of this contract, the PURCHASER shall not be obligated to complete the purchase of the property described herein or to incur any penalty by forfeiture of earnest money deposits or otherwise, unless the SELLER has delivered to the PURCHASER a written statement issued by the Federal Housing Commissioner setting forth the appraised value of the property for mortgage insurance purposes of not less than $ _____, which statement the SELLER hereby agrees to deliver to the PURCHASER promptly after such appraised value statement is made available to the SELLER. The PURCHASER shall, however, have the privilege and option of proceeding with the consummation of this contract without regard to the amount of the appraised valuation made by the Federal Housing Commissioner.

26. SALE OF PERSONAL PROPERTY
(fill in and attach list or delete entire clause)

The BUYER agrees to buy from the SELLER the articles of personal property enumerated on the attached list for the price of $ _____ and the SELLER agrees to deliver to the BUYER upon delivery of the deed hereunder, a warranty bill of sale therefor on payment of said price. The provisions of this clause shall constitute an agreement separate and apart from the provisions herein contained with respect to the real estate, and any breach of the terms and conditions of this clause shall have no effect on the provisions of this agreement with respect to the real estate.

267

27. **RELEASE BY HUSBAND OR WIFE**

The SELLER'S spouse hereby agrees to join in said deed and to release and convey all statutory and other rights and interests in said premises.

28. **BROKER AS PARTY**

The broker(s) named herein, join(s) in this agreement and become(s) a party hereto, in so far as any provisions of this agreement expressly apply to him (them), and to any amendments or modifications of such provisions to which he (they) agree(s) in writing.

29. **LIABILITY OF TRUSTEE, SHAREHOLDER, BENEFICIARY, etc.**

If the SELLER or BUYER executes this agreement in a representative or fiduciary capacity, only the principal or the estate represented shall be bound, and neither the SELLER or BUYER so executing, nor any shareholder or beneficiary of any trust, shall be personally liable for any obligation, express or implied, hereunder.

30. **CONSTRUCTION OF AGREEMENT**

* *delete "triplicate" and substitute "quadruplicate" if required. (See "Instructions in General", 1)*

_____ is to be construed as a Massachusetts contract, is to take effect as a sealed instrument, sets forth the entire contract between the parties, is binding upon and enures to the benefit of the parties hereto and their respective heirs, devises, executors, administrators, successors and assigns, and may be cancelled, modified or amended only by a written instrument executed by both the SELLER and the BUYER. If two or more persons are named herein as BUYER their obligations hereunder shall be joint and several. The captions and marginal notes are used only as a matter of convenience and are not to be considered a part of this agreement or to be used in determining the intent of the parties to it.

This instrument, executed in triplicate*

31. **ADDITIONAL PROVISIONS**

.... *Husband or Wife of Seller*

.... SELLER

.... *Husband or Wife of Buyer*

.... BUYER

.... *Broker*

268

Brokers are not lawyers. They should not be expected to know how to legally protect anybody. Everyone knows that the drafting of contracts is lawyers' work.

Again, brokers are not professional men. By Massachusetts Supreme Judicial Court determination a broker is a businessman. So, let's get one thing straight. When you, as a buyer, rush into a strange broker's office with deposit money and ask him to sign you up to a binding contract with his principal, the seller, you are not saving a lawyer's fee. You are not saving anything. As this chapter will bring out you are just making a prize chump out of yourself as you repose complete confidence in a "businessman" who is legally obligated to act in the best interests of the seller—your adversary. In the eyes of the law the broker is in an arm's-length transaction with you, and has no duty to volunteer any information to you—even those facts which you would vitally need to know to avoid catastrophe.

Take it from me—*only your own attorney* is in a position to fully and properly protect your interests when you enter into a real estate contract of sale.

Below is a typical example of the oversimplified, joker type of contract of sale form which is pushed by the typical money-mad type of broker training school. These schools are hell-bent upon making a real estate broker out of every last man and woman over 21 years of age, who can afford to pay their tuition . . . at least in easy payments. Completely in tune with their oversimplified instruction they peddle these monstrosities to their gullible students as "simplified and painless" agreement forms. When these forms are used, all the pain comes later. For all the complexities that are normally inherent in every real estate transaction, and which should be negotiated out by the parties *before signing up,* now must rear their ugly heads *after the parties are already locked into their deal.* These half-baked, new, thirty-day wonder brokers are exhorted to use these "dynamite" forms so that they can "wrap up their deal in two minutes, while their buyer is still under the ether."

By the end of this chapter you will realize how inadequate and dangerous these forms actually are. There never will be an adequate substitute for a contract of sale drawn by your own attorney who alone is in a position to completely protect your vital interest.

EXAMPLE OF OVERSIMPLIFIED CONTRACT
OF SALE

Forms* Misused by Many Brokers

* Author's list of *"Minimal* protections every buyer needs in his contract of sale" at end of this chapter shows how pitifully inadequate this often used type of form is, and why, when this so-called "painless" form is used, all the pain comes later.

AGREEMENT made this_____ day of_____ A.D. 19___

The undersigned SELLER agrees to SELL and

The undersigned BUYER agrees to BUY the property described as follows:

Total Price $ _____

Deposit herewith $ _____

Balance upon passing papers $ _____

Papers to pass on or before _____

Seller to give a good and marketble title by_____ deed.

If unable to do so, deposit to be returned and parties discharged.

Seller to give buyer possession of property on or before _____

Seller to pay commission, in accordance with Real Estate Board rates, to _____ , Broker.

If buyer defaults, he waives claim to deposit, which becomes the property of the Seller and Broker, equally, as liquidated damages.

Interest, Taxes, Fuel, Rents, Insurance to be adjusted as of date of passing papers.

All regular fixtures of the property to pass with the sale.

BUYER _____

_____

SELLER_____

BROKER _____   _____

Form ...5

MINIMAL PROTECTIONS EVERY BUYER NEEDS IN HIS CONTRACT OF SALE

1. Remember your broker is not a lawyer. He is not even your agent. He is the seller's agent. Moreover, he is out to make a business profit out of you. Only your own lawyer can properly protect your vital interests. Only he has the plain legal duty to do so.

2. Care should be exercised to ascertain that the named seller is in fact the owner. Dishonest sellers, builders and brokers frequently steal deposits from unwary buyers.

3. You, as buyer, must check to insure that the seller does not already have total encumbrances and liens exceeding the full purchase price.

4. Your deposit should be held in escrow by a stakeholder until closing day. Do not be "conned" into turning it over directly to a seller or builder unless you are positive of its safety and absolutely certain that the deal can be consummated. Recently, a greedy hard-driving bargainer drove his builder colleague and friend of twenty years to the wall, forcing him to accept a $5,000 price for a $14,000 building lot complete with foundation and utilities. This hard-driving bargain hunting buyer was in great shape until he recklessly instructed the broker, who originally planned to hold his $1,500 deposit in escrow, to endorse the deposit check over to the seller. When the seller lost the lot by bank foreclosure before the date set for the passing the buyer became infuriated. But, there was nothing he could do except become the creditor of the seller. In Massachusetts and about half the states, a seller whose title is defective may be liable in damages for the buyer's loss of his bargain, as well as for the refund of his down payment. (See Capaldi v. Burlwood Realty Corp. — 350 Mass. 756 1966.)

5. The seller's alleged gross income should be pinned down in a specific clause making the transaction subject to the seller's accountant's statement of this income for the building, for income tax purposes.

6. The seller's alleged expenses for the building should be buttoned down in the same manner as (5) above.

7. A financing clause making the agreement subject to the exact amount and type of mortgage money needed by the buyer to enable performance on closing day, should always be followed by, "failing which all deposits hereunder are to be promptly returned to the buyer." Be sure to be specific about the maximum interest rates and other bank charges you are willing to accept.

8. Make the contract subject to seller delivering a deed of good and clear record and marketable title. Permit exceptions only for those encumbrances which are specifically spelled out in the agreement and assented to by the buyer.

9. Make sure you have the election to back out and get your deposit returned, or proceed if you wish and take the insurance proceeds in case of fire or other casualty destruction before closing day. Be sure that the seller is agreeing to keep up insurance in an amount at least "sufficient to protect the buyer." Remember, the seller's actual insurance policy may no longer be high enough to protect against today's high prices.

10. The contract should be made subject to the building's conformance to zoning laws and building codes.

11. Always beware of the fine print clause, "Time is of the essence of this contract." Normally, you would be better served by a right to a reasonable extension of time for performance, if necessary.

12. The buyer buys a building as is. Therefore, the following basement guaranty clause should be inserted:

"The seller guarantees that the basement floor and walls shall be free from water leakage for a period of one year from the date of closing of title. This paragraph shall survive the delivery of the deed."

13. Same protection as (12) above for roof leaks.

14. The seller should guarantee the plumbing and heating system against defects in workmanship and materials for one year, and the heating system to have the capacity to heat all parts of the building to 70 degrees in zero weather.

15. All appliances should be guaranteed to be in working order at the time the buyer is to take possession, or they should be replaced or put in working order at seller's expense.

16. The seller should be required to supply a termite certificate.

17. Any personal property involved in the sale should be paid for separately from the total price paid for the real estate to hold down the tax assessment.

18. All betterments due right up to the closing date should be paid for by the seller.

19. Always keep your deposit money as low as possible, just in case you are forced to try to get it back.

The above suggested buyer protections are standard and minimal protections. They are not intended to be used as a substitute for your own lawyer's contract of sale, especially drafted to satisfy your particular requirements.

It is hoped that you will see by now the folly of expecting the seller's agent, the broker, to fully protect your interest. There would not be room enough on the only kind of standard printed forms he would know how to fill out. These forms are usually heavily weighted in his and the seller's favor. After all, the whole idea of the broker preparing the contract of sale is to get you, the buyer, married to the deal so that you cannot get out. So, please don't be a chump anymore. Let's keep our sellers and brokers honest.

Above all, never turn over any money, or sign anything, without your lawyer's approval.

20. The buyer must protect himself against a defaulting seller.

A suit in equity for specific performance against a defaulting seller is not always the most practical solution for the buyer. A clause similar to the following should be used:

"If the seller defaults, he agrees to pay . . ." (a specific amount of damages—usually as much as or double the buyer's deposit).

21. If necessary, special provision for specific damages if the seller delays in performance should also be provided for the buyer.

22. All parties who will have to sign the deed to the buyer on closing date must have their signatures on the antecedent purchase and sale agreement, otherwise no power on earth can make them sign the deed.

23. All the seller's oral promises should be specifically spelled out in writing. The Statute of Frauds says that any agreement to transfer real estate must be in writing and signed in order to be enforceable.

Chapter 66

SELLER AND BROKER TRICKS YOU MUST AVOID

As a buyer you must always remember that sellers will be offering to you their problem buildings and their losers. Most income property owners I have known would probably sooner sell you their wife or mother before they would part with a money-making building.

Often with the professional assistance of their brokers these sellers try to suck you in with a building statement as phony as a three dollar bill.

The sharpies and con artists who are out there trying hard to bait and trap any investor they can get are particularly gunning for the novice speculator who is trying to make a killing on a small investment.

The building statement outlined below is a recent actual sales prospectus distributed widely in the Boston area by a leading Brookline, Massachusetts investment property counseling firm. As brazen and bad as it is, it is no worse than typical of hundreds of such masterpieces of trickery, double-dealing and deceit that flood the Boston—and I presume other real estate investment markets—daily. Literally scores of income property firms are just as guilty as this one. Yet their firms continue to advertise prominently in the same misleading manner. And the firm members are considered among their knowing colleagues, and by the unwary public, to be big shots and respected leaders in their trade.

Only the brokerage name in the example below is fictitious.

BUILDING STATEMENT

DESCRIPTION:
2 frame apt. bldgs. consisting of 14 APTS. ALL 4 ROOMS
2 Oil heaters # 2 oil.

MORTGAGES:

1st	$26,402.79 int.	6%-Term: 10 yrs DR on 20 yrs
2nd	$25,000.00 int.	6% prin. 2-term: 4 yrs
3rd	$10,000.00 int.	6% prin. 2-term: 5 yrs
4th	9,470.00 int.	5%-Term: 4½ yrs.

RENT RANGE:
7 @ $80.00 mo. 5 @ $85.00 mo. 1 @ $70.00 mo. 1 @ $75.00 mo.
TOTAL ANNUAL INCOME $13,560.00
ESTIMATED EXPENSES:

Taxes	$2,046.96
1st mtg int.	1,584.17
2nd mtg int.	1,500.00
3rd mtg int.	600.00
4th mtg int.	473.50
Heat	1,750.00
Electric	150.00
Water	300.00
Insurance total	552.48
Janitor	240.00

| TOTAL ESTIMATED EXPENSES: | | | 9,197.11 |
| | | | |

TOTAL NET INCOME:			$4,362.89
PRINCIPAL SAVINGS:			
	1st mtg	$1,492.87	
	2nd mtg	504.00	
	3rd mtg	210.00	$2,206.87
CASH NET:			$2,156.02
PRICE:	$75,000.00		
CASH DOWN:	4,128.00		

The statement above looks appealing and tantalizing. Doesn't it?

After all, where can you buy a $75,000 building for only $4,000 cash down? And where can you get better than a 50 percent annual cash return on your cash investment, plus better than 100 percent total annual return on your $4,000 invested?

Does this building not meet our requirements admirably? Even if you lost the whole $4,000, by today's standards you wouldn't have lost much. You could never be wiped out.

Well, let's withhold judgment until we calmly, correctly, and honestly reconstruct this typically phony building statement. You will notice that you must learn how to read these statements between the lines.

RECONSTRUCTED STATEMENT

DESCRIPTION: Actual inspection reveals that there are, in fact, two frame buildings adjoining. And there are, in fact, 14 four-room apartments. But what buildings! They do not even look like apartment buildings. They are ancient buildings: badly located at a busy expressway exit, in a highly commercialized location of older, run-down buildings. A huge ugly illuminated billboard sits astride the roof of the two buildings. The tenants would have to be of the welfare case variety. Collection problems should be tough, and the vacancy rate high. The apartments consist of huge, barn-like, high-ceiling, old-fashioned rooms badly needing decoration, and are loaded with deferred maintenance. The #2 oil indicated means an expensive way to heat these barns.

MORTGAGES: As usual, this information is incomplete. The original face amounts of the mortgages, and their present balances due, should be stated separately. Likewise, the original terms of the mortgages and their present ages, or remaining periods to run, should be stated separately.

It is worth noting that the first mortgage, while being paid at low 20-year direct reduction payment monthly rates, was originally granted for only 10 years. This means that whenever the 10 years is up—which could be next month as far as this statement lets us know—the entire balloon balance of the mortgage can and probably will be called by the mortgagee bank.

Note that only two percent per year is being paid off on the principal balances due on the second and third mortgages, while absolutely nothing is being paid off on principal on the fourth mortgage. At this point the prospective buyer must stop to evaluate the safety of the financing. From the inadequate information given here we can only assume that this indicated financing is very unsafe. In other words, just when are these balloon balances on all these mortgages actually due; and just how is the prospective buyer going to be able to pay them off or get refinancing on such a horrible property?

RENT RANGE: The $70 to $80 monthly rents indicated for *heated* apartments show the kind of low grade neighborhood and accommodations involved. In fact these prices are so low as to be a good indication of "trouble type" apartments. In other words, modest rentals are always good—but *never* buy slum property.

TOTAL ANNUAL INCOME: The usual dream figure is given here. Just as if there would always be 100 percent occupancy, and never a vacancy in this "dump." Also, as if there would never be any rent collection losses—with this type of tenants. They must be kidding! *Also*, there is the usual "no charge" for management. I shudder to think of how many times the landlord has to go back for the rents he *does* collect from the apartments that are *not vacant*.

Accordingly, from the completely unrealistic total income figure we must subtract a minimum of 15 percent vacancy allowance for this type of building. In fact, every time I went to visit this property I found 30 percent or more actual vacancy.

So, $13,560 less 15 percent (or $2,034) for vacancy allowance and collection losses leaves $11,526. Of course, I should subtract another six percent for management expense, from the *actual collectible total rent figures of $11,526*. This deduction comes to $691.56 which leaves us with an effective, adjusted gross income of *$10,834.44*. I realize that the buyer of this kind of building will probably wish to manage the property himself, to save the usual minimum management charge. I also realize that no management firm would ever take on this particular building for only $600 per year. However, I am making this subtraction to show that it properly should be made. I also know that an investor would have to

276

spend much more than $50.00 per month, in time alone, to actually manage this turkey of a building.

ESTIMATED EXPENSES:

(a) TAXES—The tax bill indicated of $2,046.96 is far out of line and much too low for the alleged gross income figure of $13,560. The fact is that cities in my area are assessing income property between 20 percent and 30 percent of their reported gross income, the usual, typical percentage being 25 percent of the gross income. Quite obviously, where this tax bill is given as only about 15 percent of gross income, only one of two situations must be the truth. Either the seller is reporting gross income to the taxing authorities at several thousand dollars less than he is reporting his income on his selling statement, or he is paying off a friend for preferential treatment which the buyer cannot expect to get for nothing—or perhaps be able to obtain at all.

Accordingly, we must correct our tax bill on our reconstructed statement by increasing it to a more realistic amount of 25 percent of the gross income on the statement, or $3,390.

(b) MORTGAGE INTEREST—Note that the interest, only, on the four mortgages is listed on the statement. However, each and every month the new buyer would have to make payments to the first, second and third mortgages of principal as well as interest. These principal expense items for the year—completely omitted—amount to:

1st mtg. principal	$1,492.87
2nd mtg. principal	504.00
3rd mtg. principal	210.00
Total annual principal charges on mortgages	$3,206.87

(This must be added to the mortgage interest expense shown.)

Accordingly, we must add cash outlay of $3,206.87 on our reconstructed statement for annual mortgage principal payments. Please note that while, in the end, these principal payments on the mortgages represent savings, the new buyer would be obliged to pay them each year.

(c) HEAT—This type of apartment involved in our problem should cost in the Boston area between $150 and $200 per year. Since there are 14 apartments, I am going to increase the $1,750 annual heating expense indicated to $2,450.

(d) ELECTRIC—This is for hall lights and the motors on the oil burners. I am pleased to see the $150 which I shall accept. Incidentally, on 99 percent of all statements the figure is listed at only $50.00 for some unexplained reason.

(e) WATER—The $300 figure for 14 apartments means about $21.00 per year per apartment which is comparable for actual charges in the area. I shall accept this water expense figure.

(f) INSURANCE—The $552.48 figure seems low. I am certain that $1,250 would be a more realistic minimum figure for 14 units of this type. That would only be about $89.00 per unit. Remember, our "shoe-string" buyer will not be getting a special rate from a blanket policy covering many buildings. Our buyer is going to need a lot of personal liability protection. He will not be able to afford the risk of a low price $250 deductible policy.

Our buyer will have a larger investment to protect than the previous owner had.

In any event an adjusted new increased amount of $1,250 would still be a modest estimate for this kind of property.

(g) JANITOR—The $240 figure, amounting to only $20.00 per month or less than $5.00 per week, is unrealistically low. A $900 amount would not be high enough, but it would at least be more realistic.

We have now reconstructed all the expenses indicated. Before we list the many expenses *not shown*, let's see how much we must already increase the indicated total of $9,197.11 expense figure on this ridiculous statement.

NEW RECONSTRUCTED FAIR EXPENSES

Taxes	$3,390.00
Total mortgage payments	7,364.54
Heat	2,450.00
Electric	150.00
Water	300.00
Insurance	1,250.00
Janitor	600.00
Total actual expenses for those items admitted and listed.	$15,504.54

Please note that already, *before* we begin to include many real expense items *not even listed,* our reconstructed figures *so far* amount to a total expense increase of $6,607.43 annually. This, alone, is enough to completely wipe out the deliberately deceitful alleged net cash income of $4,362.89. In fact, so far, we now have a real cash deficit of $2,244.54 annually. However, this is only the beginning of the falseness, fraud, and huge annual out-of-pocket expenses really involved in this monstrous fabrication of a building statement.

278

SOME ADDITIONAL EXPENSES NOT EVEN LISTED ON THE STATEMENT

(a) *Supplies*—estimated	$240.00
(b) *Miscellaneous*—estimated	240.00
(c) *Repairs*—to component parts of the buildings plus furnishings and equipment @ 5% of alleged gross income (a very conservative figure for these buildings)	668.00

(d) *Annual Reserves for replacement of component parts of the buildings:*

—roof (total cost $5,000—20 year life)	250.00
—two boilers (total cost $6,000—20 yr. life)	300.00
—exterior paint (total cost $4,000—5 year life)	800.00

(e) *Annual Reserves for replacement of furnishings and equipment*

Note: (very limited for these ancient buildings)

—14 stoves @ $150 each—10 year life	210.00
—14 refrigerators @ $150 each—10 year life	210.00
—linoleum in halls and stairways $2,000—7 yr. life	286.00
—interior paint and decoration for 56 rooms @ $35.00 per room every two years	980.00

(f) 5% interest a bank would pay you on your cash invested	206.40

Total of some additional expense items not listed on statement:	$4,390.40

It is interesting to note that a conservative allowance just for the expenses these bandit sellers and brokers do not even bother to list on their statements comes—in this case—to $4,390.40, or actually more cash outlay than the phony alleged cash income on the statement.

Our total cash out-of-pocket *annual loss* on this particular "turkey" that was being peddled as such a winner now amounts to $6,634.94.

Will somebody please tell me where the additional cash is going to come from to retire the balloon balances on those four mortgages as they become due? Amen!

MORE SELLER AND BROKER TRICKS YOU MUST GUARD AGAINST

1. Many professional speculators deliberately buy a building where either the building or the owner, or both, are in a distress situation.

They then proceed to pack the building with students (who will wreck it) to drive up the total gross annual income. Now, they offer the building to a virgin buyer whom they call a "cherry" at a very appealing price in relation to the gross income of the building.

For this reason you must be sure that the alleged rent schedule represents fair economic rent for similar accommodations in the area.

2. The smart seller knows that you can check existing tenants yourself, and demand verified accountant statements of income for income tax purposes. So the rents you have to watch very closely are the ones claimed for the vacancies.

Just talk with the next door tenants. You may be surprised to find, as I often have, that an existing tenant is paying much less for better quarters than what you are being told you will get for the vacancy.

3. Expect increased assessment and taxes if there has been recent substantial remodeling or additions. Always check the assessment at the city hall.

4. Does the building violate the local zoning ordinances?

5. Are there complaints on the building for violation of building codes at the city building inspector's office?

6. Remember, you could be considering the purchase of a five-unit building that is actually being assessed and taxed as only three units, yet the building may actually be in only a two-family zoned area.

7. You must have a professional builder check out the property for you. Remember you are buying, as is, in a basically *caveat emptor* (let the buyer beware) legal situation.

8. Be especially on the alert for the infiltration of deleterious neighborhood influences. Assuming the building itself checks out okay, this could be the very reason the owner is selling.

9. Get it in writing! Remember all those oral promises the seller or broker made are normally washed out by the subsequent written agreement. Of course, you can always sue for damages for intentional deceit—if you can prove it. And you can usually sue for rescission of the contract and a return of your money for even *innocent* misrepresentation of a material fact. But who wants to have to win a lawsuit?

10. *Never, never* turn over money or sign anything for a seller or broker without approval from your own lawyer. All of my experience amounts to constant reaffirmation of one basic fact: Wherever a dollar is involved *no* seller or broker should ever be trusted, without advice and protection from the *only one* capable of, and inclined to, protect your interests—*your own attorney.*

Chapter 67

MAKE THE BIG SCORE THROUGH LEVERAGE

This country is full of scared little people who lacked the guts to buy or hold on to real estate investments that would have made them independently wealthy today.

These are the millions of weaklings who carry high-priced, high-cost permanent, single homes, plus recreation homes for growing numbers, like monkeys on their backs—but *never invested* five cents in income real estate. Their wives, children, mothers-in-law and others conned them into thinking they were doing the right thing, and the "big thing," but they succeeded only in preventing them from ever doing the real thing—which should have been making an easy killing in real estate.

The reason for this chapter, the tenth and final way to make your killing, is to explain the difference between real estate investment and real estate speculation; to indicate why the big score is in investment rather than speculation; and, hence, why you should never sell a winner. If you need cash you do what experienced, seasoned, sophisticated investors do—refinance.

If you buy real estate for income and long-term holding for the big score, you are an investor. If you buy for a quick resale profit you are a speculator.

Of course, many speculators do all right for themselves. But many more than you realize never get to the top or stay there for long if they do get there. This group includes the vast army of speculator builders the great majority of whom have notoriously encountered bankruptcy somewhere in their risky short-profit operations.

The big score has always been in long-term investment for income. If you invest according to the principles outlined in this book, you could never be wiped out. You would make so much more annual cash return on your cash investment than you possibly could from any other safe investment that it would well pay you to even borrow the money to get started, as from your own cash value in your life insurance policy.

It works out like this:

1. You make a $5,000 loan on the cash value in your life insurance policy (the protection of the policy is still there). Interest charges for this ideal type of borrowing your own money often run only five percent. Assuming six percent interest *the cost of your loan to get started is only $300 a year.*

2. For $30,000 you purchase your first investment, a four-family structure. *Your required cash down payment is only $3,000* because you bought F.H.A. or otherwise used buying principles outlined in earlier chapters. This leaves you $2,000 for a cash emergency reserve fund.

3. Here is the way you now make out like a bandit:

$1,000 annual net cash return from building, after all expenses, including financing (when you buy according to this book as many of my clients are doing).

less $300 annual cost of your loan to buy building.

net $700 annual net cash return from building. (This is cash you would never get each year without starting real estate investment.)

plus $1,350 average annual savings on your $27,000 twenty-year direct reduction mortgage. This is known as using the bank's money and letting your tenants pay off the loan.

plus $710 annual three percent appreciation in value of building due to inflation. This is conservatively estimated, if you buy according to this book.

The United States government has just announced the current inflation rate—average for the country—at *five percent*.

Total: $2,760 annual net returns from your first building. In addition you receive preferential tax deductions for depreciation (while your building is actually increasing in value due to creeping inflation), plus other tax shelters unavailable in any other type of investment.

One thing is certain. You will never make the profit outlined above, if you never make the investment. Remember, this is only the *beginning* to making your killing.

NEVER SELL A WINNER

The sophisticated investors I know would sooner sell their wife or mother before they would sell their buildings. There are many sound reasons for holding these fortune building properties. Some of them are as follows:

1. Every time you sell off a building you decrease your net worth and so destroy some of your borrowing power.

2. Every time you sell, you face a capital gain tax problem. When you refinance you get tax-free cash. I don't know of any better way to generate tax-free cash.

3. When you refinance you frequently retire secondary financing, thus driving your annual expenses down and your annual net profit up.

4. Refinancing often permits upgrading the value of the building, and

upgrading the rental income, through modernization and improvements of present units or even the addition of new units.

5. It takes a lot of time, effort, and money to find a winner. If you were to sell it the cost of replacement would be high and hazardous.

PYRAMID YOUR HOLDINGS

Instead of selling a winner, refinance. Then use some of the tax-free cash you get from the refinancing to make a small investment in an additional building. This is precisely the way the smart operators get big, powerful, and wealthy.

MAKE THE BIG SCORE THROUGH LEVERAGE

If you stop to analyze it, the reason you do so well with income property and so poorly with 100 percent high-cost, liability-laden single homes, is that your home represents only depletion of your present income and opportunity of ever-increasing expenses. You never can realize any regular annual income from your personal dwelling, even though inflation drives up the value of your home (as you wear it out) and allows you to live partially rent free. So your *first* income property investment is a very important and necessary step for you to take, if you ever hope to get rich.

By the same token, a four-family structure is always a better income and more profitable deal than a three-family building. As we have noted earlier, two-family buildings just do not "appraise out" for absentee owners. This phenomenon is known as leverage.

Increasing your leverage means that, just as investing $5,000 in a four-family income structure is infinitely more profitable than putting this cash into a single or two-family dwelling, in the same manner, if you could buy eight income units for the same $5,000 cash down you would be that much further ahead.

Your big gains through leverage, or getting the maximum number of income units for the same amount of cash invested, include the following advantages:

1. Higher annual net cash returns, because gross income is larger while expenses of each unit are relatively lower.

2. Larger savings through amortization of bigger, or more, mortgages.

3. More annual appreciation in value—as three percent on a total

value of $50,000 is $1,500, but three percent annual appreciation in value of a $30,000 building would be only $900.

4. Bigger income tax deduction for greater depreciation allowance on the larger valued building.

5. Larger total tax shelters.

6. Greater advantages for tax-free exchanges.

7. Greater net worth.

8. Greater borrowing power.

Why not start *now?*

<u>INCOME PROPERTY BUYER'S CHECK LIST</u>

TYPE BUILDING:

Address :

Assess: $_____ 19____ tax rate: $_____ per M_____

Mortgages: 1st. - $_____ at____ % int. & _____ **Prin.** Term:_____

Orig. Am't._____ Orig. Term:_____

2nd. - $_____ at____ % int. & _____ Prin. Term:_____

3rd. - $_____ at____ % int. & _____ Prin. Term:_____

(SEE RENT ROLL - OTHER SIDE)

Rent Range:

N o. of Apts.

Adjusted Effective, Total Annual Income $_____
(Gross Fair Rent, Less Vacancy &
Mgt. Expense)

Furnished?	No. Leases:	Taxes.....................$_____
Stoves:	Refrigs.:	1st. Mtg. Int. ....$_____
		1st. Mtg. Prin..........$_____
Sinks:	Air Cond,:	2nd. Mtg. Int............$_____
		2nd. Mtg. Prin..........$_____
Incinerator:	Disposals:	3rd. Mtg. Int............$_____
		3rd. Mtg. Prin..........$_____
No. Baths:	Type Baths:	Heat.....................$_____
		Electricity..............$_____
Type Heat:	Who Supplies Heat?	Gas......................$_____
		Water....................$_____
No. Boilers:	Type of Hot Water?	Insurance................$_____
		Janitor..................$_____
Condition:		Supplies.................$_____
		Maintenance..............$_____
Age of Prop.:	Remod.: When:	Miscellaneous............$_____
		Reserve for Parts of
Rock Bottom Price:$_____		building.................$_____
		Reserve for Furniture &
Lowest Cash Down: $_____		Equipment ....$_____

VALUE OF LAND?

Total Expenses: $_____

Net Income: $_____

Total Prin. Savings: $_____

Total Net Income: $_____

Notes: Recent Improvements? Condition of Exterior, Interior?
What Is Vacancy History of Building?
What is Remaining Economic Life of Building?
Is Price - Gross Income Ratio comparable for area?
What capitalization Rate is Justified (See Chapter 63)

Owner's Name: Address:

Home Tel. No.:   Bus. Tel. No.:   Exclusive: Date will expire:

NOTE: This enables you to start appraising the fair market value of the building. See
Chapter 63. If the building appraises out, have a builder check it out.
See your lawyer before signing anything or turning over money.

RENT ROLL

FAIR RENT	APT. NO.	Tenant	No.Rms.	Yrs. Occ.	Actual Rent	Leases (security deposits, Tax Clauses)

INCOME PROPERTY BUYER'S APPRAISAL FORM

Property address_____City_____

Legal description_____

Name of owner_____Phone_____

Address_____City_____

INCOME ANALYSIS

No. of similar units	Room Count Per Unit	Sq.Ft. Area Per Unit	NOTES (if furnished, etc)	Actual Rent Per Unit	Fair Rent Per Unit	Total Monthly Fair Rent
				$	$	$

Furniture value $_____ Effective age of building___years Gross monthly fair
Land value $_____ Remaining life of building___years rent $_____
                                                      (Multiply by 12 and enter on
                                                       line 1 below)

ANNUAL EXPENSES

FIXED CHARGES:
Real estate tax....................$_____
Personal property tax.............$_____
Insurance.........................$_____
Other.............................$_____

OPERATING EXPENSES:
Electric..........................$_____
Water ....$_____
Fuel..............................$_____
Janitor...........................$_____
Advertising and leasing...........$_____
Building maintenance..............$_____
Furniture and equipment maintenance$_____
Ground Care.......................$_____
Swimming pool service.............$_____
Snow Removal......................$_____
Supplies..........................$_____
Miscellaneous.....................$_____

RESERVE FOR REPLACEMENTS:
Building components................$_____
Furniture and equipment...........$_____
Misc..............................$_____

TOTAL ANNUAL EXPENSES............$_____

APPRAISAL PROCESS

1. ANNUAL RAW GROSS INCOME..$_____
2. Vacancy allowance
   @ ___% (of annual gross..$_____
3. ANNUAL EFFECTIVE GROSS INCOME
   (line 1 minus line 2)..... $_____
4. Management fee............ $_____
5. TRUE GROSS INCOME FROM PROPERTY
   (line 3 minus line 4).....$_____
6. Total annual expenses.....$_____
7. ANNUAL NET INCOME
   (line 5 minus line 6)....$_____
8. Expected return on Land
   investment___% of land
   value.......................$_____
9. Expected return on
   furniture investment
   ___% of furniture value.$_____
10. INCOME RESIDUAL TO BUILDING
    IMPROVEMENTS
    (line 7 minus sum of lines
    8 & 9)....................$_____
11. CAPITALIZATION:
    A. Expected rate of
       return_____%
    B. Amortization rate
       _____%
    C. Total capitalization
       rate   _____%

12. CAPITALIZED VALUE OF
    BUILDING IMPROVEMENTS
    (line 10 divided by line 11C)$_____
13. Land value.............$_____
14. CAPITALIZED VALUE OF TOTAL
    PROPERTY UNFURNISHED
    (line 12 plus line 13). $_____
15. Furniture value........ $_____
16. CAPITALIZED VALUE OF
    PROPERTY INCLUDING
    FURNITURE
    (line 14 plus line 15)...$_____
THIS IS THE FAIR MARKET VALUE

PART V

How the Broker Makes His Money

Chapter 68

WHAT THE BROKER MUST DO TO EARN A COMMISSION HE CAN ENFORCE

In most states to enforce a commission claim a broker must sustain the burden of proving that he is licensed, that he had the listing at the time of the sale, and that he was the efficient procuring cause of the sale. A few states have already added a greater burden upon the broker. In New Jersey, it is illegal for a broker to charge a commission unless the sale culminates in a closing. In Massachusetts, if there is a purchase and sale agreement, then the sale must culminate in a closing, unless the closing was prevented by the seller. In Texas the broker must prove that there was a listing in writing. Oral listings are illegal. Unfortunately for the brokers, many of the common beliefs held by them and laymen are false.

Too many brokers fail to take the precaution to obtain a listing from the seller before they introduce a buyer to him. In a highly interesting Massachusetts case an over-eager broker sold a golf course only to find his claim for a sales commission thrown out of court because he neglected to take the trouble of getting hired to make the sale.

However, the most troublesome area in most of our states concerns what constitutes the broker being the *efficient procuring cause of the sale*. The day is fast drawing to a close where any state will protect a broker in a commission claim just because he was the first broker involved, and a sale was subsequently made to his buyer by a succeeding broker or directly by the seller. In more and more states it is not enough for the broker to be the first broker, or to have been a contributing cause of the sale. In these states, if they do not in fact insist on the plaintiff

288

broker producing the actual closing, they at least require the broker to prove that he was the actual procuring cause of the sale. The majority view is that to hold otherwise would expose the seller to multi commission suits from all brokers who merely attempted to make the sale.

Courts have held that a broker could not collect his commission in the following cases: where the listing was revoked in writing two months before the seller sold directly to the buyer admittedly originally produced by the broker; where the broker had not actively worked with his buyer for a period of six months and this was considered abandonment of effort.

Chapter 69

HOW THE BROKER GETS HIS LISTINGS

1. By systematically telephoning residents area by area.
2. Following all newspaper owner ads.
3. Getting help from local businessmen who cater to large numbers of restaurant owners or managers, debit insurance men, bartenders and beauticians.
4. Getting help from church officials or club and organization officials.
5. Getting help from sellers of new development houses; their buyers could be his sellers.
6. From sign painters who may be painting "For Sale by Owner" signs."
7. Looking for "Sale" signs on the property. 27 percent of all sellers don't use brokers. Even if the house was originally given to a broker exclusively, the chances are great that the exclusive has already terminated or will soon.
8. Following up closely all houses with "Sold" signs on them, or houses reported to have been sold. Even good brokers fail to close some of their sales due to lack of financing, buyers chickening out, and so on.
9. Getting help from mortgage banker friends for tips on homeowners who are seeking appraisals or are in financial hot water, or face foreclosure, as well as appraisal rejects or buyer rejects.

10. Cultivating appraisers in the area who can give valuable tips.

11. Tips from second mortgage lenders. They can tell who is being forced to sell.

12. Asking residents or children on each block where the house is on that block that is for sale. If they confirm that no house on that block is for sale, you know to move on to the next block.

13. Asking buyers what they have seen for sale.

14. Advertising for listings.

BEST BETS FOR INCOME PROPERTY LISTINGS

1. Most income property buyers already own some investment property which they will always sell for a price—especially if they have already upgraded the property, or they seek a capital gain tax, or they are anxious to get into "something bigger." In any event your buyers are your best source of listings.

2. Whenever you see a building which you believe you can sell, ask the janitor or superintendent for the name and address and 'phone number of the owner. With janitors and "supers," like headwaiters, a five-spot will work wonders and frequently yield much valuable information.

3. Once you get to the income property owner and ask for the listing, most of them will retort that they will sell their mother for a price, indicating that they could be interested in a high offer. Don't be afraid to take overpriced listings. Most of these sellers are forced to sell eventually at fair market value.

Chapter 70

HOW THE BROKER GETS THE SELLER DOWN IN PRICE

Most listings are taken at unrealistically high prices for the following five reasons:

1. Most sellers allow themselves some lead time to try to extort an

unfair profit from an ignorant or compulsive buyer, at the expense of any willing broker who comes along.

2. Most brokers are too green about appraisal know-how when they are listing too high above fair market value.

3. Most brokers are too eager to please the seller and get an exclusive right to sell the house.

4. Most brokers list the house too rapidly to be able to justify the "right" price. Often they merely take the listing over the telephone or rush through the house.

5. Many seasoned brokers deliberately take the listing at a high price, especially if it is an open listing, then break the price with a low offer when they get a buyer. They feel that this way the house is safe from getting sold until they have enough time to come up with the right buyer and win the commission.

Obviously it is far better in the end for all concerned if the listing comes on the market at the right price—the fair market value. Next to having enough listings the most important thing that the money-making broker has is listings at the right price—a salable price. To accomplish this the broker must be prepared in advance when he goes out to take a listing. A telephone call to the assessor's office, or a personal visit when necessary, will arm the broker with invaluable information. He will know who really owns the house, what the assessed value is, what percentage of fair market value the town assessor normally uses on this type of parcel, how many square feet of land there is, what the frontage really is, and what the book and page is at the Registry of Deeds or town hall so he can find out from the state revenue stamps affixed to the deed exactly how much the present owner paid for the property (usually about $1.00 for each $500 or fraction thereof of the sales price or amount of equity transferred). Next, the good broker checks his comparable sales file to know in advance of his call how much similar parcels in the area recently sold for, and just what was actually contained in those parcels.

Now, and only now, is the listing broker in a position to intelligently and successfully take the listing. The broker should casually estimate the square footage of the lot and the assessed value and tax bill in front of the seller who will be both amazed and impressed with his professionalism and accuracy. Remember a good lawyer wins his case by burning the midnight oil *before* he goes into court.

Taking plenty of time going through the house with the seller, the broker points out all the disadvantages from a buyer's or bank or government appraiser's viewpoint.

The following list is only a sample of what should be covered and emphasized:

1. bad location due to commercial or industrial influence, and so forth
2. proximity of inferior houses
3. infiltration of inharmonious influences
4. high steps to climb
5. poor drainage on the lot
6. not enough yard space
7. lack of garage
8. no playroom or family room
9. no fireplace
10. insufficient interior wall space
11. rooms too small
12. ceilings too high
13. excessive deferred maintenance
14. old fashioned bathroom or not enough bathrooms
15. outmoded kitchen or lack of eating area in kitchen
16. inferior plumbing and heating
17. inferior wiring and electrical capacity
18. unwanted siding, such as asbestos or asphalt shingles
19. worn out roof (average good life is only twenty years)
20. water leaks
21. poor room layout such as: direct entrance into living room or kitchen, no through hall, having to enter a bedroom through another bedroom, bad location of bathroom, etc.
22. excessive bone-structure physical depreciation due to great age (appraisers generally allow only a total of fifty years for the useful economic life of a house)
23. functional obsolescence
24. shortage of closet space
25. inadequate workroom or storage space
26. lack of insulation
27. too much snow to shovel or grass to cut
28. lack of shade trees
29. absence of porches
30. absence of storm windows
31. inferior schools or great distance to schools
32. lack of transportation
33. distance to stores, churches, libraries, recreational facilities
34. declining neighborhood
35. high tax bill

The professional broker uses the above shortcomings, and much more, to his advantage in securing a realistic, salable price on a house. To do this effectively and successfully he always prefaces his bad-news remarks with compliments to Mrs. Kitooli for the cleanliness of her home, or the good behavior or good looks of her children. And the minus factors are always the opinion of the current crop of buyers and not the broker's own personal opinion.

It is extremely important for the broker to be sure that Mrs. Kitooli understands how little her neighbor's house actually sold for, compared to the high asking price.

Finally, it would be well for the broker to understand that it is far more economical to take the needed hour or two to list the house at a price at which it will sell, than to rush through in five or ten minutes and list it at a price which will break him in time and money and failure to sell.

Chapter 71

HOW THE BROKER SELLS OVERPRICED PROPERTIES

The broker advertises and sells the following points:
1. Low down payment
2. Low monthly payment
3. Any unique feature about the house
4. Arranges a take-over of a low interest rate present mortgage, including a second mortgage taken by the seller if necessary.
5. If he can't push the house, he pushes the location.
6. Gets the buyer to like the house before he lets him know what the price is.
7. Emphasizes a low tax bill (an average $9.00 a month saved on the tax bill affords an extra $1,000 on the mortgage).
8. If the buyer objects to the seller's price the broker asks him if he is prepared to make an offer and give a deposit at his price.
9. If necessary, the broker waits until the seller has used up the lead time he has allowed himself, or until he gets himself into a financial bind and begins to "see the light."
10. The successful broker accepts a commission cut only as a last

resort. He never prematurely permits this to happen. He never forgets that in a tight squeeze the fellow who holds out the longest nearly always prevails.

Chapter 72

HOW THE BROKER CONVINCES THE SELLER TO ACCEPT A FAIR OFFER

The broker emphasizes the following points to the seller:

1. If he is fortunate enough to run quickly into a fair offer, he makes sure that the seller does not feel he will get more by waiting. Before submitting the offer he makes certain that the seller knows about the many people who would want to pay less, or would not buy his house at any price. One of the biggest problems a broker can have with a seller is to sell his house too fast.

2. Makes the cash deposit as large and tempting as possible.

3. Arranges for an unusually fast closing. Emphasizes the certainty of the closing.

4. Arranges for a substantial payment—all to the seller—in the event of buyer's default.

5. Gives the seller an "out" if the buyer cannot show a letter of committal for bank financing at an early date.

6. Gets the buyer to take some furniture or furnishings not really wanted by the seller, to provide additional cash.

7. Emphasizes the buyer's need, his appreciation for the property, his inability to pay more and what an asset he will be to the seller's neighbors. Remember there are still many good and proud people left in this hard world.

8. Makes sure the seller knows that the buyer has his eye on an alternate property where he would be getting a fabulous break.

9. Emphasizes that any delay will be costly to the seller whether he realizes it or not. Time alone is worth money. So are heat bills, tax bills, maintenance, advertising and so forth.

10. The next offer could be lower as well as higher.

11. Buyers become skeptical of a house that lingers on the market. They know that if it is priced right it will sell fast.

12. Reviews thoroughly all the shortcomings and minus factors about the house as brought up by buyers who would not even go inside, or buy the house at all.

13. Writes out a check by the buyer for the full amount of the offer made out to the seller. Places it in the seller's hand. Asks him as a favor to imagine for a moment that he has deposited this check in his account at the bank, Now, ask him if, knowing what he knows about the house, would he withdraw this amount from his bank account to purchase this house?

14. If he still has not won an acceptance, reminds the seller that a bird in the hand is worth two in the bush, and asks him to sleep on it.

15. He makes sure the seller understands that legally the buyer has a right to withdraw the offer anytime before acceptance has been communicated to him.

16. He makes sure the seller fully realizes that legally an offer once rejected can never be revived; that any later change of heart and subsequent acceptance would only amount to a counter-offer which the buyer would then have the right to accept or reject?

17. Never cuts his commission except as a last resort, and it is his honest opinion that he is sure to lose the sale altogether if he doesn't.

Chapter 73

HOW THE BROKER WINS HIS FULL COMMISSION

In recent years under the present wave of consumerism, the Anti-Trust Division of the U.S. Attorney General's Office has investigated complaints about real estate broker associations fixing prices charged for brokerage commissions. The result is that it is now illegal for Realtor Boards, or anyone else, to recommend a standard brokerage fee. As a matter of law the amount of a broker's commission has always been according to the private agreement between the broker and the seller.

However, most sellers are not aware of this and do not question the customary standard charge of 6 or 7% asked by the broker.

As a practical matter, the seller usually allows the broker to set the selling price of the house for sale. The broker determines the rock bottom price that he thinks the seller will take, then he adds his regular commission, plus a little leverage for the buyer who wants something knocked off the price. This type of buyer requires this "preacher's discount." Most brokers avoid "net listings" which give a guaranteed net amount to the seller. Thus, they collect their standard percentage on the actual sale price which is nearly always less than the "asking" price. And this is the practice no matter how low the actual sale price is.

Many brokers generally refuse to list a house at a price less than what will provide their standard commission to them. However, most of them will cut their commission at the end of negotiations if they are forced to in order to save the sale.

Often brokers will tell the seller that they are "not allowed" to take less than a regular, standard commission, and that if they do they will certainly be blackballed by their local broker association. Generally, these broker trade associations called, "Realtor Boards" permit their broker members to take off one percent for a builder, and consider it pardonable for a broker to take off one percent for an exclusive listing.

Finally, brokers realize that they must get full commissions in order to survive, and that if they hold out long enough either the seller or buyer will give in and agree on a price including the broker's full commission. After all the seller and buyer do not want to lose the deal either.

Chapter 74

HOW THE BROKER HANDLES BUYERS

The broker knows that he is the legal agent of the seller and owes his principal, *the seller*, a fiduciary duty to act in *his* best interest, *not the buyer's best interest*. He knows that the law considers him to be in an "arms length transaction" with the buyer. However, as a practical matter, the broker depends on the buyer to provide him his living and often "gets in bed with the buyer," often at the expense of the seller.

The following tips, gleaned from much front line experience, which I have used in training thousands of brokers on the best ways to handle buyers should provide a useful insight to all buyers and sellers.

1. Have the best possible salesman, or the manager, answer that telephone inquiry or handle that "walk-in."

2. Get the buyer relaxed before you start working him over. Take his coat. Offer him a comfortable seat, a cigarette, a cold drink in summer, a cup of hot coffee in winter. If he is coming in over the telephone, be friendly, cooperative, alert. Do not evade him. Answer directly. Remember, he has to relax and let his guard down before you can start selling him anything.

3. His first image of you is a mighty important one, usually a lasting picture of you, and may be the only one he will ever bother to get of you if you are not very careful and on the ball.

4. Remember that being friendly, cooperative and trying to create a good first impression does not mean abject capitulation or giving up without a fight.

5. Never tell the buyer over the telephone, or in the office, so much about the house that he feels no need to go out and see it. Don't keep talking so much that you are bound to hit upon some fact that will convince him he doesn't want the house.

6. Remember, you must show the house in order to sell it. The most eager buyer in the world is not going to buy the house without seeing it, but he can easily decide not to see it. Accordingly, everything you say or do must be calculated to get the buyer out to see the house as soon as possible—before the house is sold, or the buyer is sold by a harder-working broker.

7. Never unnecessarily delay or postpone a showing just to suit your convenience. Next Tuesday afternoon may be easier for you, but it may also be too late to sell the house. The buyer or the house or both may not be around by then.

8. Qualify the buyer whenever possible and as much as possible before taking him out of the office. To facilitate this all-important screening process direct him to meet you at your office if he is telephoning in.

9. Take him out in your car, or you go in his car, if at all possible.

10. Presell him on the house before you get there. Inspection should merely be for the purpose of confirming what you have already advised him, for example that this house is the best buy in a $25,000 three-bedroom ranch in your town this year.

11. Lead him through the property. End up in the most favorable spot in or outside the house.

12. Keep the owner out of the way. He may talk too much.

13. Ask the buyer if he likes the house. If he says no, ask him why. Then try to remove the now known impediment to the sale. If you can't do this, move on to your preselected "play-off" house that now appears to be more suitable for him. If he says he likes the house, ask him to go right back to your office so you can make arrangements for him to get the house before someone else in the office, or some other broker, sells it, and it is too late.

14. If he says he likes it, but not at the seller's price, suggest that you go right back to the office and draw up an offer at his price.

15. When you pull up to a stop in front of your office, get out of the car fast and go inside. Remember you can't sell him in the car, only in the office. And he can always change his mind about coming inside, due to the lateness of the hour, his family not being with him, or just plain fear which creeps up on every buyer the moment he begins to think about buying. If you start entering the office, he will follow you in.

16. When you get inside go to the closing room, free from interruption, and start writing out an offer blank or a purchase and sale agreement.

17. Don't stop filling it in until he makes you stop. Don't say anything—just start writing. If he has not started to talk by now, fill in the full price. He has to either sign it or tell you what price he wants you to start at.

18. If the buyer's offer seems low, tell him you are willing to go to the seller and ask him to come down in price as long as the buyer understands that he may have to come up to get the house. Tell the buyer that it is your job as the broker to negotiate the sale, and that negotiation usually means a compromise where both parties give in something to effect a sale. Assure him that you will do your very best for him.

19. When the seller greets you with open arms, kisses you and quickly accepts the buyer's low offer it is all right for you to feel pleasantly surprised, and promptly leave for your office before the seller changes his mind. Just don't expect the buyer to be overjoyed at a fast acceptance of his low offer. He is likely to feel that he did not come in low enough, become unhappy, and perhaps even try to back off the deal in an effort to wring some further concession from an apparently desperate seller. There is something about human nature that causes many people to want to take every advantage of their fellow man, push him to the wall and exact the last pound of flesh. Accordingly in circumstances like these the seasoned broker waits overnight to explain to the buyer

the next day how long and hard he had to fight with the seller to get him to accept this low offer.

20. It is most important to move the buyer along fast and keep getting him further committed so that it becomes harder for him to back out of the deal than it would be to go forward to a final closing.

21. Remember that if the buyer ever gets a chance to bring in an expert to advise him, that the expert may be Uncle Tim, "who bought a house once himself." In any event, the expert will nearly always try to prove to the buyer how lucky he was to come to him so that he could save the buyer from utter disaster. All you can do is try to move the buyer along so fast that he feels committed or *is* committed before Uncle Tim gets into the act.

22. It is a waste of time, as a rule, to show the house to the husband alone. It is usually twice as difficult to please both the husband and wife together on a first showing. Normally, it is much easier to show and sell the wife alone. Then she sells her husband. This is better than you having to sell him. It is a lot easier for him to say no to you than to his own wife.

23. Always show the buyer clearly that you are fully and properly protecting him on the offer form, or in the contract to buy. For example, he deserves the protection of a financing escape clause which gives him an out if he can't raise the amount of mortgage he will need. Also, excessive and burdensome default penalties should be avoided if there is no actual fault on his part. It would be best if you did not plan on taking anything for yourself unless the deal is consummated. I have always operated on this basis and I know that it has paid me not only in personal satisfaction, but in business as well.

24. Never place the buyer's mortgage for him just to control the sale or win a finder's fee from the bank, unless you can do at least as well as the terms the buyer could get for himself.

25. Hold the deposit in escrow and spell out to the buyer the following: If the deposit money were paid directly to the seller or builder, he might use it, only to run into trouble when he finds out later that the bank or the V.A. or the F.H.A. rejected the deal, or that he himself cannot perform. With the money in escrow and a fairly drawn contract of sale the buyer is protected, and is entitled to the return of his deposit.

Chapter 75

HOW THE BROKER CLOSES THE DEAL

The broker uses the following arguments to close the seller:

1. He tells the seller that he cannot safely commit himself to a contract to buy his new house without knowing for sure that he has his present house sold. Asks him if he can afford to risk having to pay for two houses at the same time.

2. How much longer can he afford putting off the contract to buy his new house without losing it?

3. Suppose he has to move to his new job, alone, and leave the family behind?

4. That he is facing a tax increase which will make his house that much harder to sell later.

5. That if he has to leave his house empty, all the defects will become glaringly apparent, and it will be harder to sell.

6. If the husband has already been transferred and moved on alone, does she want to remain behind any longer than necessary? Will even a little more money later on really be worth it?

7. That the next offer could be lower as well as higher.

8. That some brokers are already charging 7 percent sales commission, but he is still holding to 6 percent until he is forced to go up.

9. That the prices on new houses are going up 15 percent this year. If he has not sold his house yet, how can he expect to get 15 percent more for his present house?

10. That as this country's commitments to contain communism increase—as they certainly shall—shortages and other restrictions on the availability of new housing are bound to develop. Why not get his new house now while he can?

11. That certain inflation ahead may bar him from being able to afford his new house, but by buying now he could cash in on this inflation.

12. That mortgage money is getting tighter than ever, since the banks can lend their money more profitably in other types of loans. And rates are bound to go up on new mortgages. This can also cause buyers to offer him even less later on.

13. That any delay will mean a new paint job, new roof or new heating system, etc.

14. That the market is getting tighter and buyers just aren't coming out. And it looks like it is going to get worse before it gets better.

15. That a bird in the hand is worth two in the bush. Bread that we throw away today, we may wish for tomorrow.

16. That if we reject this offer now from the buyer to try to force him up, we may lose him altogether, since he could then decide to forget the whole thing. And there would be no chance to go back to the seller for further instructions.

17. That the buyer's bank has already told him that he is paying top dollar (or too much) now.

18. That this is the first buyer willing to make any offer at any price.

19. That if he had the amount of this offer safely in his bank account, he would never draw it out to buy his house.

20. That after all he does not have to accept the offer, or the deposit. You can always return it to the buyer and let him buy something else.

21. That the buyer has to know one way or the other as he has another opportunity pending.

22. That the V.A. will probably appraise the property for even less than this offer.

23. That the F.H.A. will probably appraise the house for even less.

24. That this is a conventional deal with a big cash down payment and nothing could prevent a fast closing.

25. That the buyer will increase his deposit substantially immediately upon acceptance of the offer.

26. That maybe the buyer would pay him extra cash for some of the things he planned to leave anyway.

27. That the fair market value of his house—that is, what an informed buyer will be willing to pay him—has nothing to do with his original cost, or what his new home will cost.

28. That he cannot expect to regain the whole cost of all the repairs and improvements he has added.

29. That, after all, he did raise his family in his house and has enjoyed free rent for many years.

30. That a house normally has only a fifty-year total economic life, and that the remaining economic life of his house is very short indeed. That his house by appraisal standards is loaded with bone structure depreciation, deferred maintenance and functional obsolescence.

31. That the neighborhood is declining in value.

32. That banks just aren't taking older houses anymore, or asbestos siding or locations adjacent to commercial or industrial influences.

33. Asks the seller to give him something to go back to the buyer with, rather than lose him altogether.

The broker uses the following arguments to close the buyer.

1. Appeals to his built-in conviction that, after all, you get what you

pay for, a higher price in the beginning usually means a lower price in the end, and that it pays in the long run to spend a little more and get the best quality. Explain how this is particularly true in real estate purchases where so much depends on good location and good condition.

2. Emphasizes the superior resale value of his intended purchase.

3. Explains how a 15 percent rise in new homes this year is placing an ever-increasing price on all real estate. Therefore, any delay will be costly.

4. Mortgage money is getting scarcer all the time and rates will have to go up further.

5. Inevitable inflation will guarantee higher prices later. Any delay will represent a double loss to the buyer in that he will have to pay more later while in the meantime he is losing out on certain appreciation in value.

6. In any event he will really be living rent free, and can always sell for more later. So why wait?

7. Rent money is spent money that goes down the drain, while mortgage payments generate equity, income tax deductions and appreciation in value.

8. Real estate is the best hedge there ever was against inflation.

9. The house may not have everything the buyer was looking for, but neither would a more expensive one, or even a new custom-built house.

10. At least the buyer knows what he is getting here, but if he builds he can never be sure what problems or price he may end up with.

11. There is nothing wrong with a high price, just so it can be justified.

12. Never quote a price alone, without giving the buyer plenty of reasons why he is getting a big bargain, such as:
   a. lowest cost per square foot of house available in the area.
   b. most valuable lot available at the price he is paying, in addition to the house itself being a bargain even if the site were less desirable than it is.
   c. unusual amenities (extra, pleasant benefits like fine neighbors, good view, etc.)
   d. the very thing he wants most—a private sumptuous bath with the master bedroom, or a fireplaced den, or a back yard made for outdoor barbecues, etc.

13. Emphasize the advantage of a low down payment to conserve his cash.

14. Explain how a longer term mortgage will bring the monthly payment within reach, and why the average mortgage lasts only six years, anyway.

302

15. Show how a small increase in present mortgage rates is more than offset by a higher price later so that it still pays him to act now.

16. Explain how, if he is buying G.I. or F.H.A., he will be protected by the fair market value price set by the government. If the value turns out to be less than the price, he will have the option of getting the house for the lower price or his deposit back—in accordance with the escape clause you are inserting in his contract.

17. When the buyer tells you that the price is too high, don't be afraid to ask him what he is basing his estimate of value on. Then explain how the bank or the V.A. or the F.H.A. has already determined that the fair market value of this house is equal to, or even greater than, the asking price.

18. No matter what the buyer's objection to closing, once he knows about it he is only one short step away from being able to close the sale. All he has to do is make a deal with the buyer that if the reason for his objecting to buy were removed he would proceed to close the transaction. Then he removes the objectionable factor if he possibly can.

19. He tells the buyer that he knows more about the deal now than he will ever know again; that, therefore, he has more facts and information on which to base an intelligent decision than he will ever have again. Make sure he knows that if he does not buy now, somebody else will be sure to buy it and then it will be gone. And if he turns this house down, at this price, he simply would not know where to begin trying to show him anything else that would make any sense at all.

20. Finds out the *main* reason why this buyer is out looking for a house. It may be a burning desire for more space, more privacy, better opportunities for his children; or it may be as simple a thing as time being of the essence. Now he shows the buyer why this house provides a better answer to his main reason for buying than any other property possibly could. Then he asks for immediate action before the house is gone.

21. Never, never asks the buyer to think it over.

22. If all else fails, asks him if he is prepared to make an offer at the price he thinks it is worth. If he does give him an offer, no matter how low it may seem, rushes to the seller as fast as he can—in person—and starts using the arguments for the seller as outlined in the beginning of this chapter.

Chapter 76

HOW THE BROKER CAN LOSE HIS LICENSE

All of the States have real estate broker and salesmen licensing boards which regulate their licensees and provide grounds for revocation or suspensions of their licenses. Every buyer and seller should be familiar with these grounds, just in case they are being hurt by a broker. A typical list of the acts which would cause a broker to be disqualified follows:

ACTS WHICH ARE CAUSE FOR SUSPENSION OR REVOCATION OF A BROKER LICENSE IN TEXAS

1. Knowingly making a substantial misrepresentation; or
2. Making any false promise with intent to influence, persuade, or induce; or
3. Pursuing a continued and flagrant course of misrepresentation or the making of false promises through agents, salesmen, advertising, or otherwise; or
4. Failure to make clear to all parties to a transaction for which party he is acting, or receiving compensation from more than one party, except with the full knowledge and consent of all parties; or
5. Failing within a reasonable time to account for or remit moneys coming into his possession which belong to others, or commingling of moneys belonging to others with his own funds; or
6. Paying commission or fees to or dividing commission or fees with anyone not licensed as a real estate broker or salesman in this State or any other state, or attorney-at-law in this State or any other state; or
7. Using any misleading or untruthful advertising including the use of any trade name or insignia of membership of any real estate organization of which he is not a member; or
8. Accepting, receiving, or charging any undisclosed commission, rebate or direct profit on expenditures made for a principal; or
9. Soliciting, selling or offering for sale real property under a scheme or program that constitutes a lottery or deceptive practice; or
10. Acting in the dual capacity of broker and undisclosed principal in any transaction; or

11. Guaranteeing, authorizing or permitting any person to guarantee future profits which may result from a resale of real property; or

12. Placing a sign on any property offering it for sale or rent without the consent of the owner or his authorized agent; or

13. Inducing or attempting to induce any party to a contract of sale or lease to break such contract for the purpose of substituting in lieu thereof a new contract; or

14. Negotiating or attempting to negotiate the sale, exchange, lease, or rental of any real property with an owner or lessor, knowing that such owner or lessor had a written outstanding contract, granting exclusive agency in connection with such property, with another real estate broker; or

15. Offering real property for sale or for lease without the knowledge and consent of the owner or his authorized agency, or on any terms other than those authorized by the owner or his authorized agent; or

16. Publishing, or causing to be published, any advertisement including, but not limited to advertising by newspaper, radio, television, or display which is misleading or which is likely to deceive the public, or which in any manner whatsoever tends to create a misleading impression or which fails to carry plainly the name of the broker causing the advertisement to be published; or

17. Having knowingly withheld from or inserted in a statement of account or invoice, any statement that made it inaccurate in any material particular; or

18. Publishing or circulating any unjustified or unwarranted threats of legal proceedings, or other actions; or

19. Establishing an association, by employment or otherwise, with an unlicensed person who is expected or required to act as a real estate licensee or aiding or abetting or conspiring with any person to circumvent the requirements of this Act; or

20. Failing or refusing upon demand to furnish copies of any document pertaining to any transaction dealing with real estate to any person whose signature is affixed thereto; or

21. Failing to advise a purchaser in writing before the closing of the transaction concerned, that said purchaser should either have the abstract, covering real estate which is the subject of the contract, examined by an attorney of the purchaser's own selection; or be furnished with or obtain a policy of title insurance; or

22. Conduct which constitutes dishonest dealings, bad faith, untrustworthiness or incompetency; or

23. Disregarding or violating any provision of this Act; or

24. Failing within a reasonable time to deposit moneys, received as

escrow agent in a real estate transaction, either in trust with a title company authorized to do business in this State, or in a custodial, trust, or escrow account maintained for such purpose in a banking institution authorized to do business in this State; or

25. Disbursing moneys deposited in a custodial, trust, or escrow account in accordance with Subsection (24) above, before the transaction concerned has been consummated or finally terminated otherwise; or

26. Failing or refusing upon demand to produce any document, book, or record in his possession concerning any real estate transaction transacted by him for inspection by the Real Estate Commission or its authorized personnel or representative; or

27. Failing without just cause to surrender into the rightful owner, upon demand, any document or instrument coming into his possession.

Normally, a license board is not empowered to act against a broker in the absence of a signed written complaint by an aggrieved party. The broker is always entitled to a hearing. If the board finds against him, he may appeal their decision in the state courts. The suspension or revocation is in effect, however, pending a court appeal.

Normally, a buyer or seller aggrieved by a broker should appeal first to his State's licensing board before starting litigation in the courts against the broker. The reason for this is that once a lawyer is handling your case the Licensing Board will not interfere and will expect you to go to court for satisfaction.

Since brokers usually fear inspection and investigation by their Licensing Board, appeals to these Boards, in writing and signed, can be very effective deterrents against brokers.

INDEX

net, 40, 47, 105
open, 40, 103
Local real estate taxes, 134

M

Maintenance of home
  publications on, 92
  responsibility for, 71
Management, importance of good, 224
Massachusetts law on fact disclosure, 9
Massachusetts Realty Trust, 221
Merchandise
  buyer's rights and remedies for, 149
  sales contract for, 146
Minority groups, open housing for, 151
Money, finding investment, 229
Mortgage, mortgages. *See also*
  Financing, Lender, Refinancing.
  bank policy on, 28
  cancellation insurance, 132
  conditions, 171
  costs, 28
  costs, calculating, 85
  costs, comparison of, 84
  costs, questions related to, 62
  and costs, relationship of, 62
  financing, conventional, 117
  financing, FHA, 118
  financing, methods of, 117
  financing, V. A., 120
  finder's fees for, 121
  foreclosure, 171
  payments, obligations on, 71
  personnel and financing help, 28
  points for, 121
  search for, 59
  selecting, 28, 62
Multiple
  line insurance, 130
  listing, use of, 40, 41
  unit property, profit from, 185
  unit property, purchasing, 33
  unit property, selling, 50
  unit property, types of, 209

N

National Association of Real Estate
  Boards Code of Ethics, 27
Navigable waterfront rights, 160
Negligence, liability for product, 148
Neighborhood, checking the, 52
Net listing, 40, 47, 105
Net net lease for commercial buildings, 237
Nursing homes, investment in, 212

O

Obligations
  of buyer, 71, 94
  property, 150
  of seller, 100
Offer
  acceptance and broker, 294
  making an, 20
Office buildings, investment in, 212
Open listing, use of, 40, 103
Overpricing, dangers of, 100
Owner, owners
  contract laws for property, 140
  and contractor, relationship of, 143
  and household employees, relationship of, 144
  protection against builder, 140, 141
  responsibility for workers, 140
Ownership
  of income property, types of, 220
  types of, 161

P

Partnership, nature of, 220
Payments, mortgage, 71
Personal rights and liabilities, 168
Points for mortgages, 121
Possession of land, adverse, 156
Price
  and appraisal, 3
  bracket, changing purchase, 35
  of buying, calculating, 85, 86
  buying at lowest, 246
  and fair market value, 3